THE ZONE CONTINUUM™

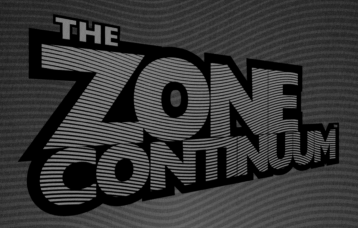

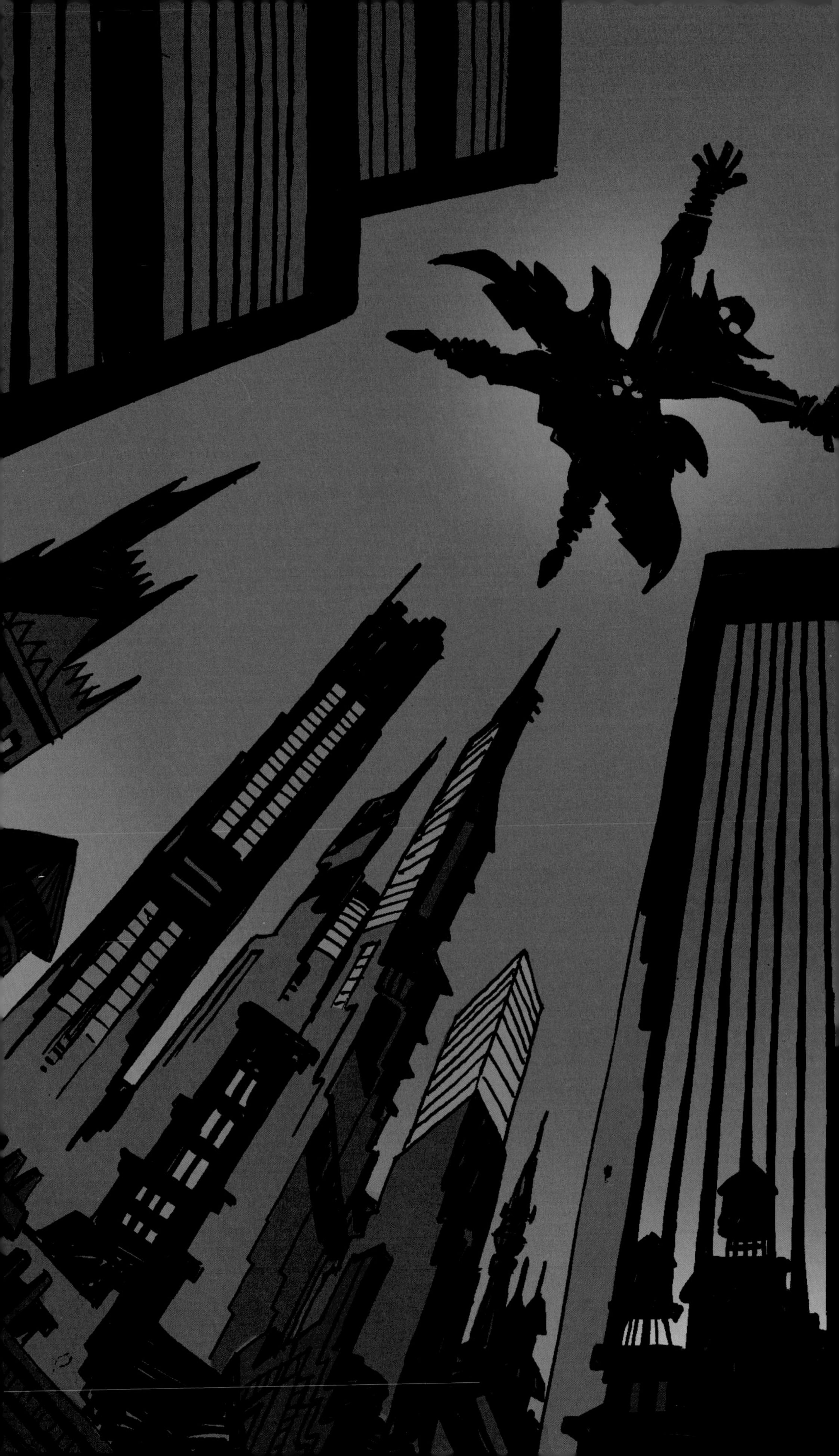

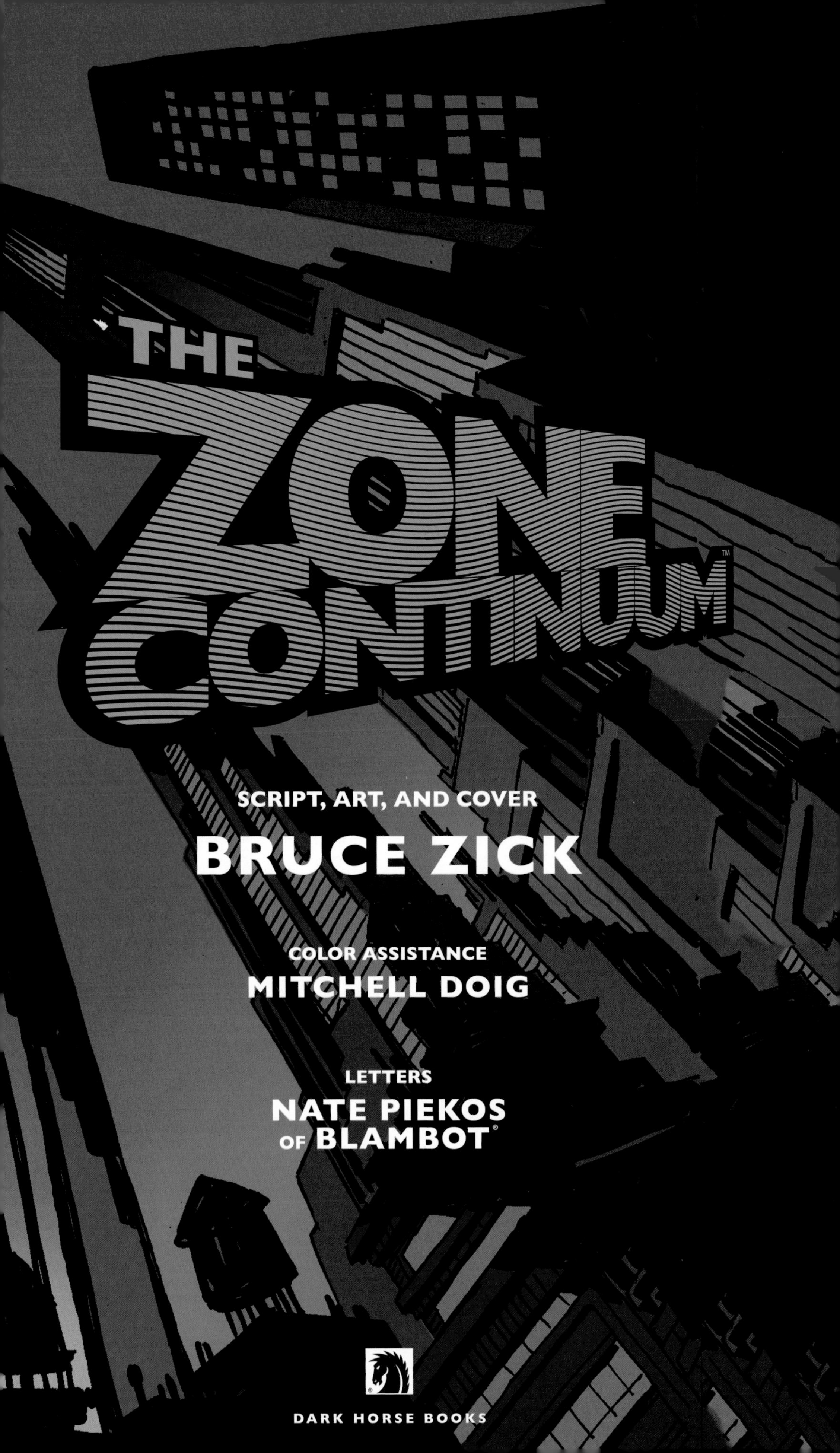

THE ZONE CONTINUUM™

SCRIPT, ART, AND COVER

BRUCE ZICK

COLOR ASSISTANCE

MITCHELL DOIG

LETTERS

NATE PIEKOS OF BLAMBOT®

DARK HORSE BOOKS

president & publisher
MIKE RICHARDSON

designer
JUSTIN COUCH

editor
IAN TUCKER

digital art technician
CHRISTIANNE GOUDREAU

THE ZONE CONTINUUM

Dark Horse Books. A division of Dark Horse Comics, Inc. 10956 SE Main Street, Milwaukie, OR 97222

DarkHorse.com

To find a comics shop in your area, call the Comic Shop Locator Service toll-free at 1-888-266-4226. International Licensing: (503) 905-2377

First edition: February 2016   ISBN 978-1-61655-950-2

10 9 8 7 6 5 4 3 2 1
Printed in China

Neil Hankerson, Executive Vice President • Tom Weddle, Chief Financial Officer • Randy Stradley, Vice President of Publishing • Michael Martens, Vice President of Book Trade Sales • Matt Parkinson, Vice President of Marketing • David Scroggy, Vice President of Product Development • Dale LaFountain, Vice President of Information Technology • Cara Niece, Vice President of Production and Scheduling • Ken Lizzi, General Counsel • Davey Estrada, Editorial Director • Dave Marshall, Editor in Chief • Scott Allie, Executive Senior Editor • Chris Warner, Senior Books Editor • Cary Grazzini, Director of Print and Development • Lia Ribacchi, Art Director • Mark Bernardi, Director of Digital Publishing

Maybe because of those Steve Ditko *Spider-Man* scenes, or maybe because of my studies of New York City. Every time I saw a rooftop, with those stout water towers, old brick chimneys, vents, pipes, ductworks, exhaust fans, gargoyle statues, and art deco cornices, I thought—this is a world unto itself, unique from the everyday streets where we live.

That got me to thinking that someday I would do a story that takes place high over the city. Later, I thought what a neat idea it would be to have someone's headquarters in an abandoned water tower.

That's how *The Zone Continuum* started.

The story grew organically from there. Who lived in this urban jungle? A secret race of ancients—the Dar—were stranded there, never to walk the streets again. But why? Because, of course, they were trapped in Zones. I like metaphors, and this one is a doozy. Aren't we all trapped by barriers of our own making or imposed upon us by others? Wouldn't we all like to be free of restrictions and able to soar?

Next came the idea that Talon and his wife, Paris, live in separate Zones, thanks to the 1945 atomic bomb tests of the Manhattan Project, which fractured the Zone Continuum and subdivided Zone 27 into two. Paris could only survive in the newly formed, adjacent Zone 26, so they could never be together again. Yes, another metaphor, true to many a relationship. Partners live in their own worlds of limitations—or Zones, if you will—and they struggle to coexist in happiness.

Lastly, I felt the need to center the story around the crises of a world ravaged by pollution. Should humanity be allowed to continue their destructive ways, or should they be eradicated so that the planet may be restored? That is the question the characters must face.

The Zone Continuum was originally a four-book series printed by Gary Reed and Caliber Press, and I'm eternally grateful to Gary for taking a chance. It was a labor of love, and unfortunately the Zones came to an end as I left the comic book field to focus more fully on the animation business.

But I never could forget the story. I was determined, somehow, someway, to bring the series back. Now, thanks to Mike Richardson at Dark Horse Comics, and my old friend Ira Weintraub, the series has returned.

So, welcome, dear readers. If you're familiar with the original books, welcome back, and thanks for waiting so long (twenty-two years!). If you're new to the story, welcome as well, and thanks for giving it a shot. I value each and every reader, and I hope to hear from you.

Lastly, maybe, just maybe, you'll pay more attention to the next rooftop you see and appreciate it in an entirely new way. And don't be surprised if you see or hear something strange up there— maybe there's more truth to this story than you might imagine.

CHAPTER ONE

THE CHALLENGE

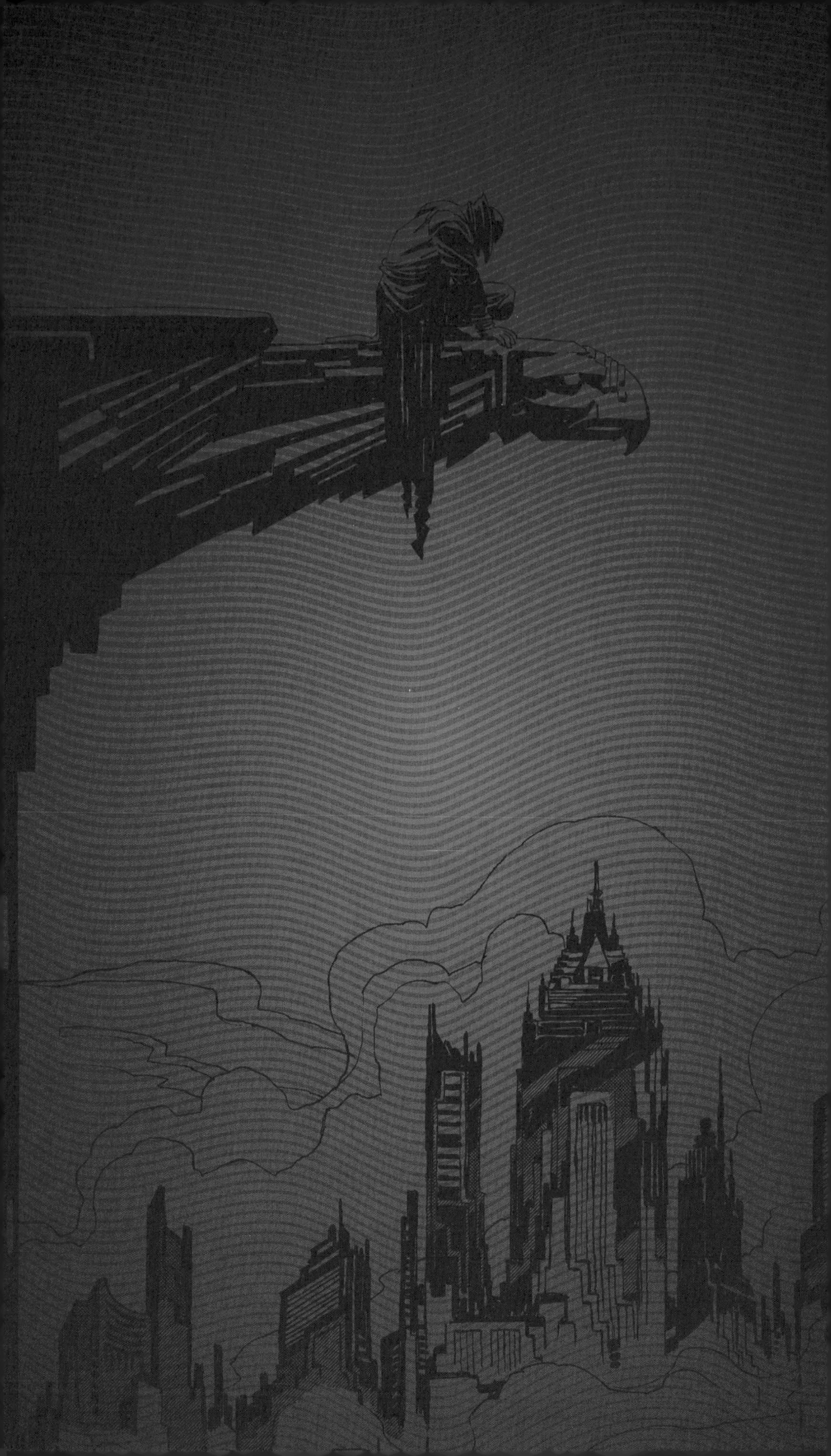

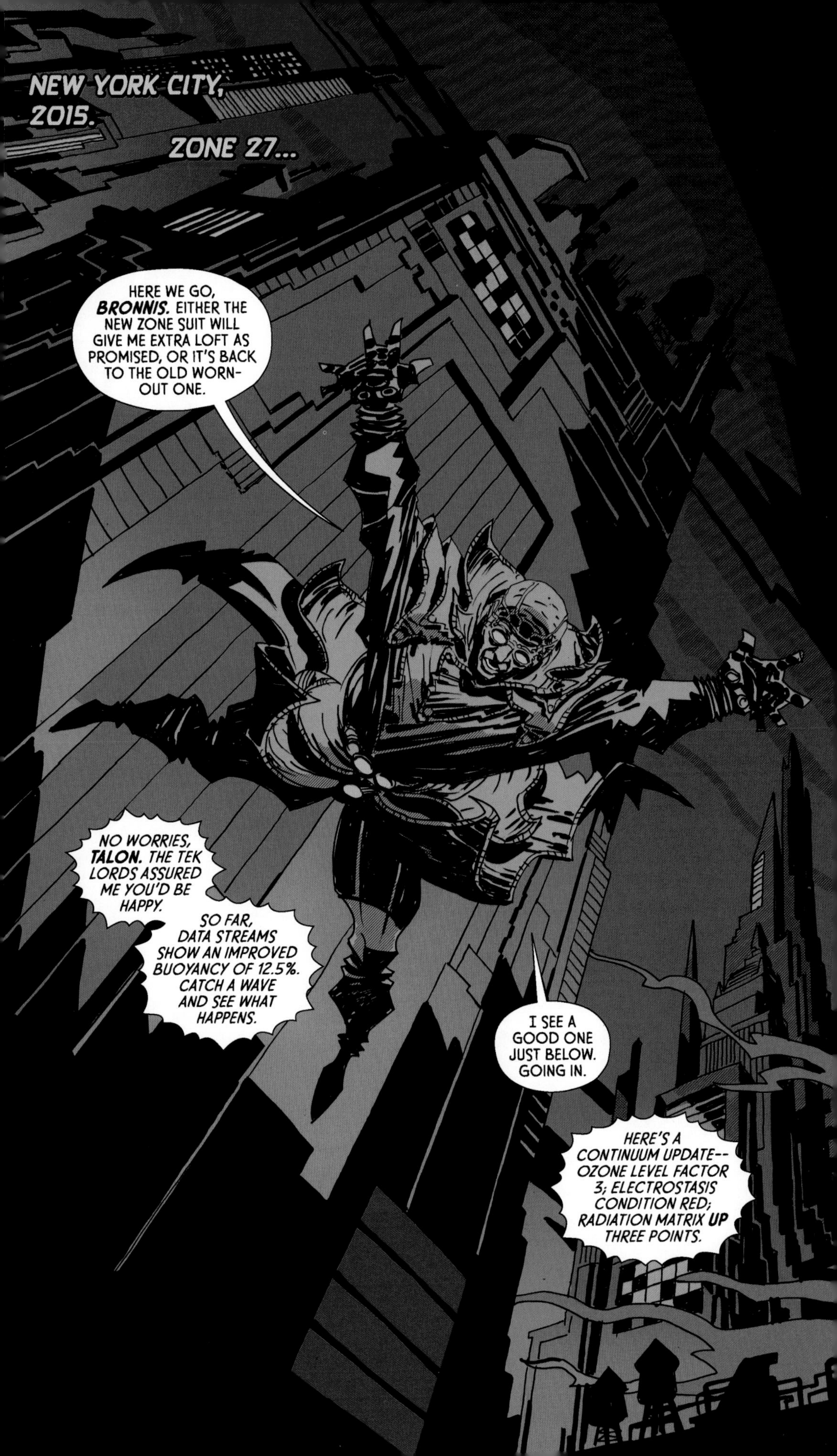
NEW YORK CITY, 2015.
ZONE 27...
HERE WE GO, BRONNIS. EITHER THE NEW ZONE SUIT WILL GIVE ME EXTRA LOFT AS PROMISED, OR IT'S BACK TO THE OLD WORN-OUT ONE.
NO WORRIES, TALON. THE TEK LORDS ASSURED ME YOU'D BE HAPPY.
SO FAR, DATA STREAMS SHOW AN IMPROVED BUOYANCY OF 12.5%. CATCH A WAVE AND SEE WHAT HAPPENS.
I SEE A GOOD ONE JUST BELOW. GOING IN.
HERE'S A CONTINUUM UPDATE-- OZONE LEVEL FACTOR 3; ELECTROSTASIS CONDITION RED; RADIATION MATRIX UP THREE POINTS.

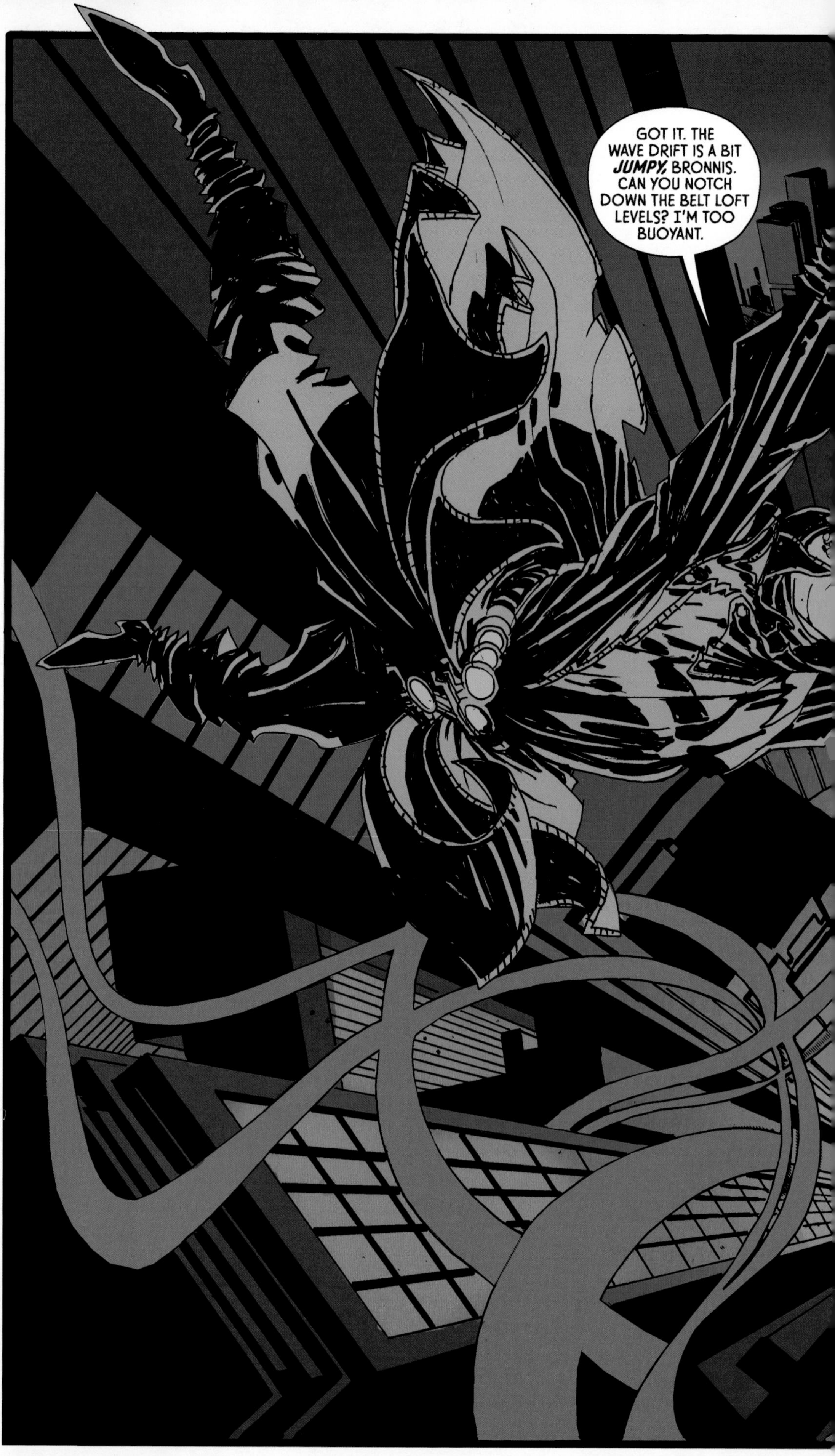
GOT IT. THE WAVE DRIFT IS A BIT *JUMPY,* BRONNIS. CAN YOU NOTCH DOWN THE BELT LOFT LEVELS? I'M TOO BUOYANT.

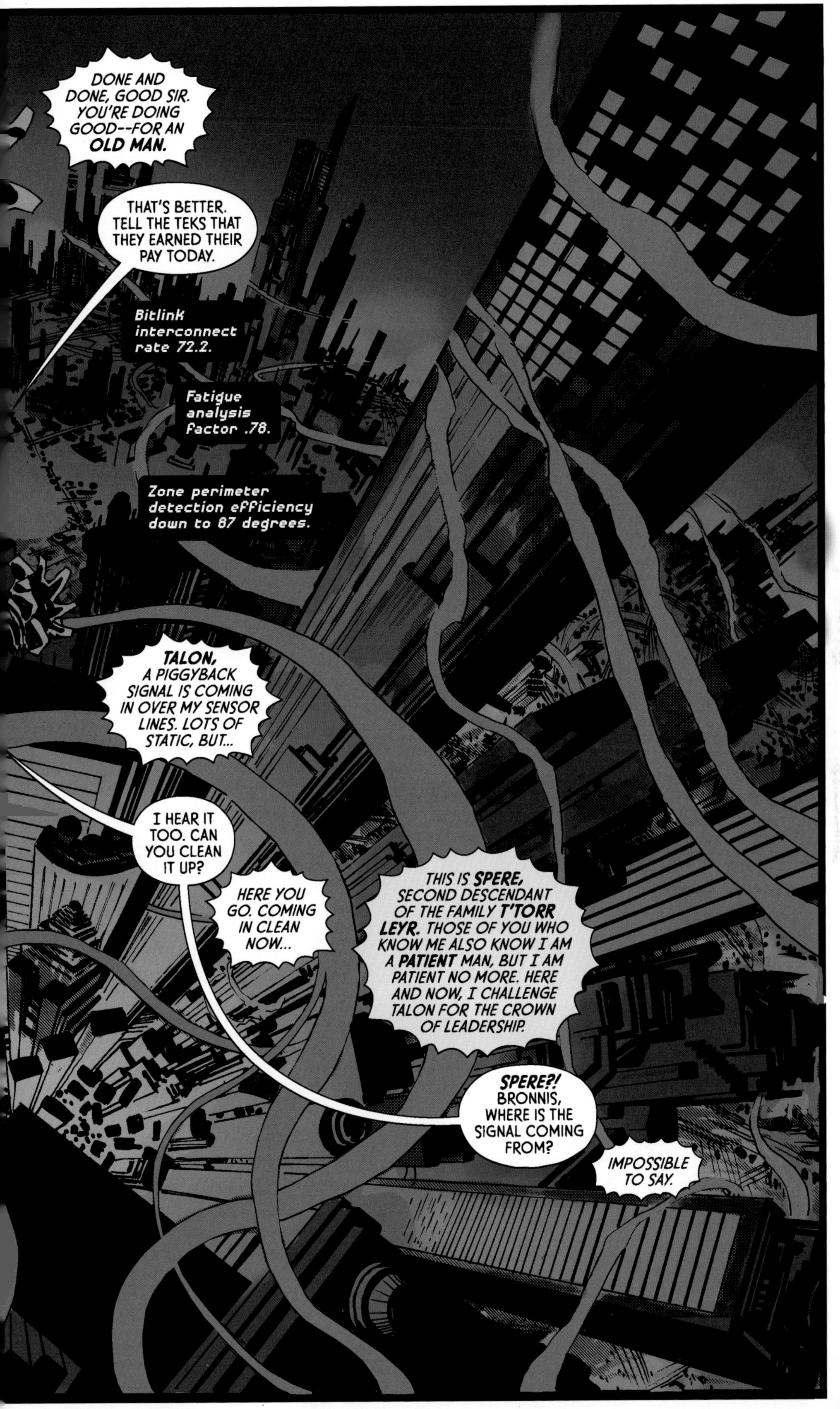
DONE AND DONE, GOOD SIR. YOU'RE DOING GOOD--FOR AN OLD MAN.
THAT'S BETTER. TELL THE TEKS THAT THEY EARNED THEIR PAY TODAY.
Bitlink interconnect rate 72.2.
Fatigue analysis factor .78.
Zone perimeter detection efficiency down to 87 degrees.
TALON, A PIGGYBACK SIGNAL IS COMING IN OVER MY SENSOR LINES. LOTS OF STATIC, BUT...
I HEAR IT TOO. CAN YOU CLEAN IT UP?
HERE YOU GO. COMING IN CLEAN NOW...
THIS IS SPERE, SECOND DESCENDANT OF THE FAMILY T'TORR LEYR. THOSE OF YOU WHO KNOW ME ALSO KNOW I AM A PATIENT MAN, BUT I AM PATIENT NO MORE. HERE AND NOW, I CHALLENGE TALON FOR THE CROWN OF LEADERSHIP.
SPERE?! BRONNIS, WHERE IS THE SIGNAL COMING FROM?
IMPOSSIBLE TO SAY.

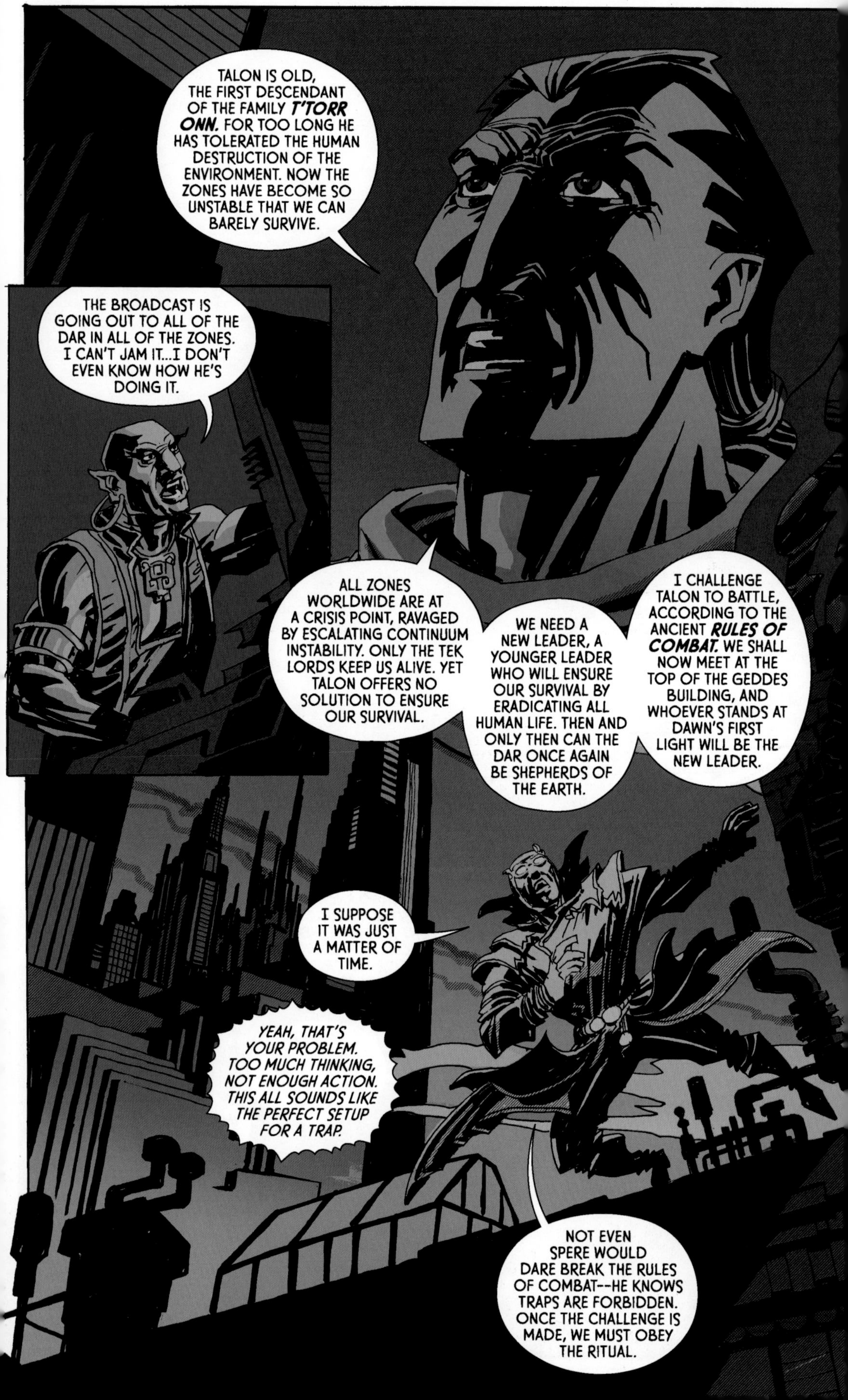

TALON IS OLD, THE FIRST DESCENDANT OF THE FAMILY *T'TORR ONN.* FOR TOO LONG HE HAS TOLERATED THE HUMAN DESTRUCTION OF THE ENVIRONMENT. NOW THE ZONES HAVE BECOME SO UNSTABLE THAT WE CAN BARELY SURVIVE.
THE BROADCAST IS GOING OUT TO ALL OF THE DAR IN ALL OF THE ZONES. I CAN'T JAM IT...I DON'T EVEN KNOW HOW HE'S DOING IT.
ALL ZONES WORLDWIDE ARE AT A CRISIS POINT, RAVAGED BY ESCALATING CONTINUUM INSTABILITY. ONLY THE TEK LORDS KEEP US ALIVE. YET TALON OFFERS NO SOLUTION TO ENSURE OUR SURVIVAL.
WE NEED A NEW LEADER, A YOUNGER LEADER WHO WILL ENSURE OUR SURVIVAL BY ERADICATING ALL HUMAN LIFE. THEN AND ONLY THEN CAN THE DAR ONCE AGAIN BE SHEPHERDS OF THE EARTH.
I CHALLENGE TALON TO BATTLE, ACCORDING TO THE ANCIENT *RULES OF COMBAT.* WE SHALL NOW MEET AT THE TOP OF THE GEDDES BUILDING, AND WHOEVER STANDS AT DAWN'S FIRST LIGHT WILL BE THE NEW LEADER.
I SUPPOSE IT WAS JUST A MATTER OF TIME.
YEAH, THAT'S YOUR PROBLEM. TOO MUCH THINKING, NOT ENOUGH ACTION. THIS ALL SOUNDS LIKE THE PERFECT SETUP FOR A TRAP.
NOT EVEN SPERE WOULD DARE BREAK THE RULES OF COMBAT--HE KNOWS TRAPS ARE FORBIDDEN. ONCE THE CHALLENGE IS MADE, WE MUST OBEY THE RITUAL.

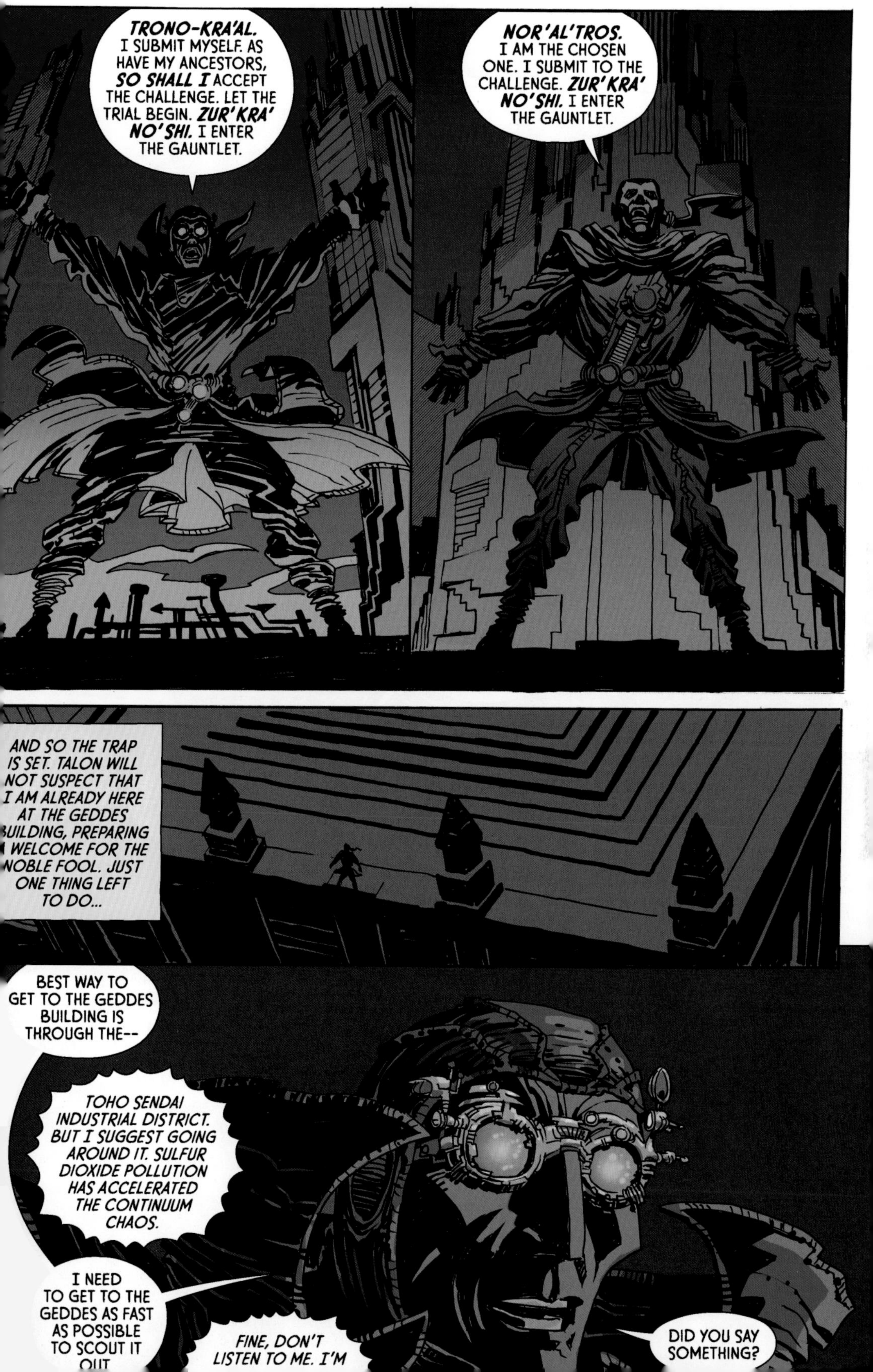

TRONO-KRA'AL. I SUBMIT MYSELF. AS HAVE MY ANCESTORS, SO SHALL I ACCEPT THE CHALLENGE. LET THE TRIAL BEGIN. ZUR'KRA' NO'SHI. I ENTER THE GAUNTLET.
NOR'AL'TROS. I AM THE CHOSEN ONE. I SUBMIT TO THE CHALLENGE. ZUR'KRA' NO'SHI. I ENTER THE GAUNTLET.
AND SO THE TRAP IS SET. TALON WILL NOT SUSPECT THAT I AM ALREADY HERE AT THE GEDDES BUILDING, PREPARING WELCOME FOR THE NOBLE FOOL. JUST ONE THING LEFT TO DO...
BEST WAY TO GET TO THE GEDDES BUILDING IS THROUGH THE--
TOHO SENDAI INDUSTRIAL DISTRICT. BUT I SUGGEST GOING AROUND IT. SULFUR DIOXIDE POLLUTION HAS ACCELERATED THE CONTINUUM CHAOS.
I NEED TO GET TO THE GEDDES AS FAST AS POSSIBLE TO SCOUT IT OUT.
FINE, DON'T LISTEN TO ME. I'M
DID YOU SAY SOMETHING?

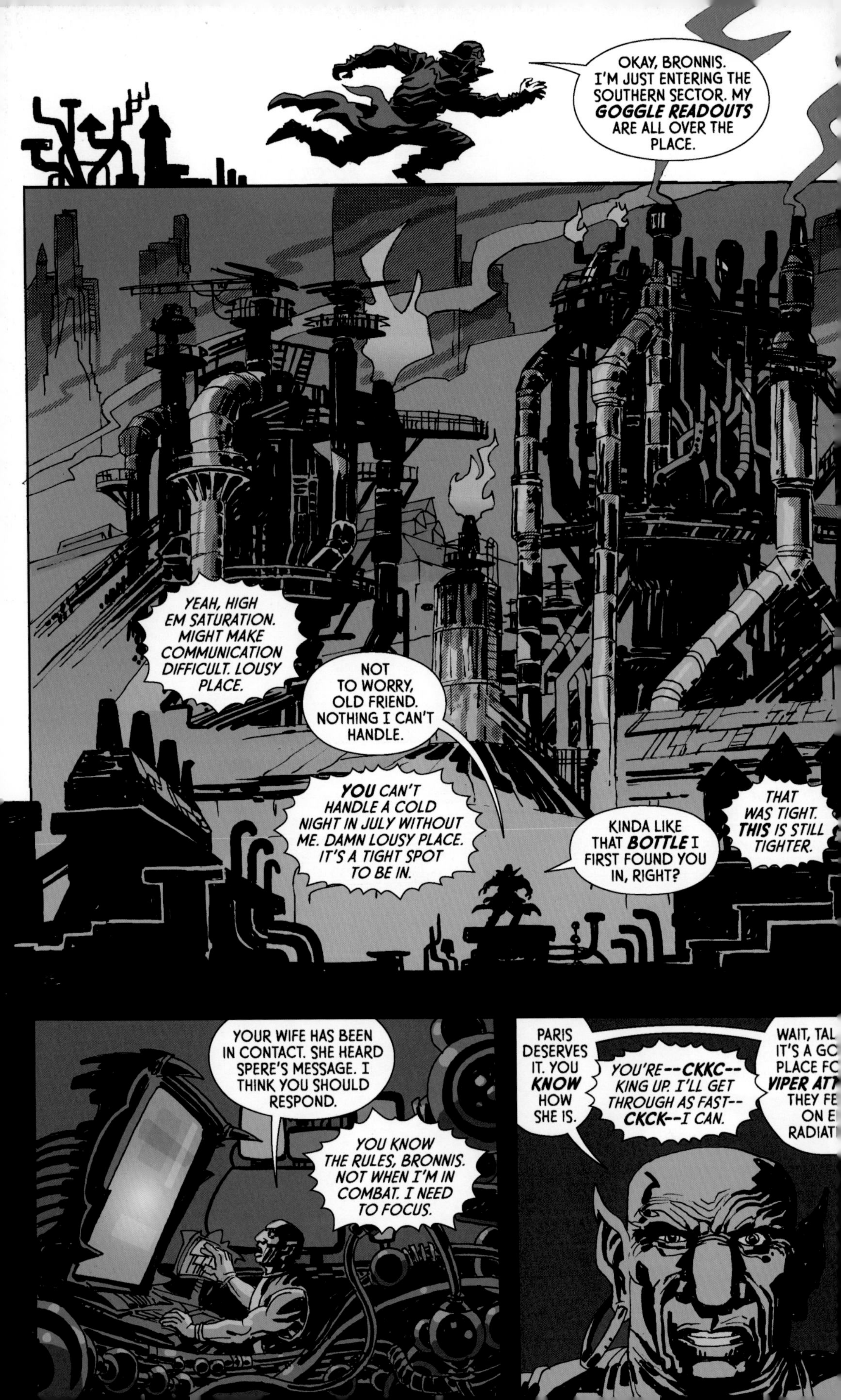
OKAY, BRONNIS. I'M JUST ENTERING THE SOUTHERN SECTOR. MY GOGGLE READOUTS ARE ALL OVER THE PLACE.
YEAH, HIGH EM SATURATION. MIGHT MAKE COMMUNICATION DIFFICULT. LOUSY PLACE.
NOT TO WORRY, OLD FRIEND. NOTHING I CAN'T HANDLE.
YOU CAN'T HANDLE A COLD NIGHT IN JULY WITHOUT ME. DAMN LOUSY PLACE. IT'S A TIGHT SPOT TO BE IN.
KINDA LIKE THAT BOTTLE I FIRST FOUND YOU IN, RIGHT?
THAT WAS TIGHT. THIS IS STILL TIGHTER.
YOUR WIFE HAS BEEN IN CONTACT. SHE HEARD SPERE'S MESSAGE. I THINK YOU SHOULD RESPOND.
YOU KNOW THE RULES, BRONNIS. NOT WHEN I'M IN COMBAT. I NEED TO FOCUS.
PARIS DESERVES IT. YOU KNOW HOW SHE IS.
YOU'RE--CKKC--KING UP. I'LL GET THROUGH AS FAST--CKCK--I CAN.

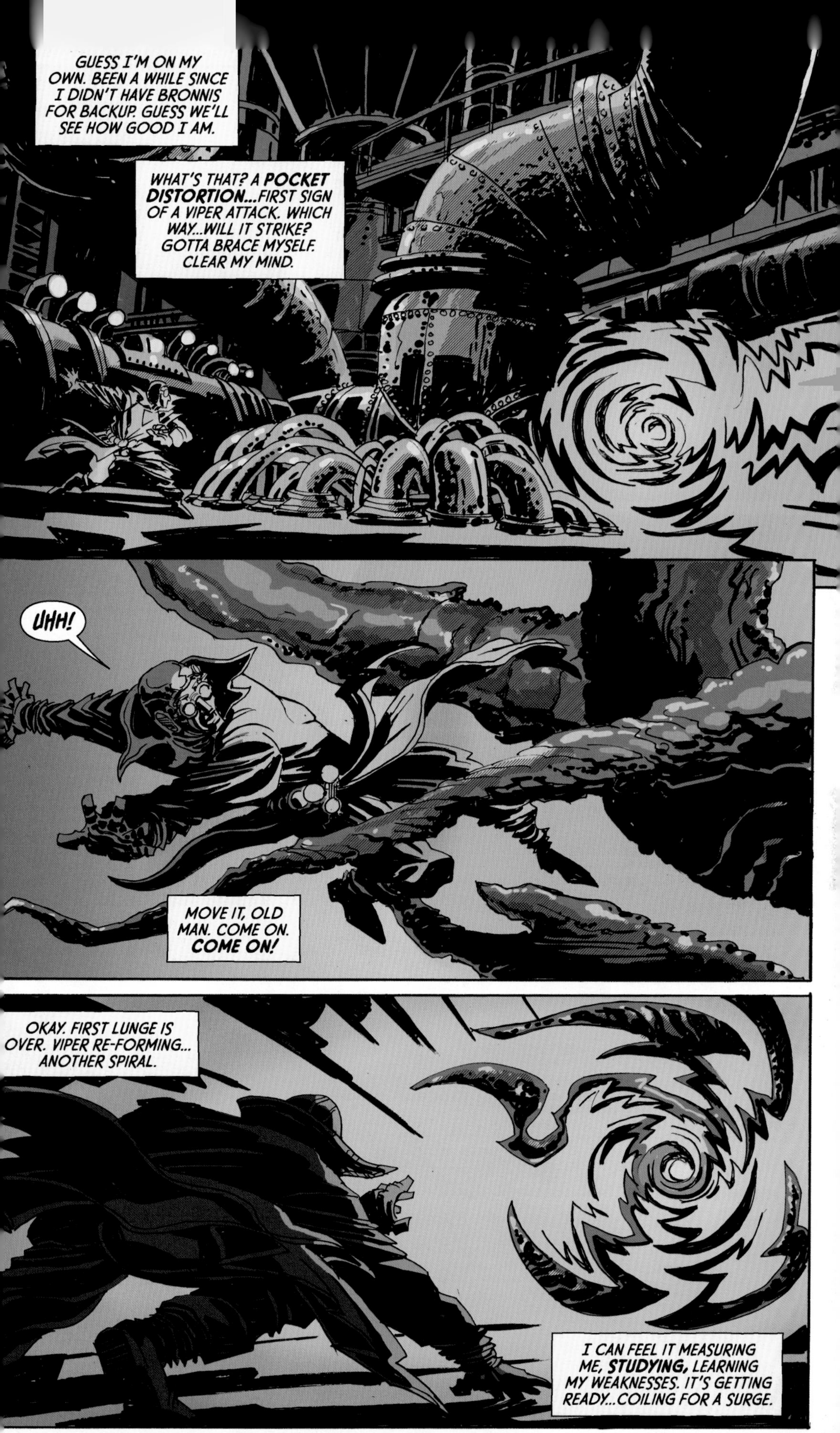
GUESS I'M ON MY OWN. BEEN A WHILE SINCE I DIDN'T HAVE BRONNIS FOR BACKUP. GUESS WE'LL SEE HOW GOOD I AM.
WHAT'S THAT? A **POCKET DISTORTION...** FIRST SIGN OF A VIPER ATTACK. WHICH WAY...WILL IT STRIKE? GOTTA BRACE MYSELF. CLEAR MY MIND.
UHH!
MOVE IT, OLD MAN. COME ON. **COME ON!**
OKAY. FIRST LUNGE IS OVER. VIPER RE-FORMING... ANOTHER SPIRAL.
I CAN FEEL IT MEASURING ME, **STUDYING,** LEARNING MY WEAKNESSES. IT'S GETTING READY...COILING FOR A SURGE.

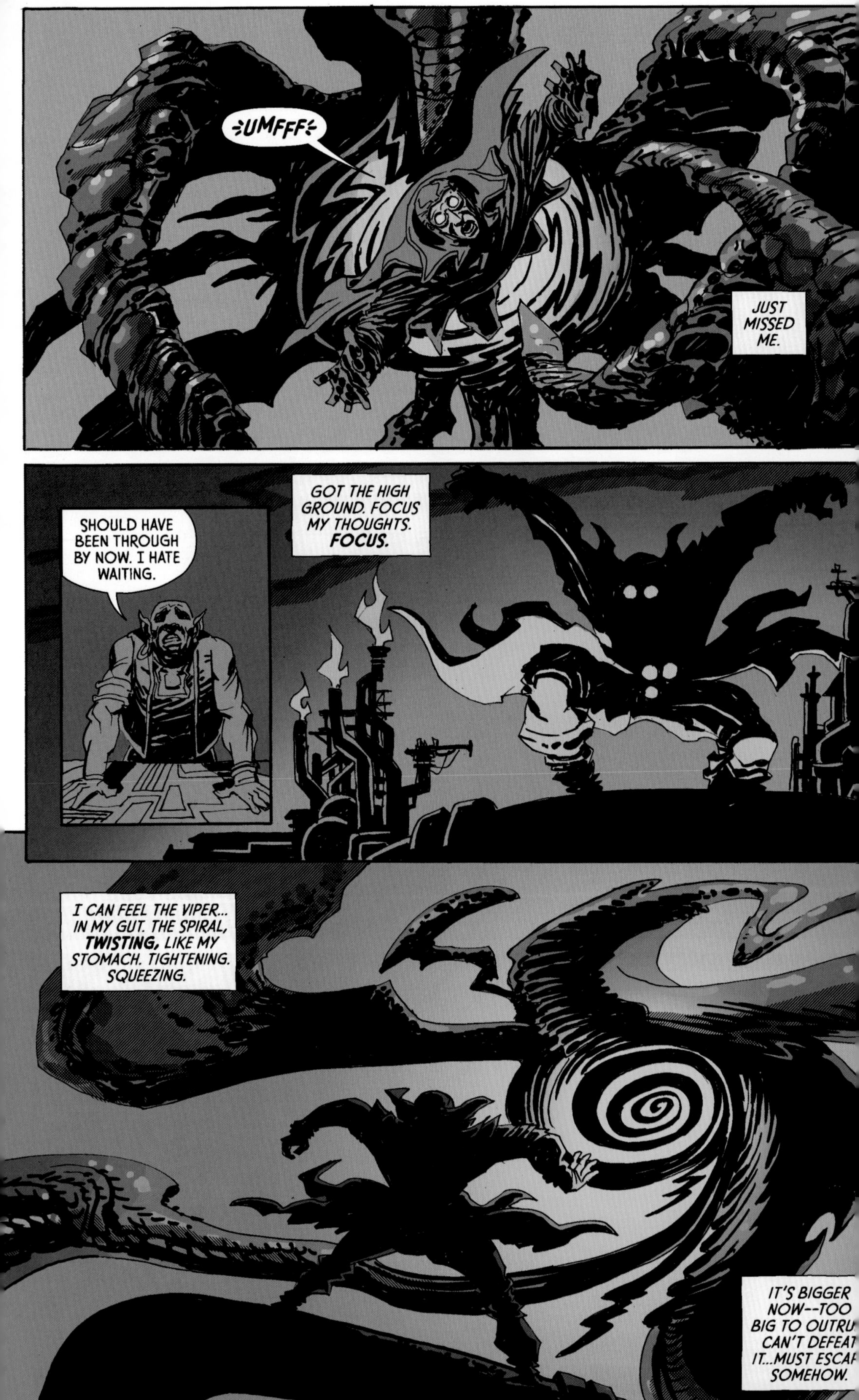

UMFFF
JUST MISSED ME.
GOT THE HIGH GROUND. FOCUS MY THOUGHTS. **FOCUS.**
SHOULD HAVE BEEN THROUGH BY NOW. I HATE WAITING.
I CAN FEEL THE VIPER... IN MY GUT. THE SPIRAL, **TWISTING,** LIKE MY STOMACH. TIGHTENING. SQUEEZING.
IT'S BIGGER NOW--TOO BIG TO OUTRU CAN'T DEFEAT IT...MUST ESCAP SOMEHOW.

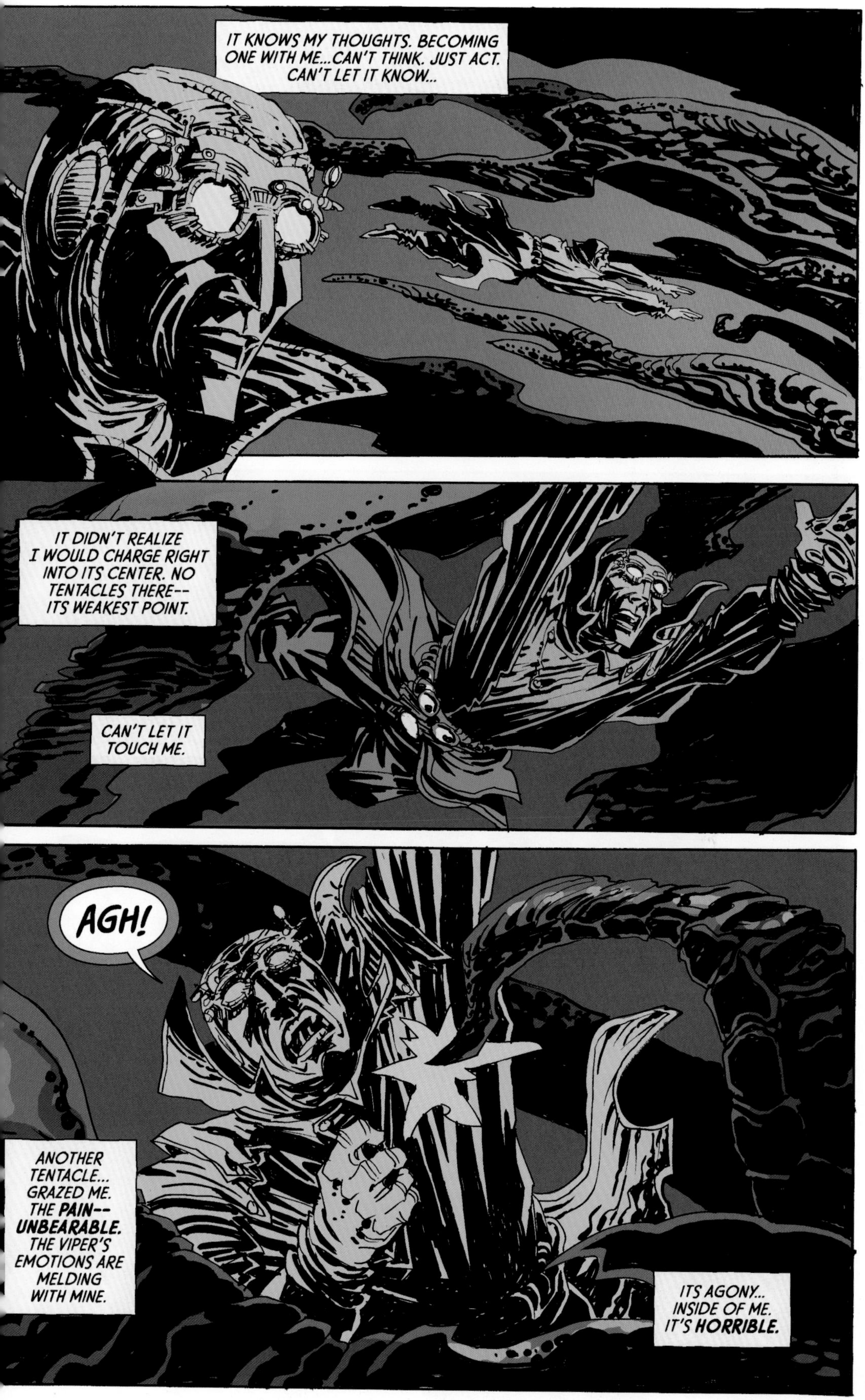
IT KNOWS MY THOUGHTS. BECOMING ONE WITH ME...CAN'T THINK. JUST ACT. CAN'T LET IT KNOW...
IT DIDN'T REALIZE I WOULD CHARGE RIGHT INTO ITS CENTER. NO TENTACLES THERE-- ITS WEAKEST POINT.
CAN'T LET IT TOUCH ME.
AGH!
ANOTHER TENTACLE... GRAZED ME. THE **PAIN--** **UNBEARABLE.** THE VIPER'S EMOTIONS ARE MELDING WITH MINE.
ITS AGONY... INSIDE OF ME. IT'S **HORRIBLE.**

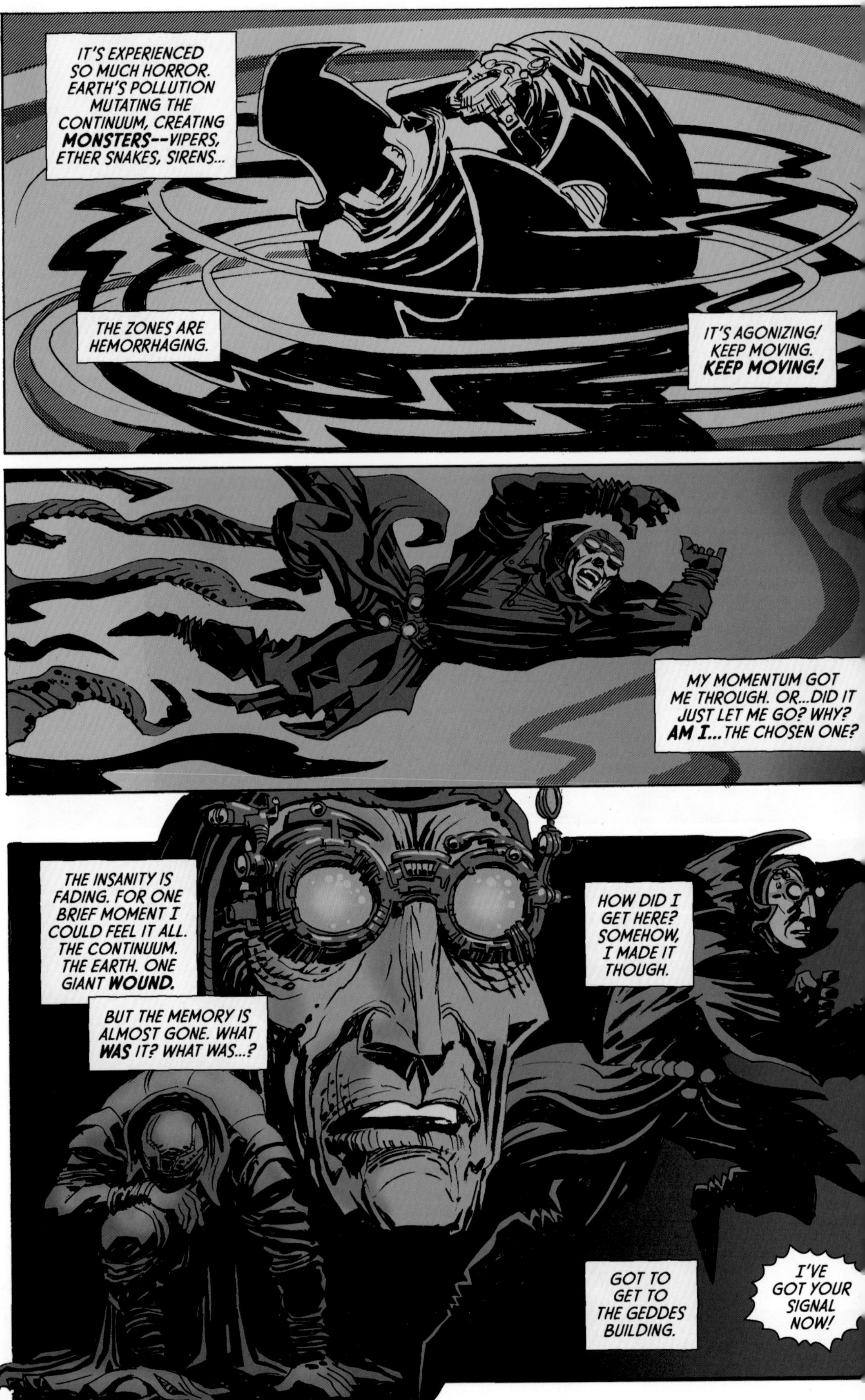

IT'S EXPERIENCED SO MUCH HORROR. EARTH'S POLLUTION MUTATING THE CONTINUUM, CREATING **MONSTERS**--VIPERS, ETHER SNAKES, SIRENS...
THE ZONES ARE HEMORRHAGING.
IT'S AGONIZING! KEEP MOVING. **KEEP MOVING!**
MY MOMENTUM GOT ME THROUGH. OR...DID IT JUST LET ME GO? WHY? **AM I...** THE CHOSEN ONE?
THE INSANITY IS FADING. FOR ONE BRIEF MOMENT I COULD FEEL IT ALL. THE CONTINUUM. THE EARTH. ONE GIANT **WOUND.**
BUT THE MEMORY IS ALMOST GONE. WHAT **WAS** IT? WHAT WAS...?
HOW DID I GET HERE? SOMEHOW, I MADE IT THOUGH.
GOT TO GET TO THE GEDDES BUILDING.
I'VE GOT YOUR SIGNAL NOW!

TALON--YOUR BIO-READOUTS-- SOMEHOW...YOU'VE AGED A THOUSAND YEARS.

I CAN PROGRAM A NEURALNET REPAIR PROTOCOL TO YOUR SUIT'S MED NODES, GIVE YOU AN ADRENAL SURGE THAT SHOULD RESTORE YOU.

THANKS, BRONNIS. I--

WAITAMINNIT. NEW DATA STREAM UPDATE COMING IN.

TALON, IT'S BAD. *REALLY* BAD.

SERVER FARM UPTAKE IN INDIA HAS DOUBLED THE SIZE OF THE DIGITAL MATRIX DIMENSION. PLUS THE MOUNT ETNA ERUPTIONS... IT'S ALL CAUSING A FRACTURE IN THE CONTINUUM.

HERE IT IS. ZONE 27 IS RISING ANOTHER TEN FEET. THAT WOULD PUT THE LOWEST BOUNDARY AT 160 FEET ABOVE SEA LEVEL.

DAMN.

GETTING TOO SMALL...

HOW MUCH LONGER BEFORE ZONE 27 RISES ABOVE THE TALLEST BUILDINGS?

THEN WHAT? WE LIVE IN THE CLOUDS?

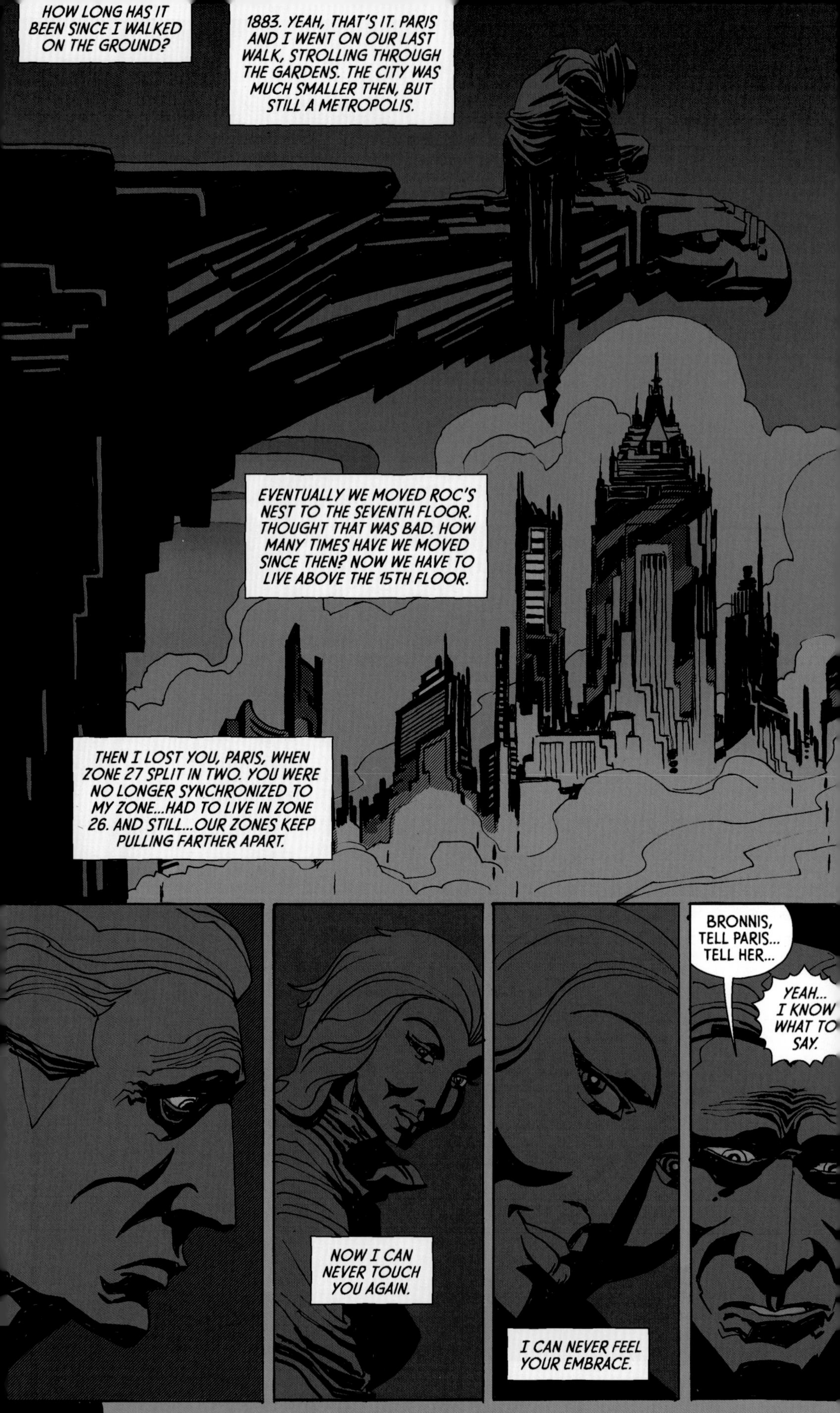
HOW LONG HAS IT BEEN SINCE I WALKED ON THE GROUND?
1883. YEAH, THAT'S IT. PARIS AND I WENT ON OUR LAST WALK, STROLLING THROUGH THE GARDENS. THE CITY WAS MUCH SMALLER THEN, BUT STILL A METROPOLIS.
EVENTUALLY WE MOVED ROC'S NEST TO THE SEVENTH FLOOR. THOUGHT THAT WAS BAD. HOW MANY TIMES HAVE WE MOVED SINCE THEN? NOW WE HAVE TO LIVE ABOVE THE 15TH FLOOR.
THEN I LOST YOU, PARIS, WHEN ZONE 27 SPLIT IN TWO. YOU WERE NO LONGER SYNCHRONIZED TO MY ZONE...HAD TO LIVE IN ZONE 26. AND STILL...OUR ZONES KEEP PULLING FARTHER APART.
NOW I CAN NEVER TOUCH YOU AGAIN.
I CAN NEVER FEEL YOUR EMBRACE.
BRONNIS, TELL PARIS... TELL HER...
YEAH... I KNOW WHAT TO SAY.

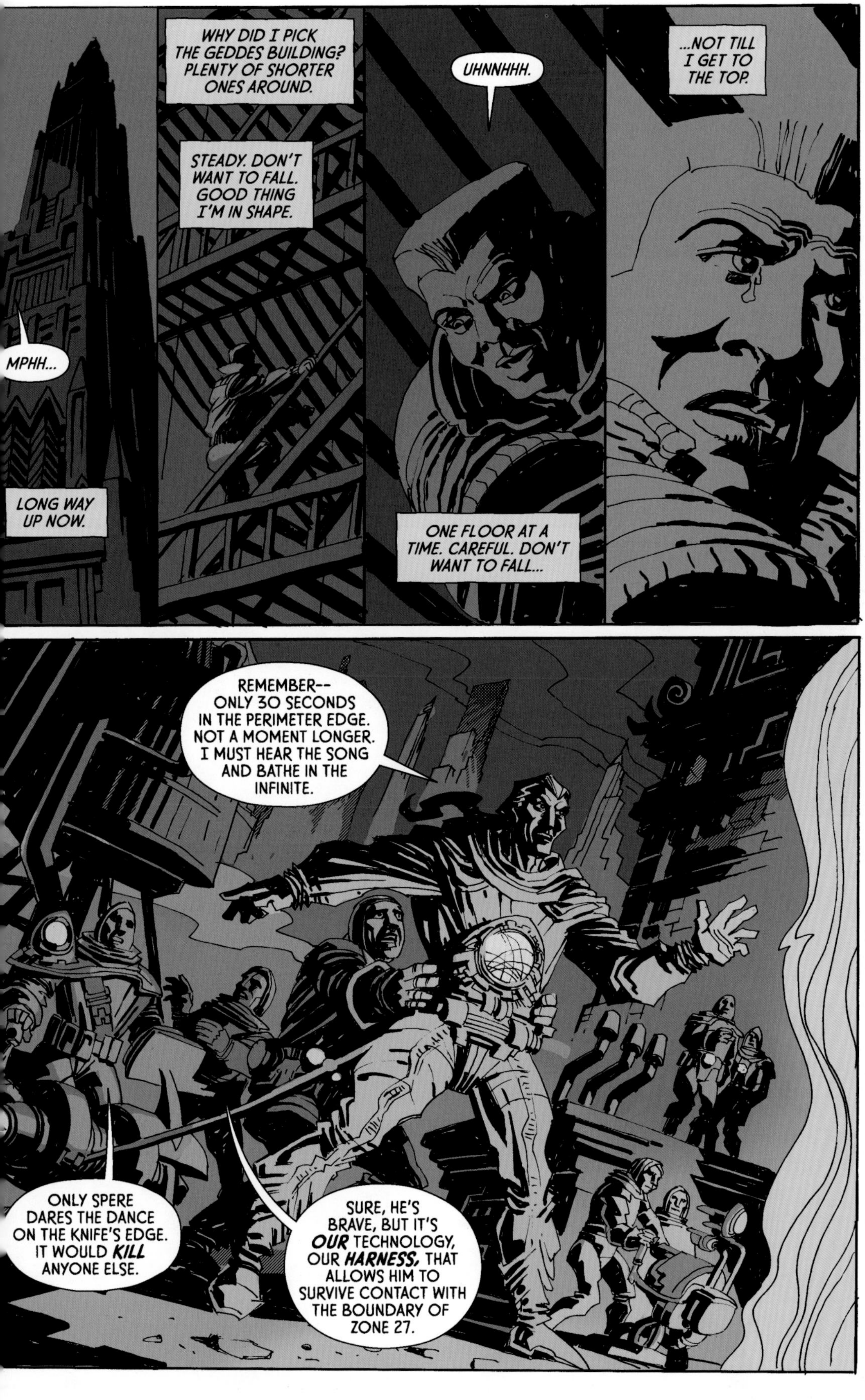
MPHH...
LONG WAY UP NOW.
WHY DID I PICK THE GEDDES BUILDING? PLENTY OF SHORTER ONES AROUND.
STEADY. DON'T WANT TO FALL. GOOD THING I'M IN SHAPE.
UHNNHHH.
ONE FLOOR AT A TIME. CAREFUL. DON'T WANT TO FALL...
...NOT TILL I GET TO THE TOP.
REMEMBER-- ONLY 30 SECONDS IN THE PERIMETER EDGE. NOT A MOMENT LONGER. I MUST HEAR THE SONG AND BATHE IN THE INFINITE.
ONLY SPERE DARES THE DANCE ON THE KNIFE'S EDGE. IT WOULD KILL ANYONE ELSE.
SURE, HE'S BRAVE, BUT IT'S OUR TECHNOLOGY, OUR HARNESS, THAT ALLOWS HIM TO SURVIVE CONTACT WITH THE BOUNDARY OF ZONE 27.

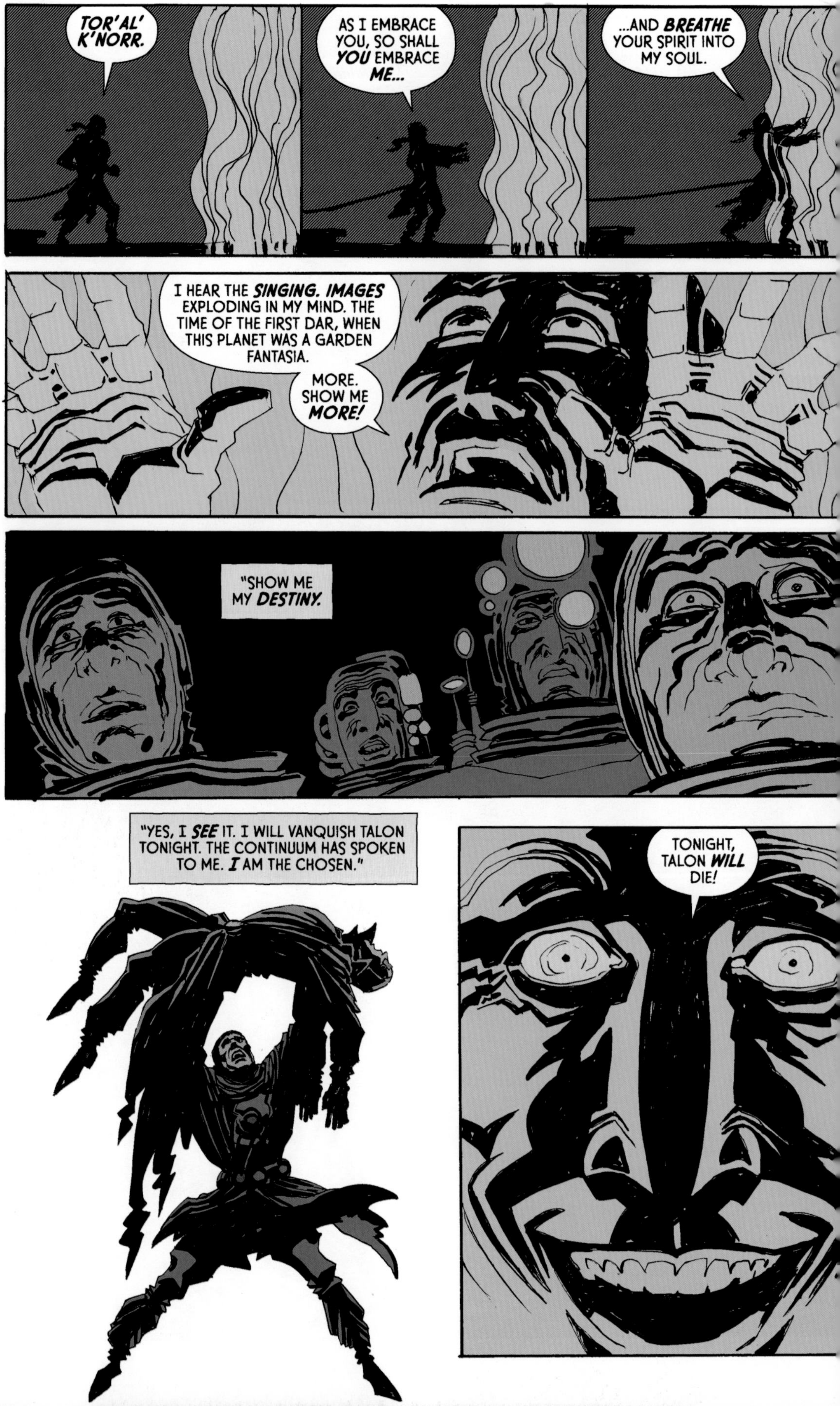
TOR'AL' K'NORR.
AS I EMBRACE YOU, SO SHALL YOU EMBRACE ME...
...AND BREATHE YOUR SPIRIT INTO MY SOUL.
I HEAR THE SINGING. IMAGES EXPLODING IN MY MIND. THE TIME OF THE FIRST DAR, WHEN THIS PLANET WAS A GARDEN FANTASIA.
MORE. SHOW ME MORE!
"SHOW ME MY DESTINY.
"YES, I SEE IT. I WILL VANQUISH TALON TONIGHT. THE CONTINUUM HAS SPOKEN TO ME. I AM THE CHOSEN."
TONIGHT, TALON WILL DIE!

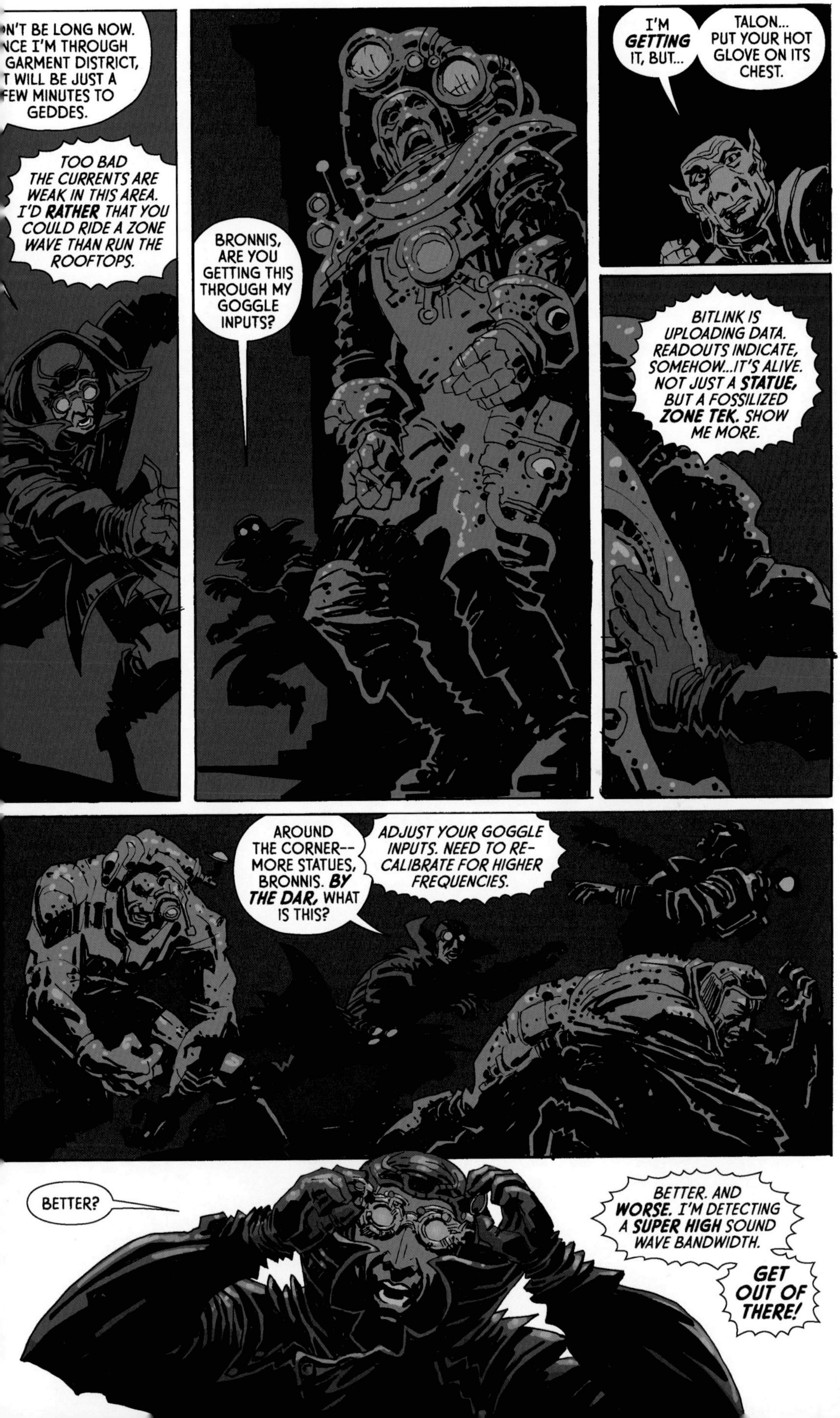

N'T BE LONG NOW. NCE I'M THROUGH GARMENT DISTRICT, T WILL BE JUST A FEW MINUTES TO GEDDES.
TOO BAD THE CURRENTS ARE WEAK IN THIS AREA. I'D RATHER THAT YOU COULD RIDE A ZONE WAVE THAN RUN THE ROOFTOPS.
BRONNIS, ARE YOU GETTING THIS THROUGH MY GOGGLE INPUTS?
I'M GETTING IT, BUT...
TALON... PUT YOUR HOT GLOVE ON ITS CHEST.
BITLINK IS UPLOADING DATA. READOUTS INDICATE, SOMEHOW...IT'S ALIVE. NOT JUST A STATUE, BUT A FOSSILIZED ZONE TEK. SHOW ME MORE.
AROUND THE CORNER-- MORE STATUES, BRONNIS. BY THE DAR, WHAT IS THIS?
ADJUST YOUR GOGGLE INPUTS. NEED TO RE-CALIBRATE FOR HIGHER FREQUENCIES.
BETTER?
BETTER. AND WORSE. I'M DETECTING A SUPER HIGH SOUND WAVE BANDWIDTH.
GET OUT OF THERE!

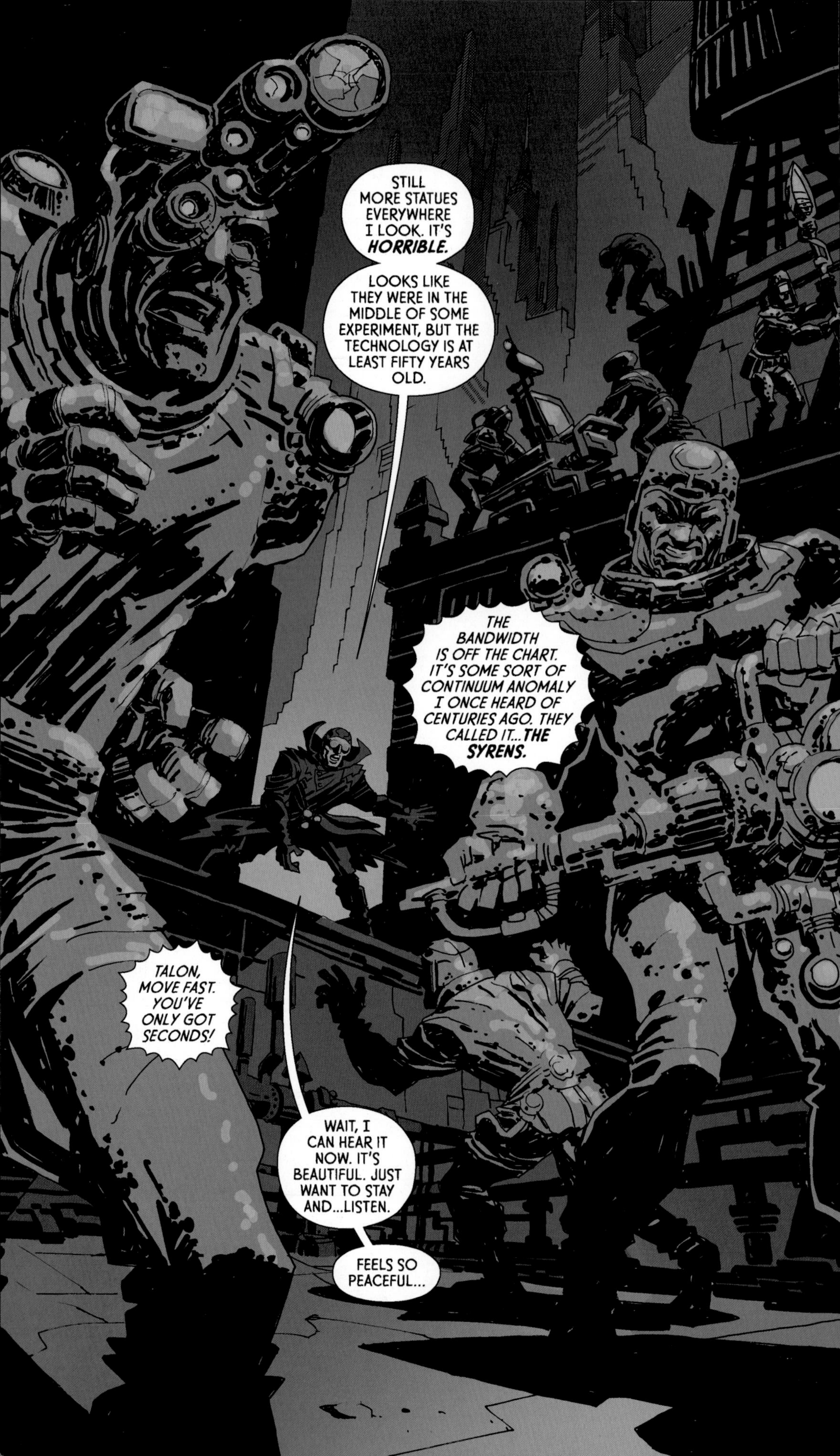
STILL MORE STATUES EVERYWHERE I LOOK. IT'S HORRIBLE.
LOOKS LIKE THEY WERE IN THE MIDDLE OF SOME EXPERIMENT, BUT THE TECHNOLOGY IS AT LEAST FIFTY YEARS OLD.
THE BANDWIDTH IS OFF THE CHART. IT'S SOME SORT OF CONTINUUM ANOMALY I ONCE HEARD OF CENTURIES AGO. THEY CALLED IT...THE SYRENS.
TALON, MOVE FAST. YOU'VE ONLY GOT SECONDS!
WAIT, I CAN HEAR IT NOW. IT'S BEAUTIFUL. JUST WANT TO STAY AND...LISTEN.
FEELS SO PEACEFUL...

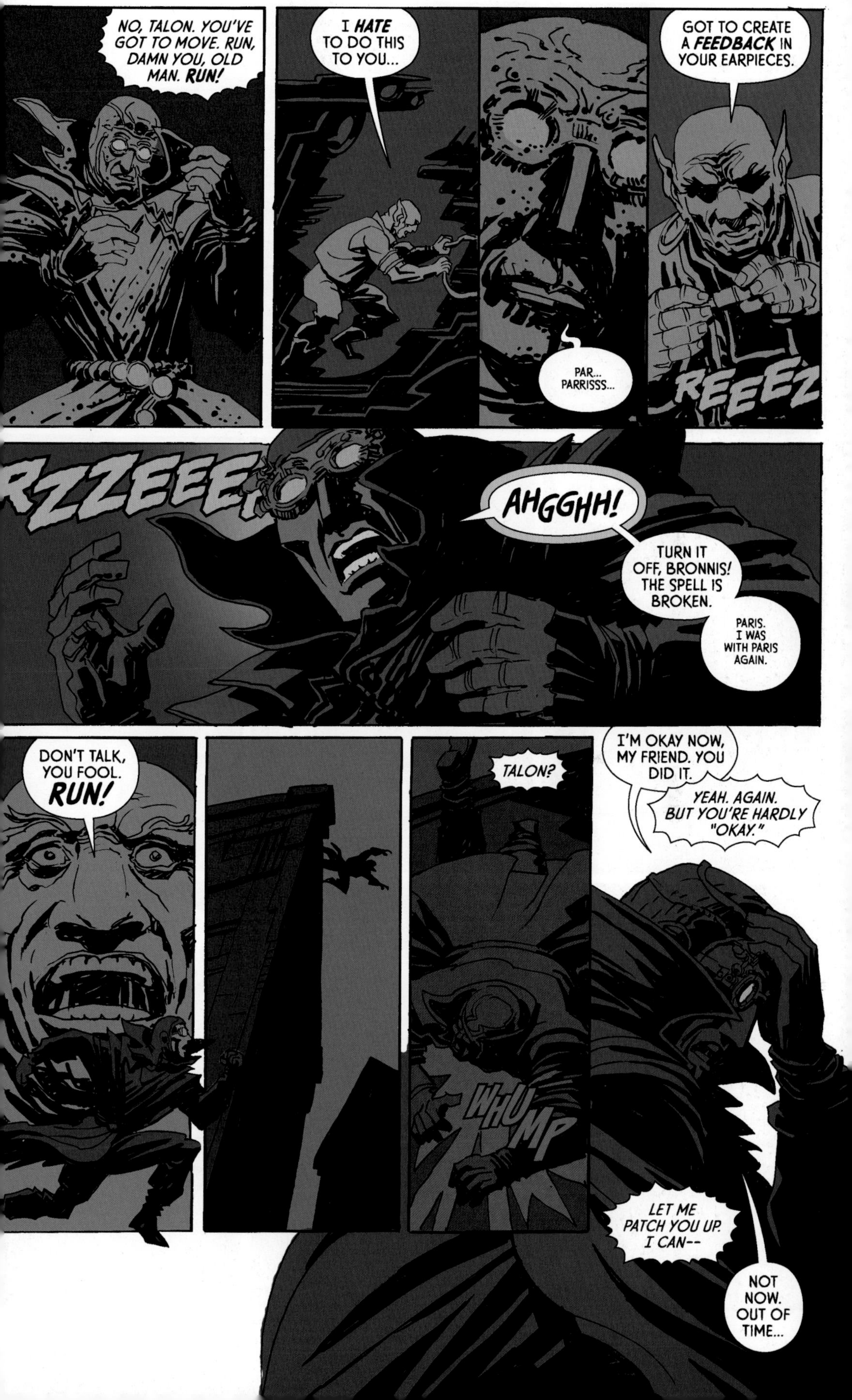
NO, TALON. YOU'VE GOT TO MOVE. RUN, DAMN YOU, OLD MAN. RUN!
I HATE TO DO THIS TO YOU...
PAR... PARRISSS...
GOT TO CREATE A FEEDBACK IN YOUR EARPIECES.
REEEZ
RZZEEE
AHGGHH!
TURN IT OFF, BRONNIS! THE SPELL IS BROKEN.
PARIS. I WAS WITH PARIS AGAIN.
DON'T TALK, YOU FOOL. RUN!
TALON?
WHUMP
I'M OKAY NOW, MY FRIEND. YOU DID IT.
YEAH. AGAIN. BUT YOU'RE HARDLY "OKAY."
LET ME PATCH YOU UP. I CAN--
NOT NOW. OUT OF TIME...

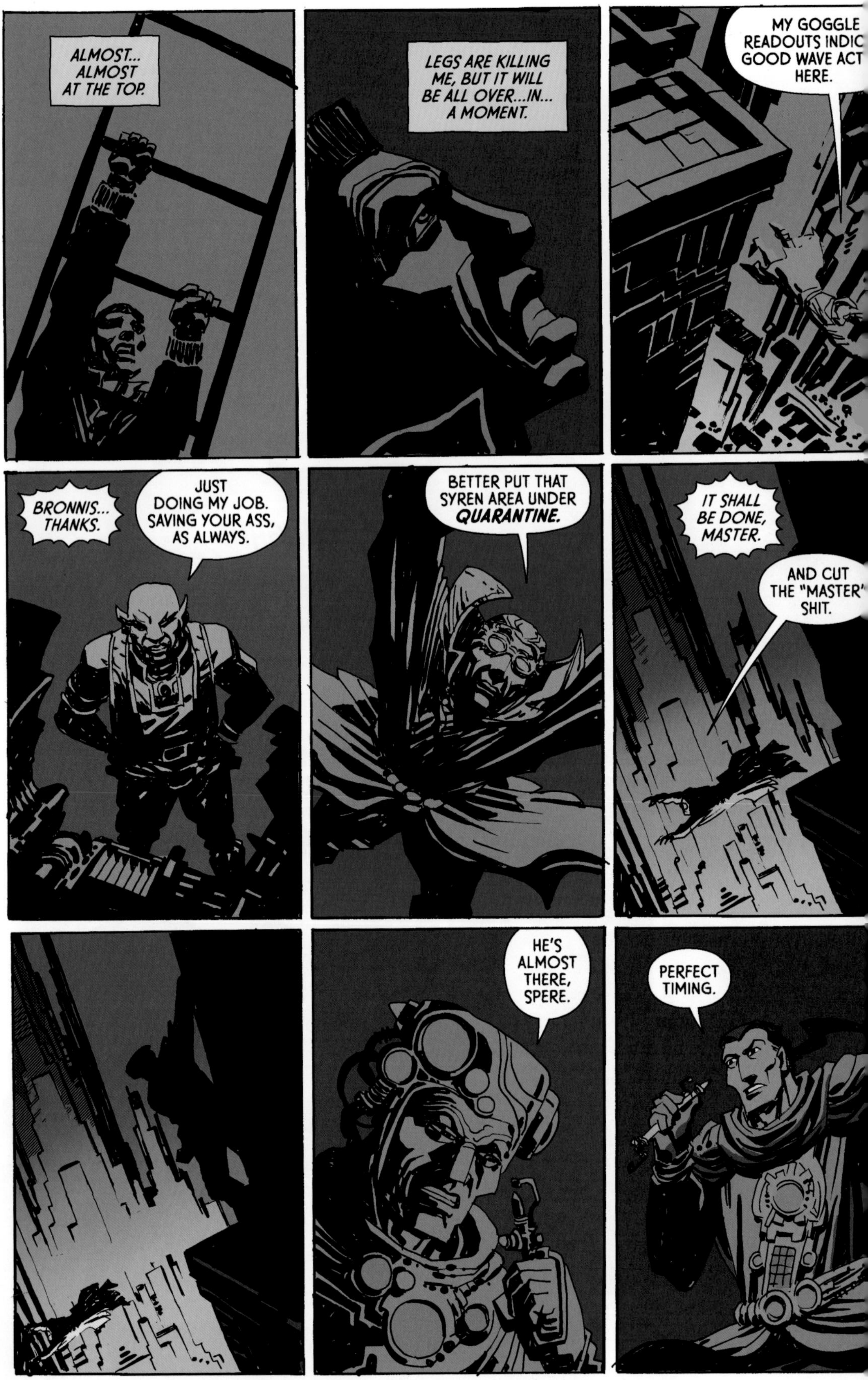
ALMOST... ALMOST AT THE TOP.
LEGS ARE KILLING ME, BUT IT WILL BE ALL OVER...IN... A MOMENT.
MY GOGGLE READOUTS INDIC GOOD WAVE ACT HERE.
BRONNIS... THANKS.
JUST DOING MY JOB. SAVING YOUR ASS, AS ALWAYS.
BETTER PUT THAT SYREN AREA UNDER QUARANTINE.
IT SHALL BE DONE, MASTER.
AND CUT THE "MASTER" SHIT.
HE'S ALMOST THERE, SPERE.
PERFECT TIMING.

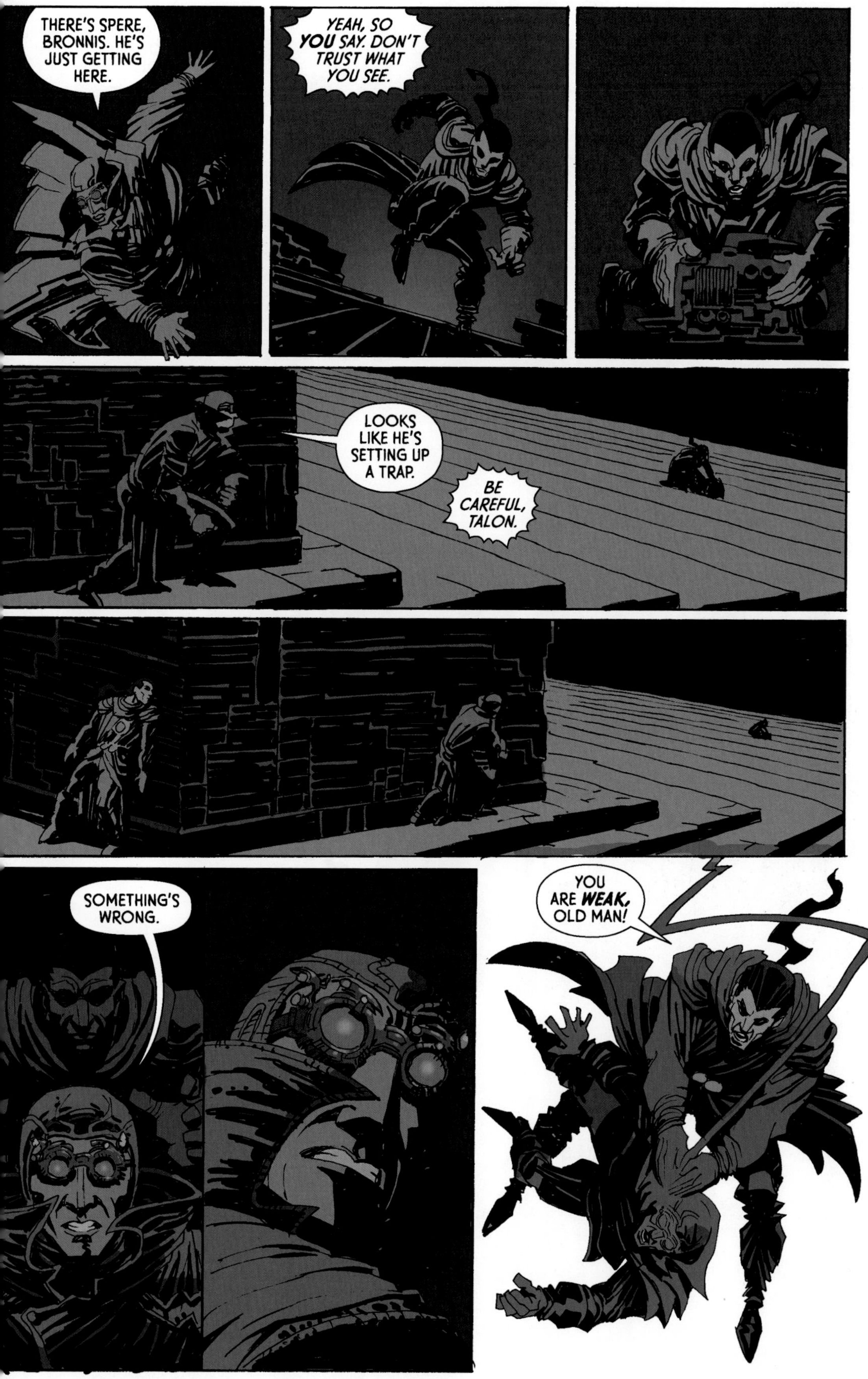
THERE'S SPERE, BRONNIS. HE'S JUST GETTING HERE.
YEAH, SO *YOU* SAY. DON'T TRUST WHAT YOU SEE.
LOOKS LIKE HE'S SETTING UP A TRAP.
BE CAREFUL, TALON.
SOMETHING'S WRONG.
YOU ARE *WEAK*, OLD MAN!

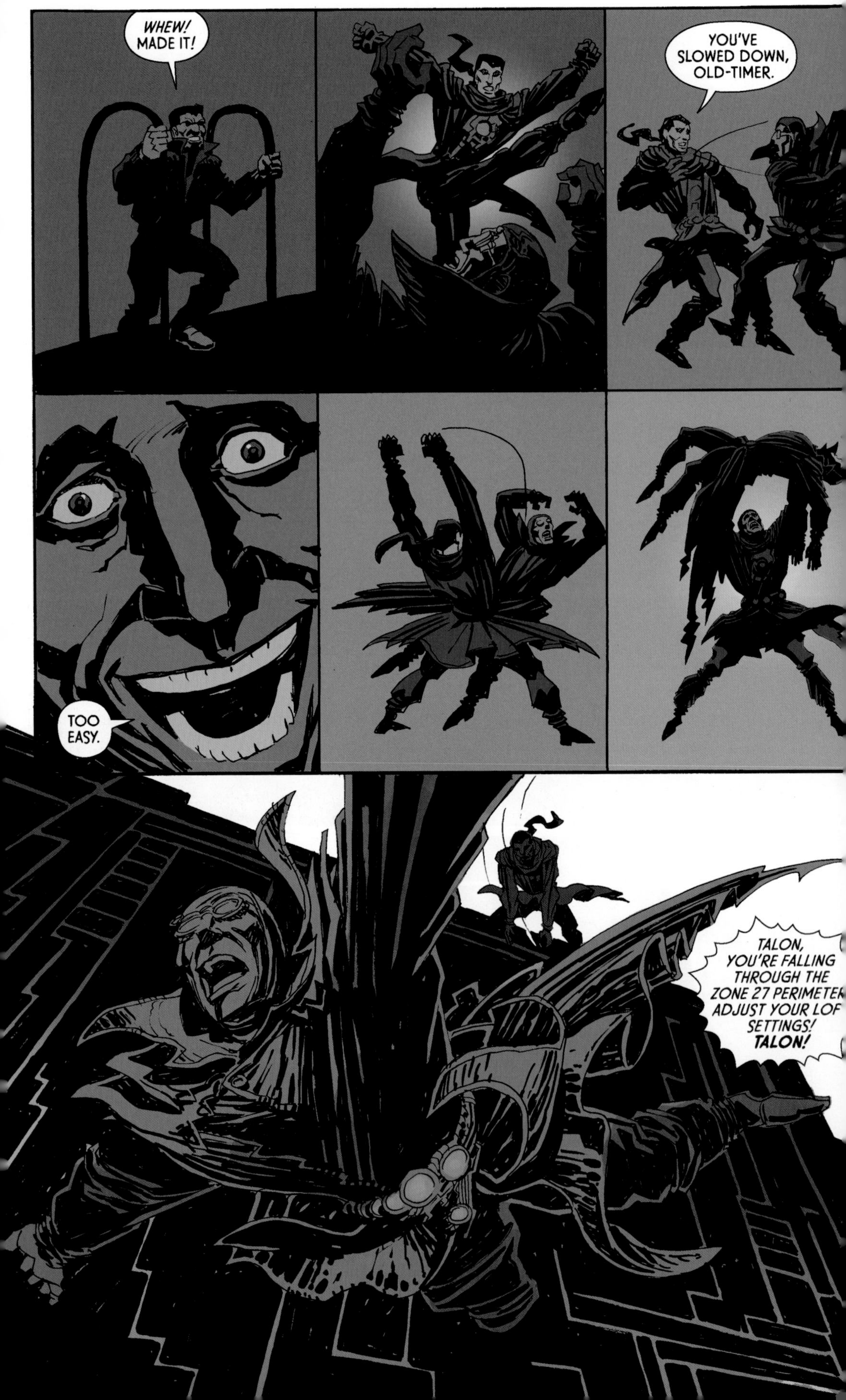
WHEW! MADE IT!
YOU'VE SLOWED DOWN, OLD-TIMER.
TOO EASY.
TALON, YOU'RE FALLING THROUGH THE ZONE 27 PERIMETER ADJUST YOUR LOF SETTINGS! TALON!

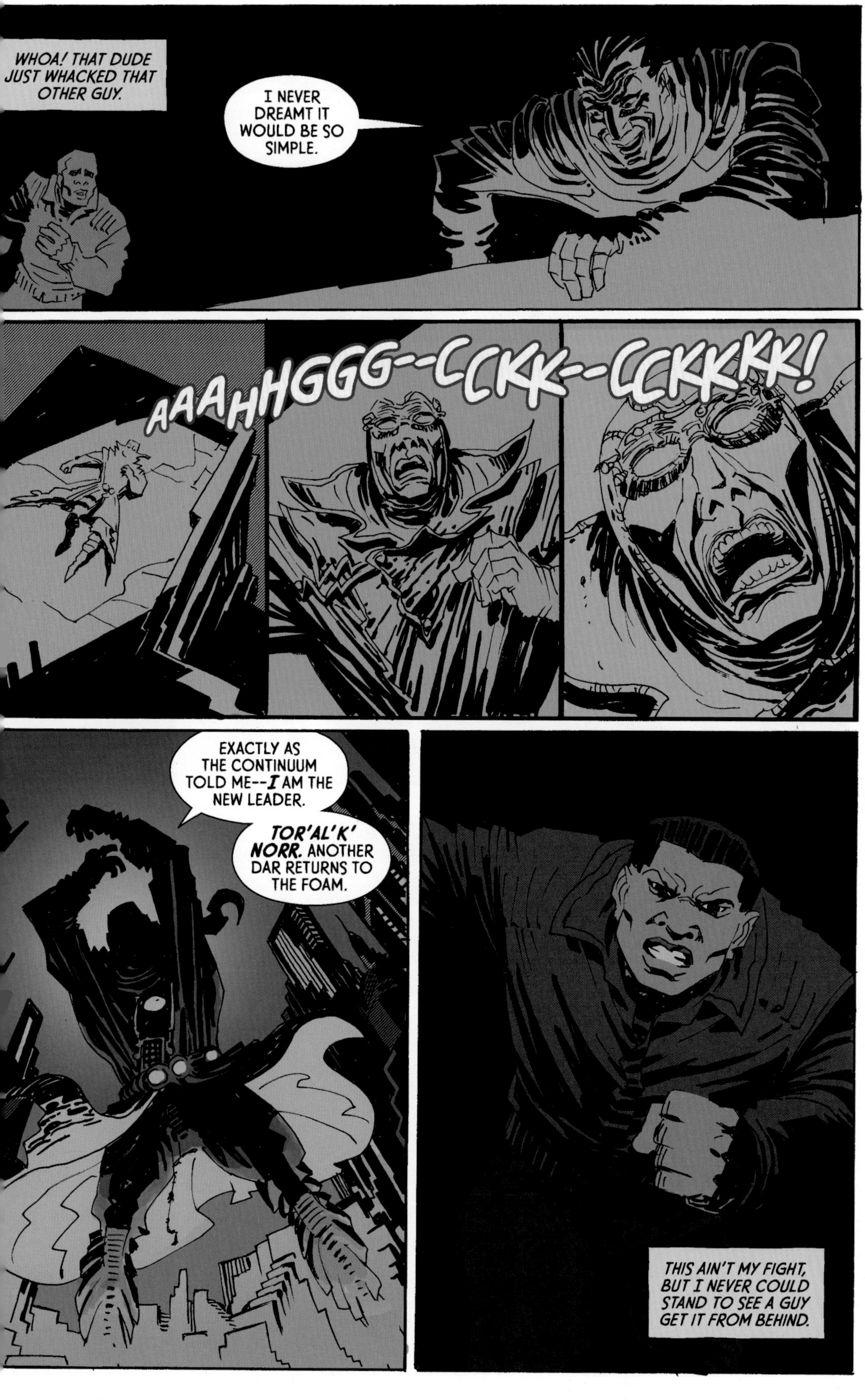
WHOA! THAT DUDE JUST WHACKED THAT OTHER GUY.
I NEVER DREAMT IT WOULD BE SO SIMPLE.
AAAHHGGG--CCKK--CCKKKK!
EXACTLY AS THE CONTINUUM TOLD ME--*I* AM THE NEW LEADER.
TOR'AL'K' NORR. ANOTHER DAR RETURNS TO THE FOAM.
THIS AIN'T MY FIGHT, BUT I NEVER COULD STAND TO SEE A GUY GET IT FROM BEHIND.

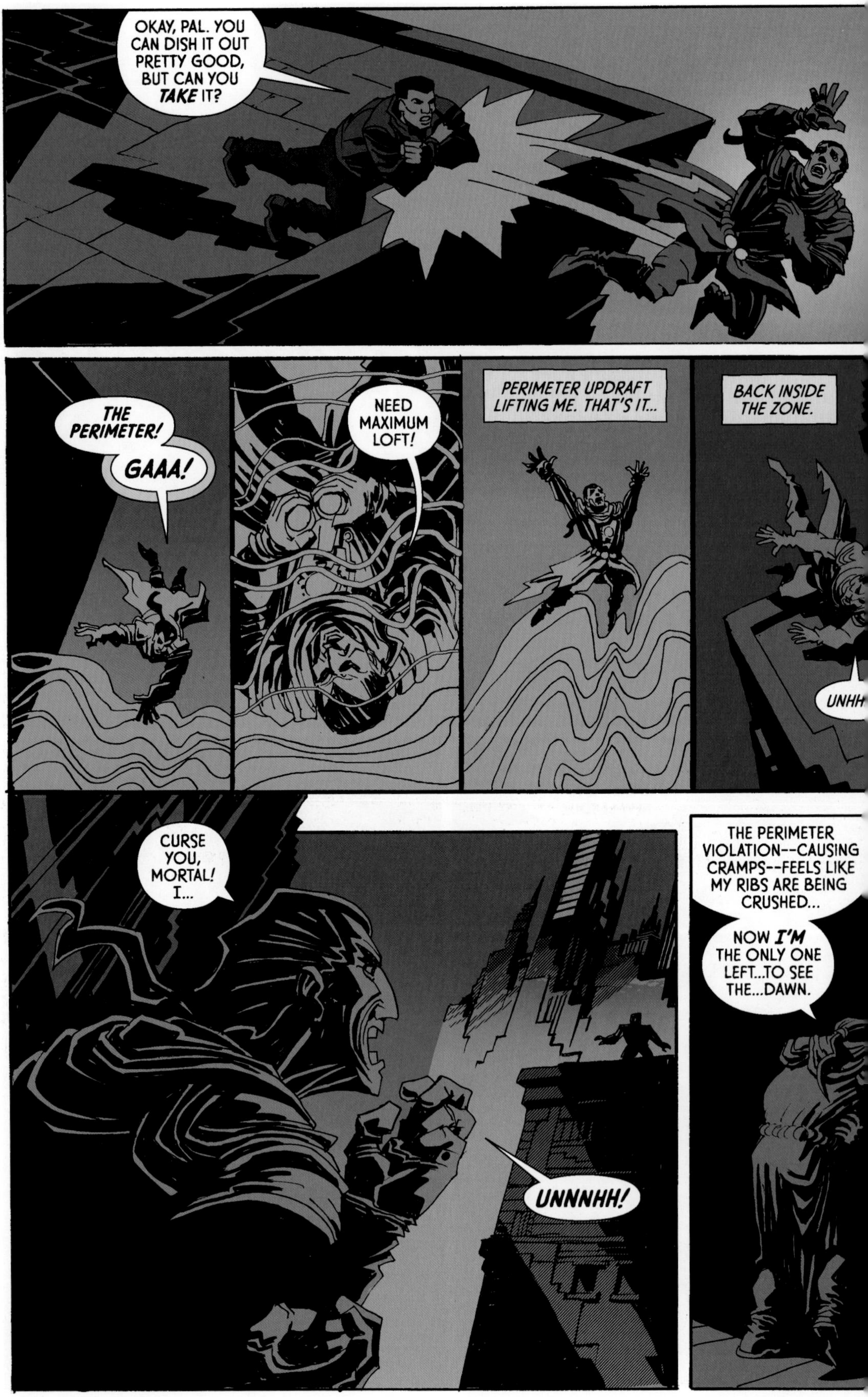
OKAY, PAL. YOU CAN DISH IT OUT PRETTY GOOD, BUT CAN YOU *TAKE* IT?
THE PERIMETER!
GAAA!
NEED MAXIMUM LOFT!
PERIMETER UPDRAFT LIFTING ME. THAT'S IT...
BACK INSIDE THE ZONE.
UNHH
CURSE YOU, MORTAL! I...
UNNNHH!
THE PERIMETER VIOLATION--CAUSING CRAMPS--FEELS LIKE MY RIBS ARE BEING CRUSHED...
NOW *I'M* THE ONLY ONE LEFT...TO SEE THE...DAWN.

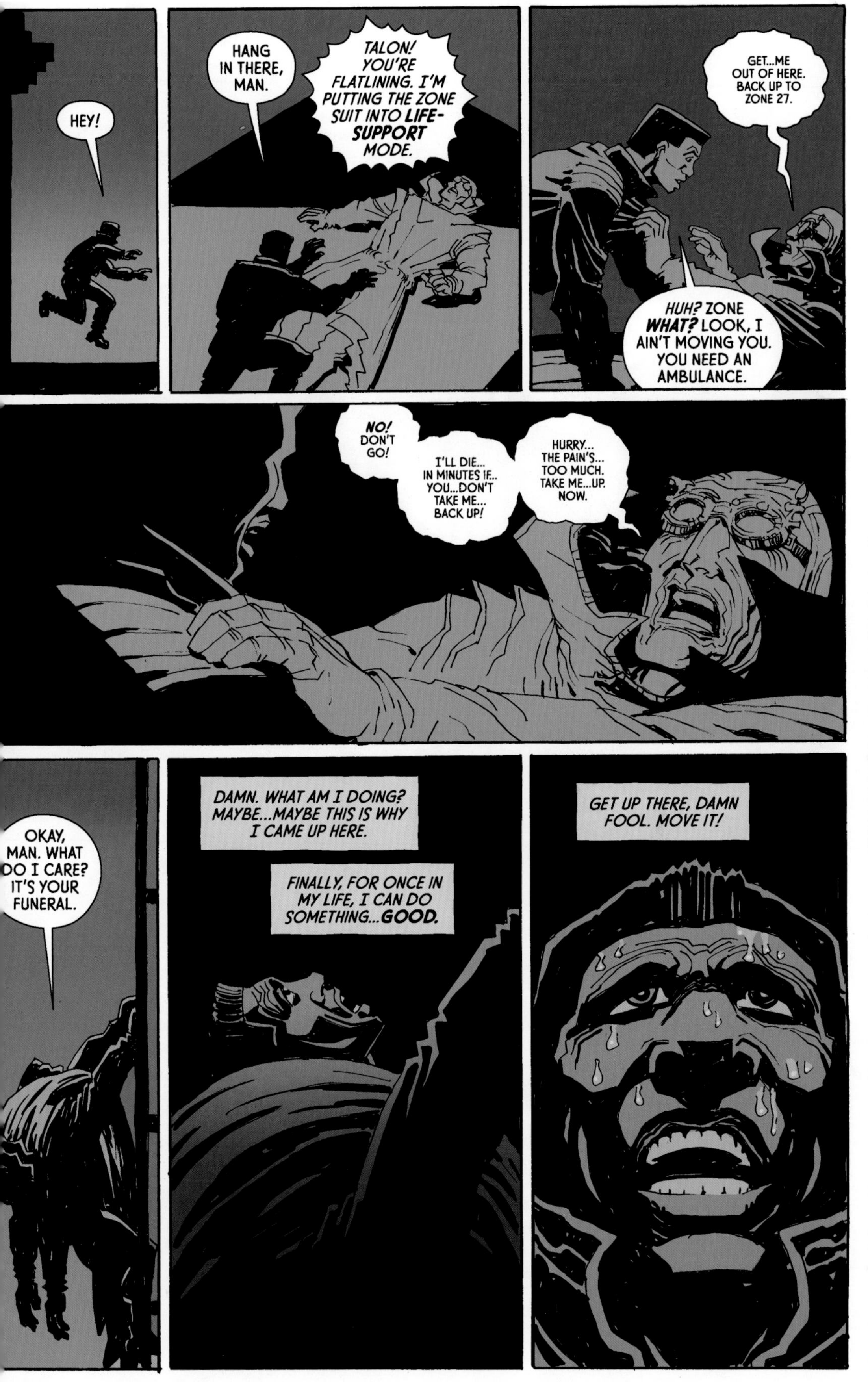
HEY!
HANG IN THERE, MAN.
TALON! YOU'RE FLATLINING. I'M PUTTING THE ZONE SUIT INTO LIFE-SUPPORT MODE.
GET...ME OUT OF HERE. BACK UP TO ZONE 27.
HUH? ZONE WHAT? LOOK, I AIN'T MOVING YOU. YOU NEED AN AMBULANCE.
NO! DON'T GO!
I'LL DIE... IN MINUTES IF.. YOU...DON'T TAKE ME... BACK UP!
HURRY... THE PAIN'S... TOO MUCH. TAKE ME...UP. NOW.
OKAY, MAN. WHAT DO I CARE? IT'S YOUR FUNERAL.
DAMN. WHAT AM I DOING? MAYBE...MAYBE THIS IS WHY I CAME UP HERE.
FINALLY, FOR ONCE IN MY LIFE, I CAN DO SOMETHING...GOOD.
GET UP THERE, DAMN FOOL. MOVE IT!

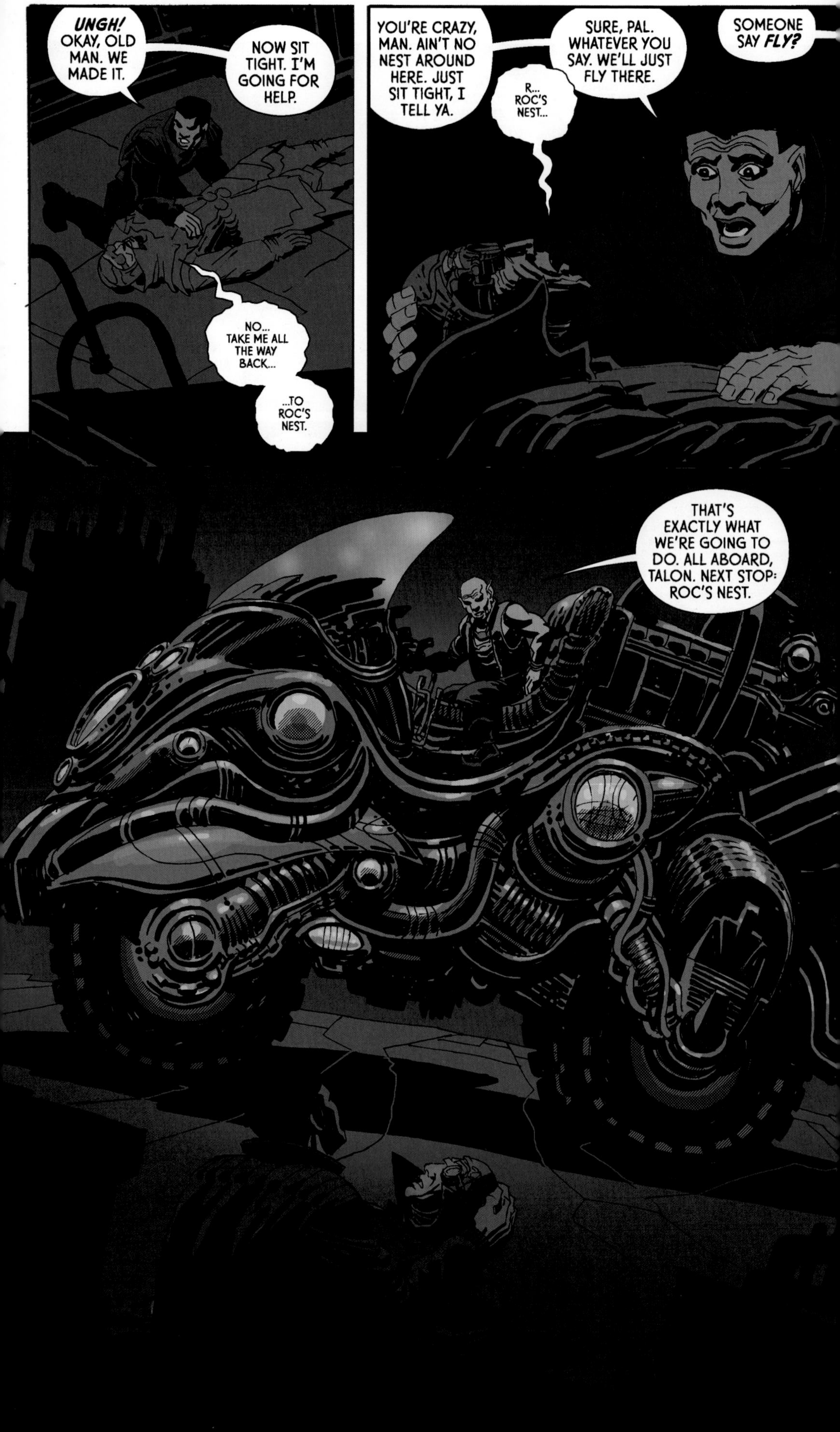
UNGH! OKAY, OLD MAN. WE MADE IT.
NOW SIT TIGHT. I'M GOING FOR HELP.
NO... TAKE ME ALL THE WAY BACK...
...TO ROC'S NEST.
YOU'RE CRAZY, MAN. AIN'T NO NEST AROUND HERE. JUST SIT TIGHT, I TELL YA.
R... ROC'S NEST...
SURE, PAL. WHATEVER YOU SAY. WE'LL JUST FLY THERE.
SOMEONE SAY FLY?
THAT'S EXACTLY WHAT WE'RE GOING TO DO. ALL ABOARD, TALON. NEXT STOP: ROC'S NEST.

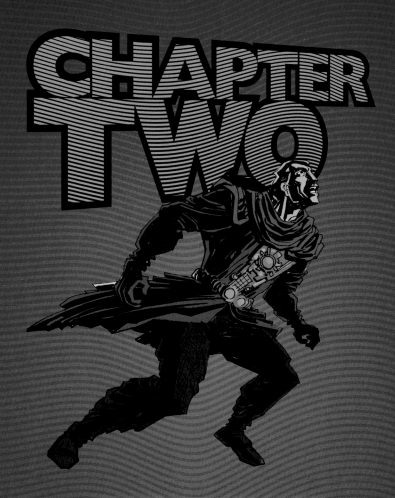

CHAPTER TWO

DEATH AND LIFE

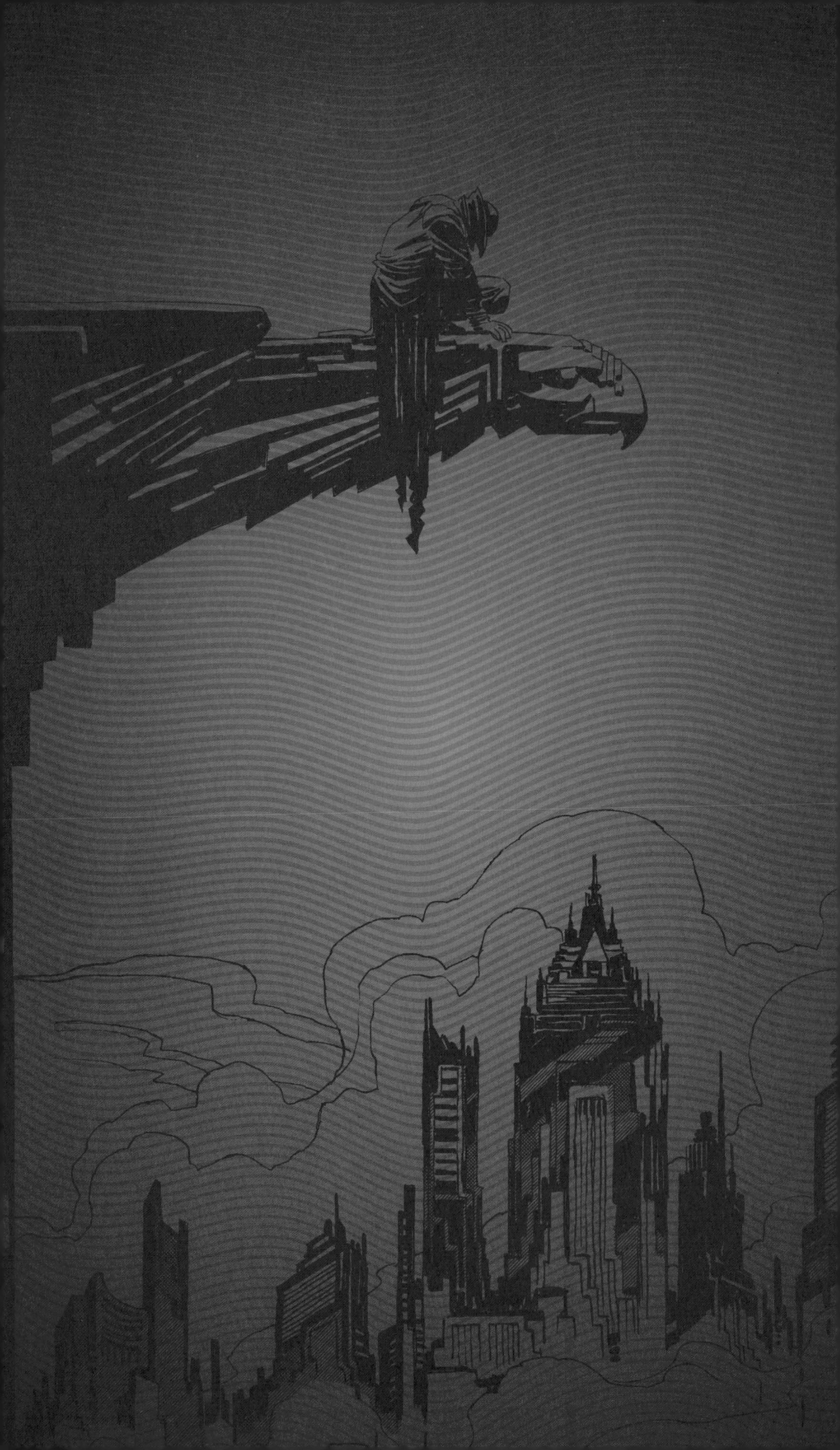

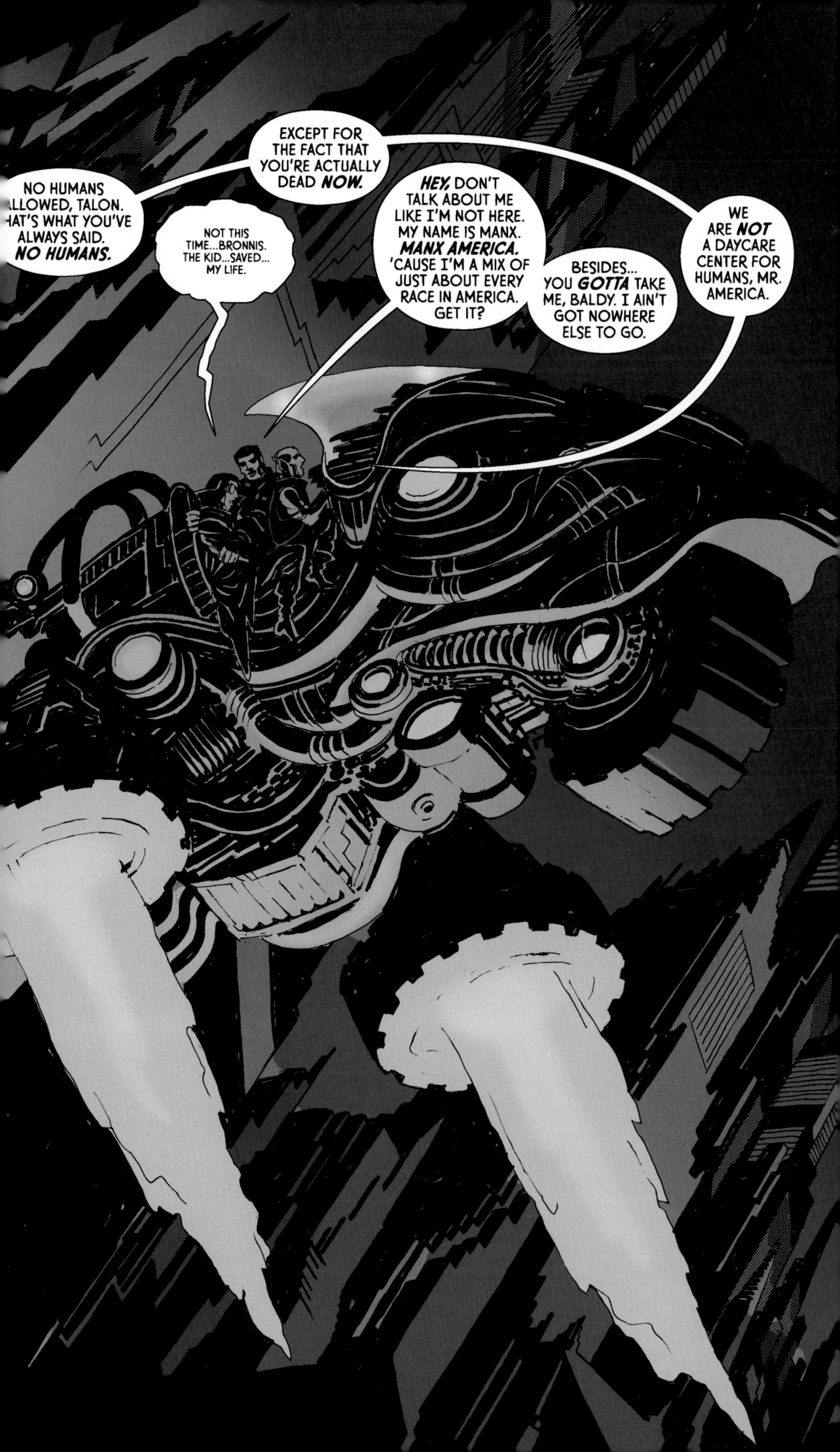
NO HUMANS LLOWED, TALON. HAT'S WHAT YOU'VE ALWAYS SAID. ***NO HUMANS.***
EXCEPT FOR THE FACT THAT YOU'RE ACTUALLY DEAD ***NOW.***
NOT THIS TIME...BRONNIS. THE KID...SAVED... MY LIFE.
HEY, DON'T TALK ABOUT ME LIKE I'M NOT HERE. MY NAME IS MANX. ***MANX AMERICA.*** 'CAUSE I'M A MIX OF JUST ABOUT EVERY RACE IN AMERICA. GET IT?
BESIDES... YOU ***GOTTA*** TAKE ME, BALDY. I AIN'T GOT NOWHERE ELSE TO GO.
WE ARE ***NOT*** A DAYCARE CENTER FOR HUMANS, MR. AMERICA.

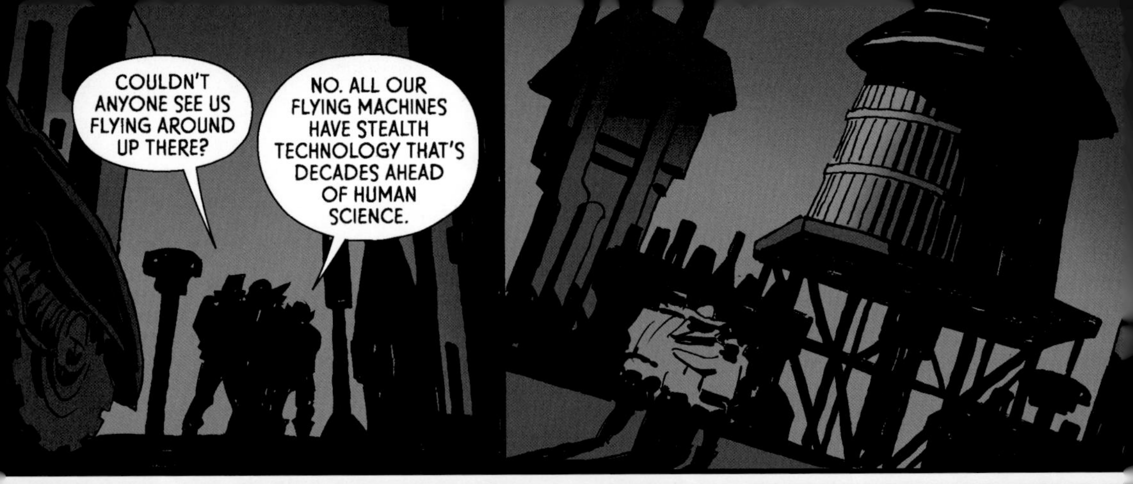
COULDN'T ANYONE SEE US FLYING AROUND UP THERE?
NO. ALL OUR FLYING MACHINES HAVE STEALTH TECHNOLOGY THAT'S DECADES AHEAD OF HUMAN SCIENCE.
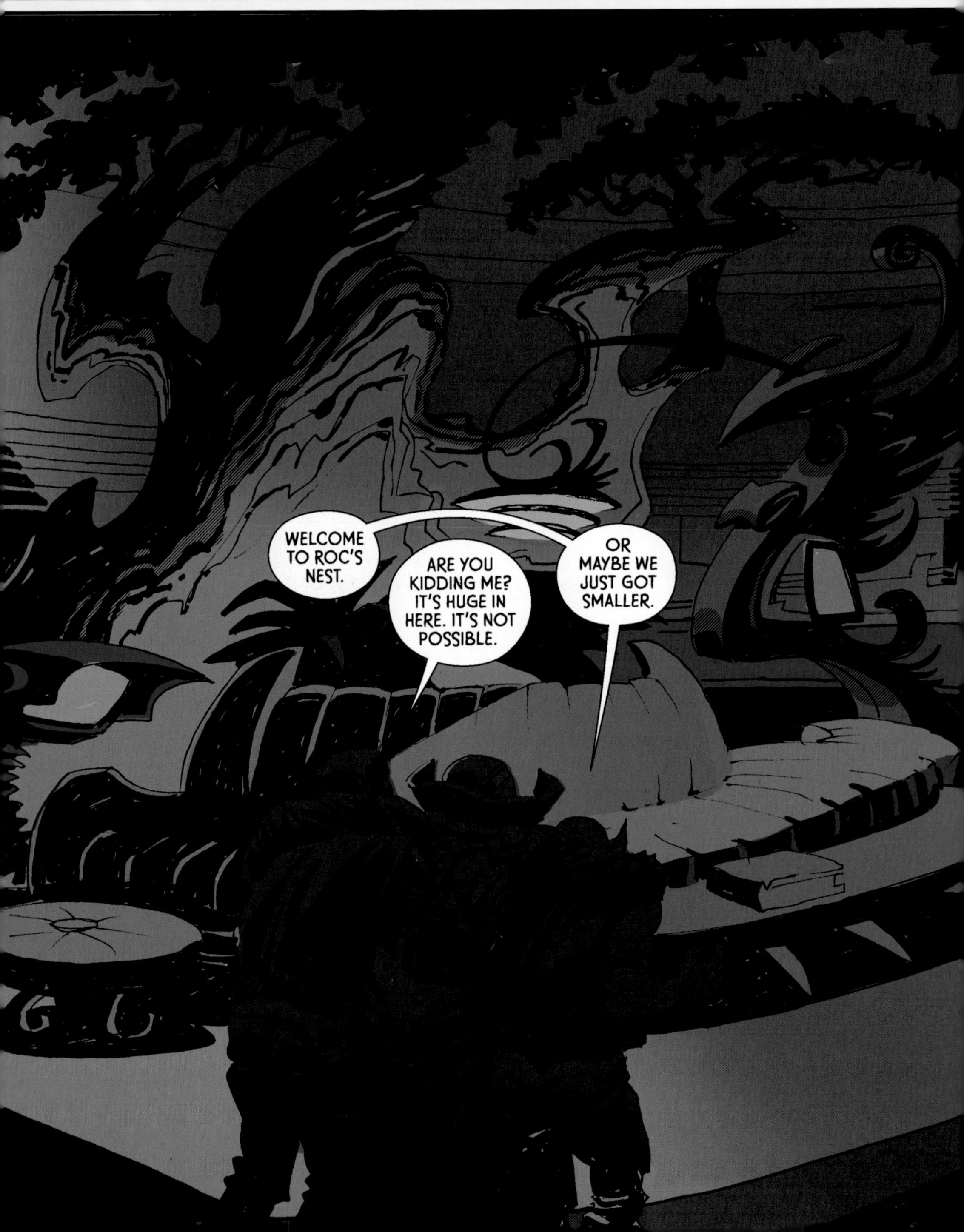
WELCOME TO ROC'S NEST.
ARE YOU KIDDING ME? IT'S HUGE IN HERE. IT'S NOT POSSIBLE.
OR MAYBE WE JUST GOT SMALLER.

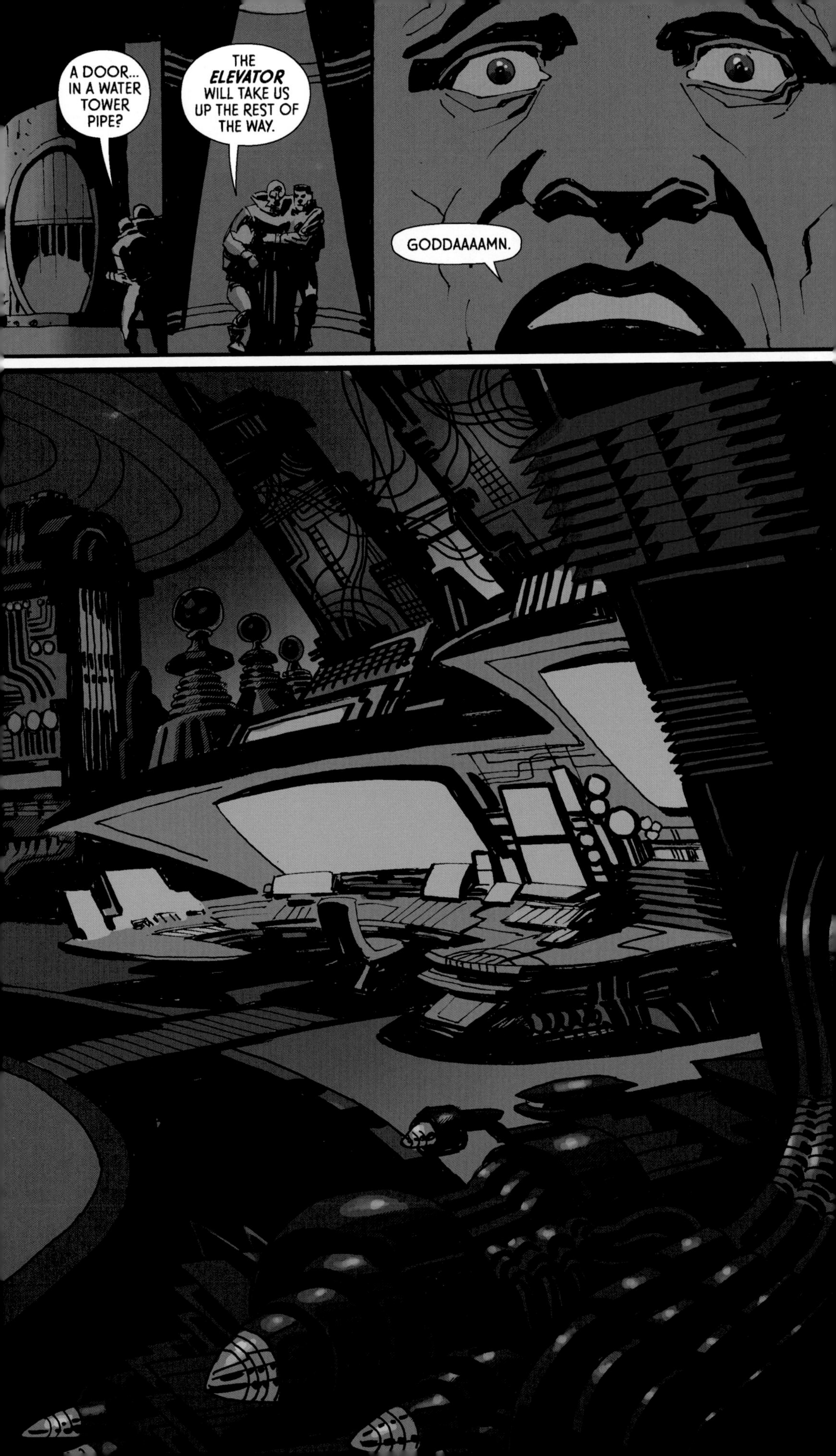
A DOOR... IN A WATER TOWER PIPE?
THE ELEVATOR WILL TAKE US UP THE REST OF THE WAY.
GODDAAAAMN.

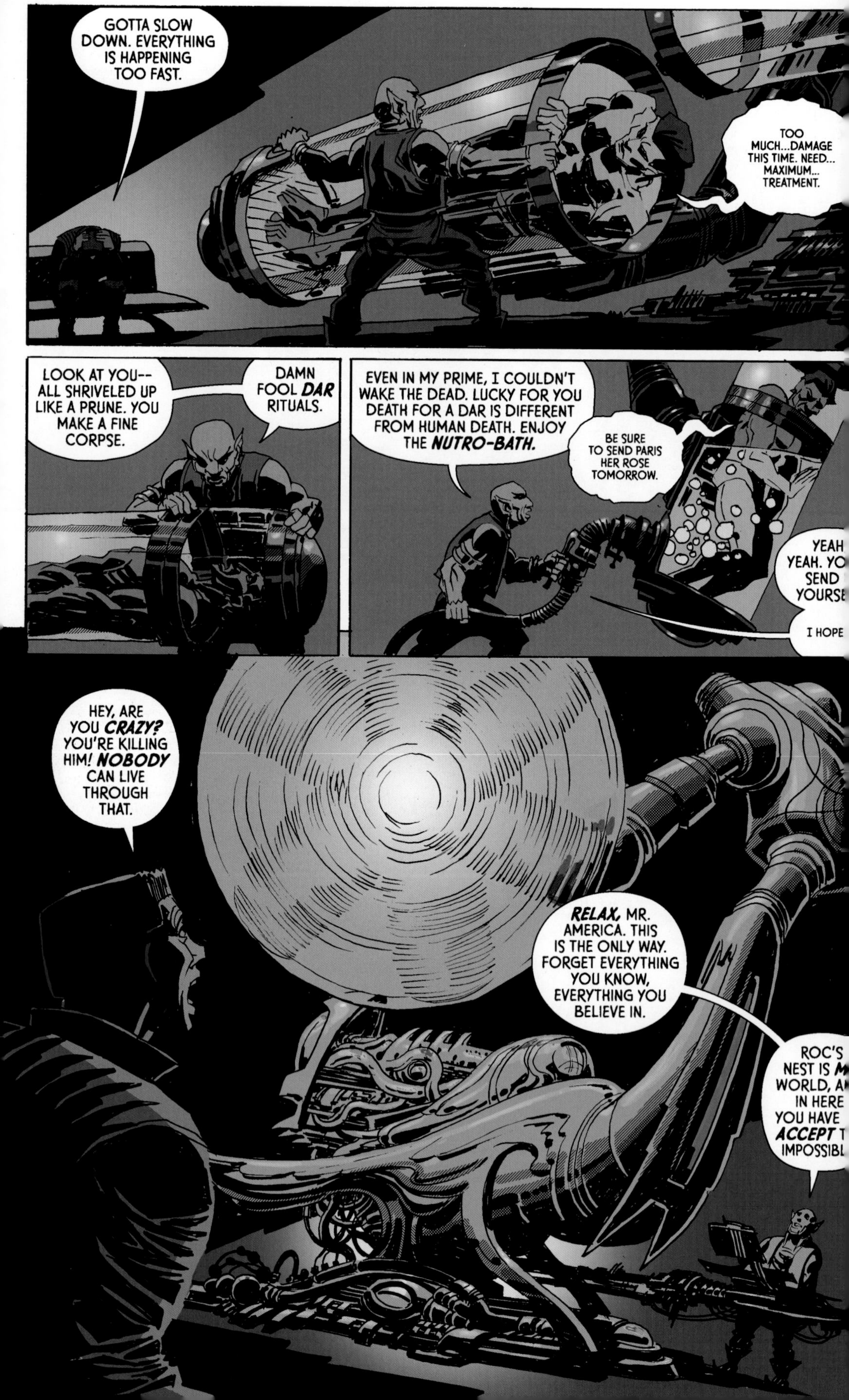

GOTTA SLOW DOWN. EVERYTHING IS HAPPENING TOO FAST.
TOO MUCH...DAMAGE THIS TIME. NEED... MAXIMUM... TREATMENT.
LOOK AT YOU-- ALL SHRIVELED UP LIKE A PRUNE. YOU MAKE A FINE CORPSE.
DAMN FOOL **DAR** RITUALS.
EVEN IN MY PRIME, I COULDN'T WAKE THE DEAD. LUCKY FOR YOU DEATH FOR A DAR IS DIFFERENT FROM HUMAN DEATH. ENJOY THE **NUTRO-BATH.**
BE SURE TO SEND PARIS HER ROSE TOMORROW.
YEAH YEAH.
HEY, ARE YOU **CRAZY?** YOU'RE KILLING HIM! **NOBODY** CAN LIVE THROUGH THAT.
RELAX, MR. AMERICA. THIS IS THE ONLY WAY. FORGET EVERYTHING YOU KNOW, EVERYTHING YOU BELIEVE IN.
ROC'S NEST IS
IN HERE YOU HAVE

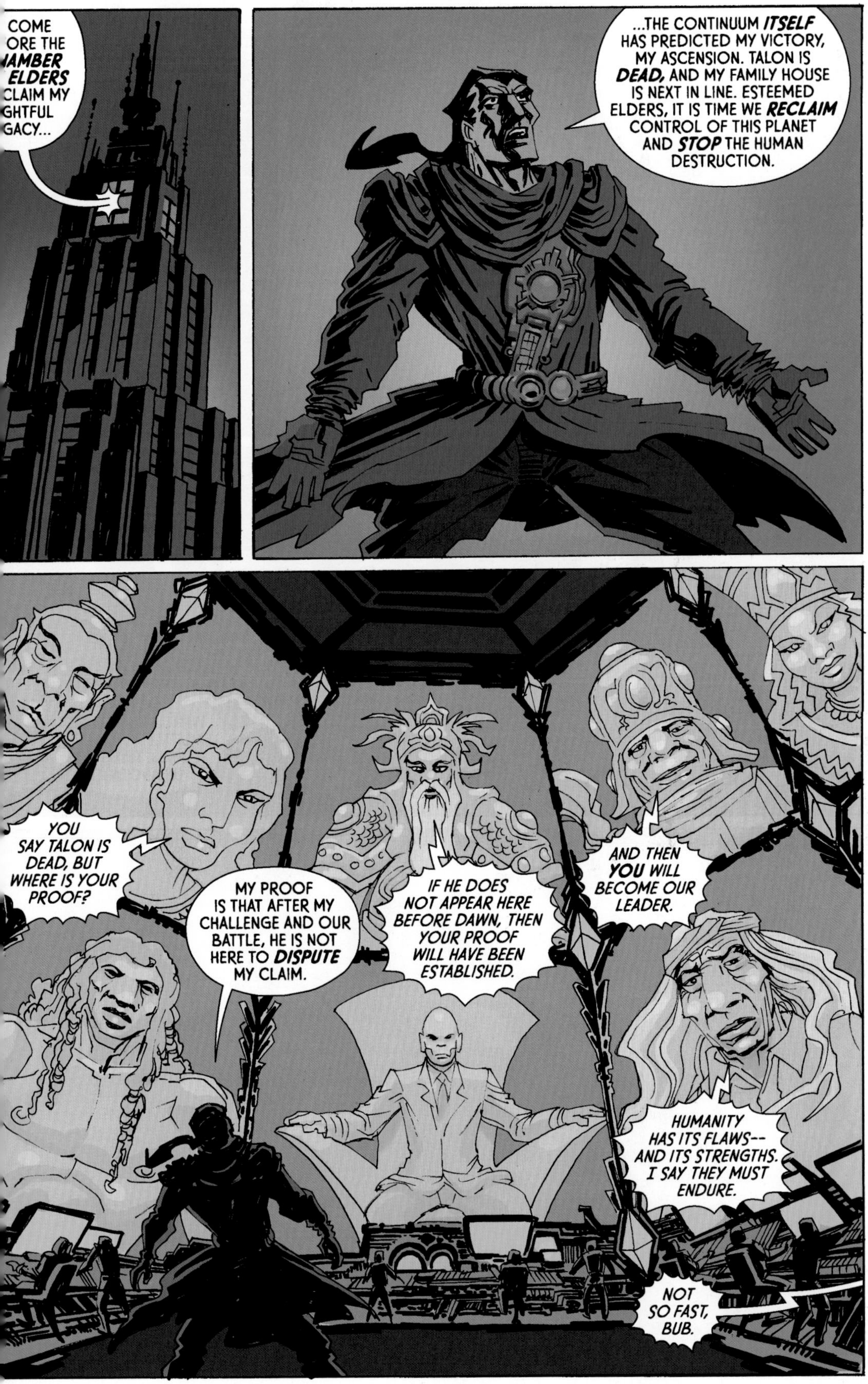
COME
ORE THE
AMBER
ELDERS
CLAIM MY
GHTFUL
GACY...
...THE CONTINUUM ITSELF HAS PREDICTED MY VICTORY, MY ASCENSION. TALON IS DEAD, AND MY FAMILY HOUSE IS NEXT IN LINE. ESTEEMED ELDERS, IT IS TIME WE RECLAIM CONTROL OF THIS PLANET AND STOP THE HUMAN DESTRUCTION.
YOU SAY TALON IS DEAD, BUT WHERE IS YOUR PROOF?
MY PROOF IS THAT AFTER MY CHALLENGE AND OUR BATTLE, HE IS NOT HERE TO DISPUTE MY CLAIM.
IF HE DOES NOT APPEAR HERE BEFORE DAWN, THEN YOUR PROOF WILL HAVE BEEN ESTABLISHED.
AND THEN YOU WILL BECOME OUR LEADER.
HUMANITY HAS ITS FLAWS--AND ITS STRENGTHS. I SAY THEY MUST ENDURE.
NOT SO FAST, BUB.

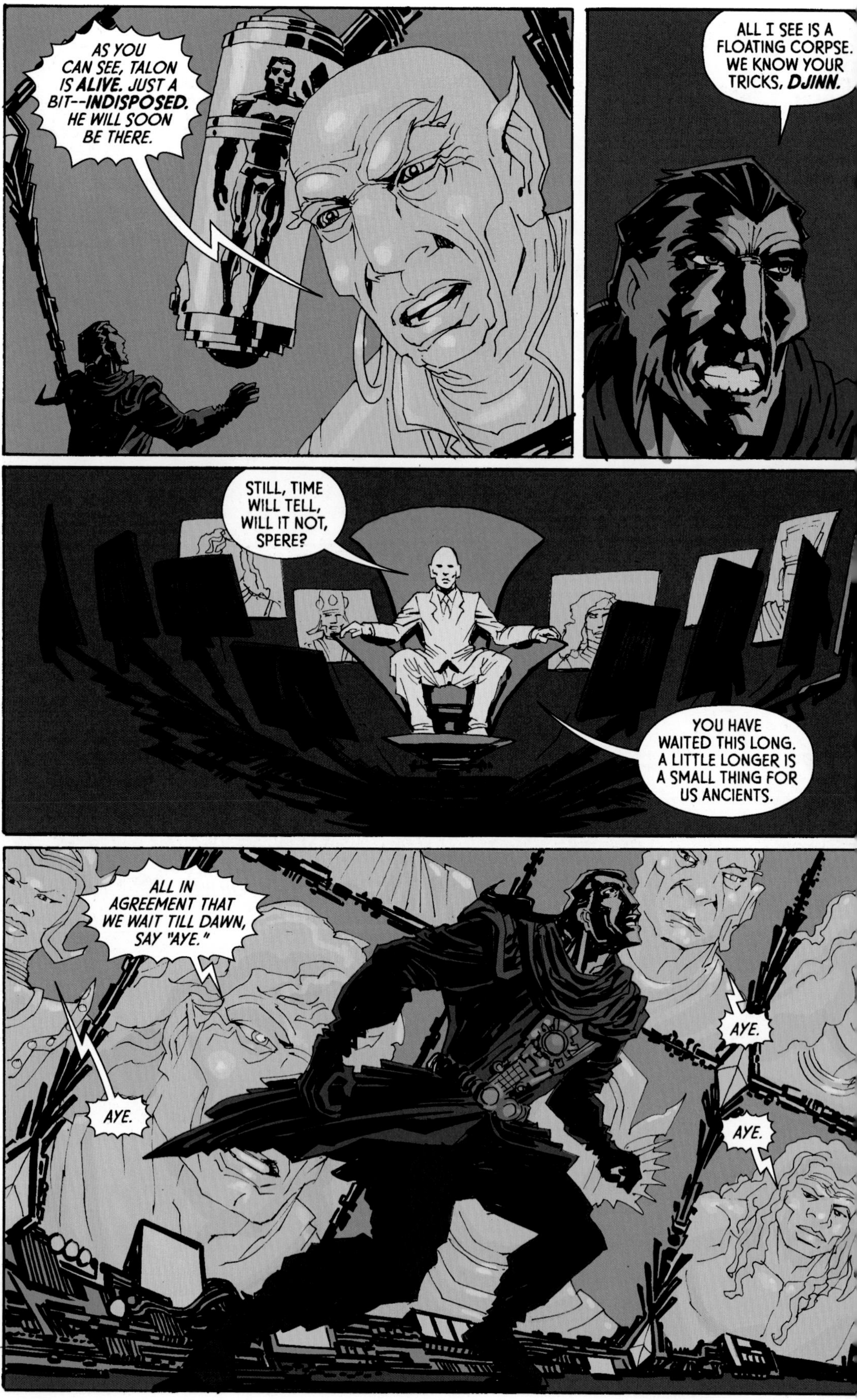
AS YOU CAN SEE, TALON IS ALIVE. JUST A BIT--INDISPOSED. HE WILL SOON BE THERE.
ALL I SEE IS A FLOATING CORPSE. WE KNOW YOUR TRICKS, DJINN.
STILL, TIME WILL TELL, WILL IT NOT, SPERE?
YOU HAVE WAITED THIS LONG. A LITTLE LONGER IS A SMALL THING FOR US ANCIENTS.
ALL IN AGREEMENT THAT WE WAIT TILL DAWN, SAY "AYE."
AYE.
AYE.
AYE.

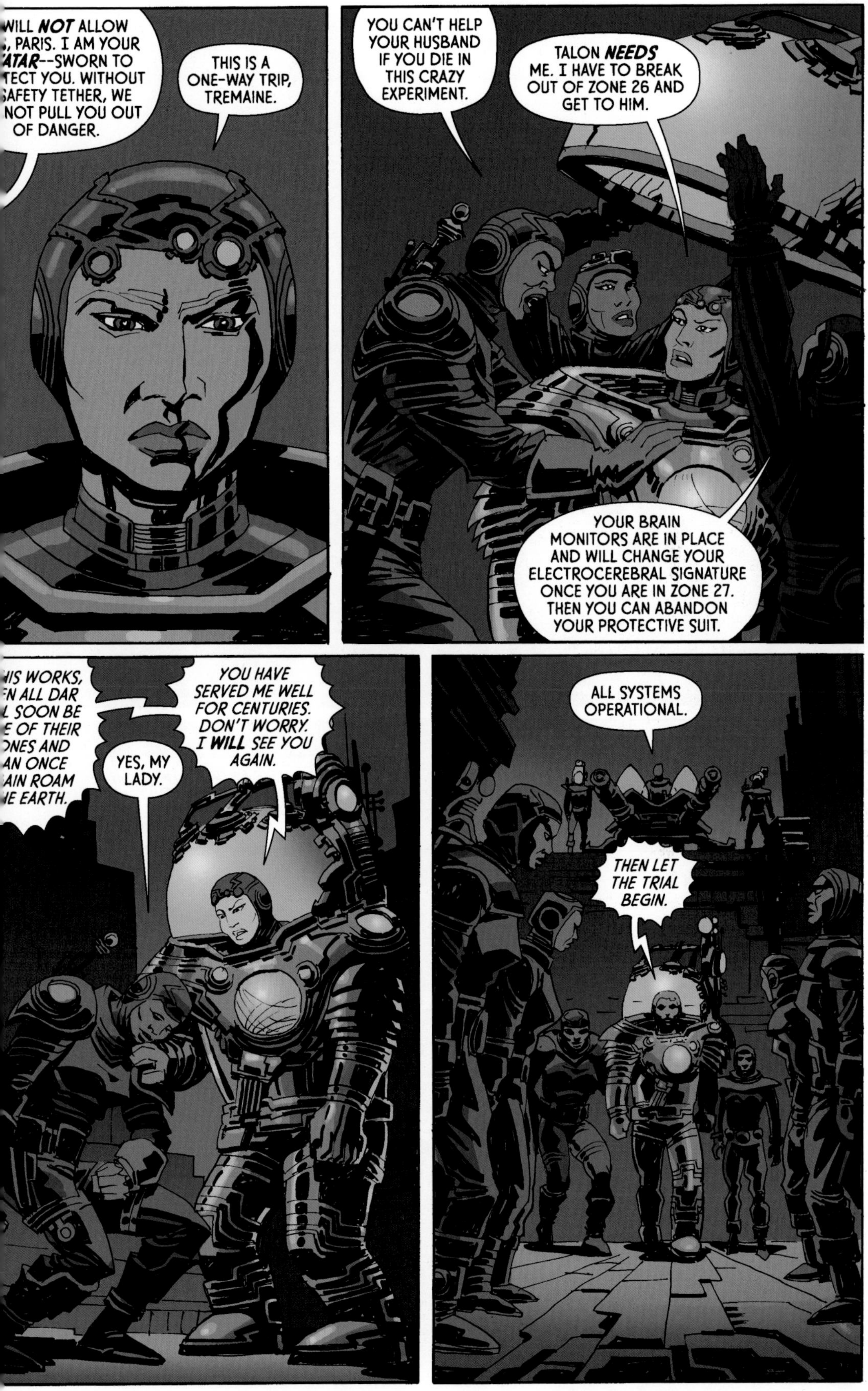

WILL NOT ALLOW , PARIS. I AM YOUR ATAR--SWORN TO TECT YOU. WITHOUT SAFETY TETHER, WE NOT PULL YOU OUT OF DANGER.
THIS IS A ONE-WAY TRIP, TREMAINE.
YOU CAN'T HELP YOUR HUSBAND IF YOU DIE IN THIS CRAZY EXPERIMENT.
TALON NEEDS ME. I HAVE TO BREAK OUT OF ZONE 26 AND GET TO HIM.
YOUR BRAIN MONITORS ARE IN PLACE AND WILL CHANGE YOUR ELECTROCEREBRAL SIGNATURE ONCE YOU ARE IN ZONE 27. THEN YOU CAN ABANDON YOUR PROTECTIVE SUIT.
IIS WORKS, N ALL DAR L SOON BE E OF THEIR ONES AND AN ONCE AIN ROAM IE EARTH.
YOU HAVE SERVED ME WELL FOR CENTURIES. DON'T WORRY. I WILL SEE YOU AGAIN.
YES, MY LADY.
ALL SYSTEMS OPERATIONAL.
THEN LET THE TRIAL BEGIN.

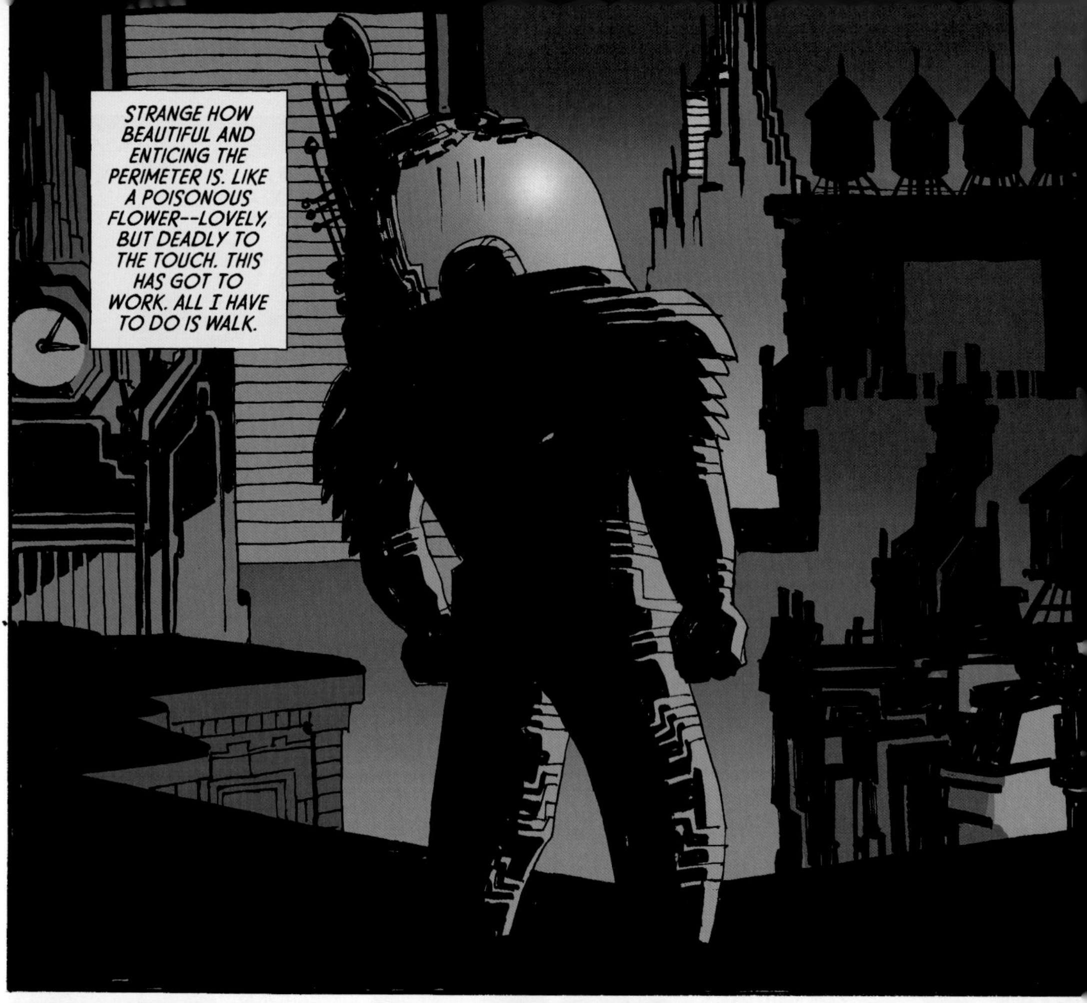
STRANGE HOW BEAUTIFUL AND ENTICING THE PERIMETER IS. LIKE A POISONOUS FLOWER--LOVELY, BUT DEADLY TO THE TOUCH. THIS HAS GOT TO WORK. ALL I HAVE TO DO IS WALK.

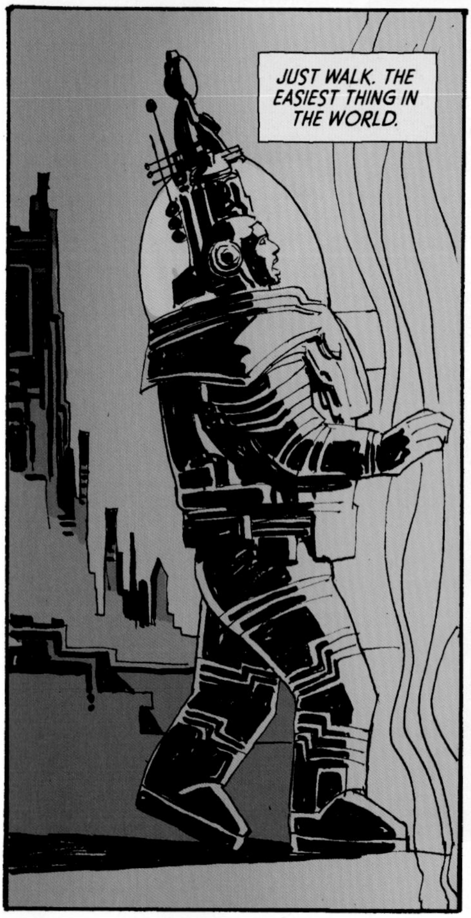
JUST WALK. THE EASIEST THING IN THE WORLD.

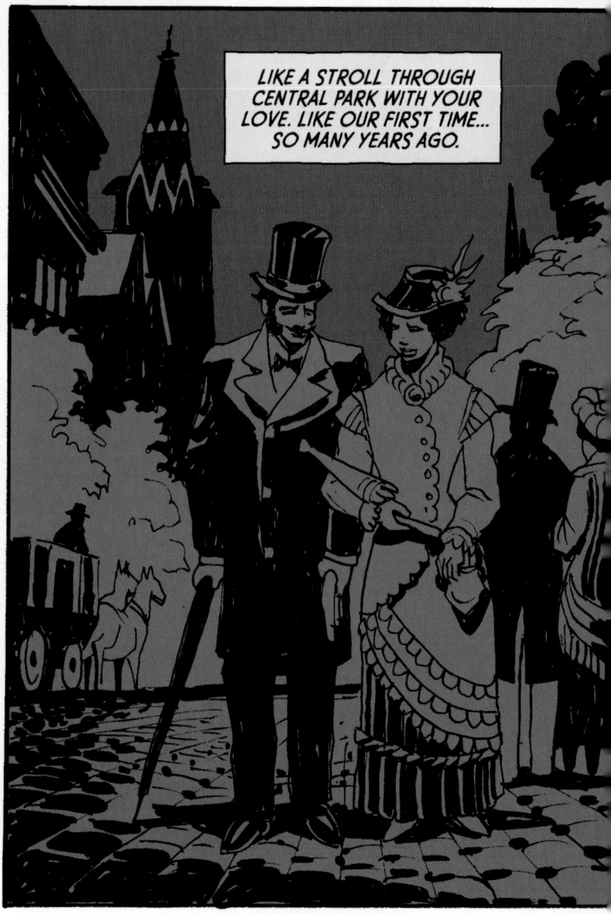
LIKE A STROLL THROUGH CENTRAL PARK WITH YOUR LOVE. LIKE OUR FIRST TIME... SO MANY YEARS AGO.

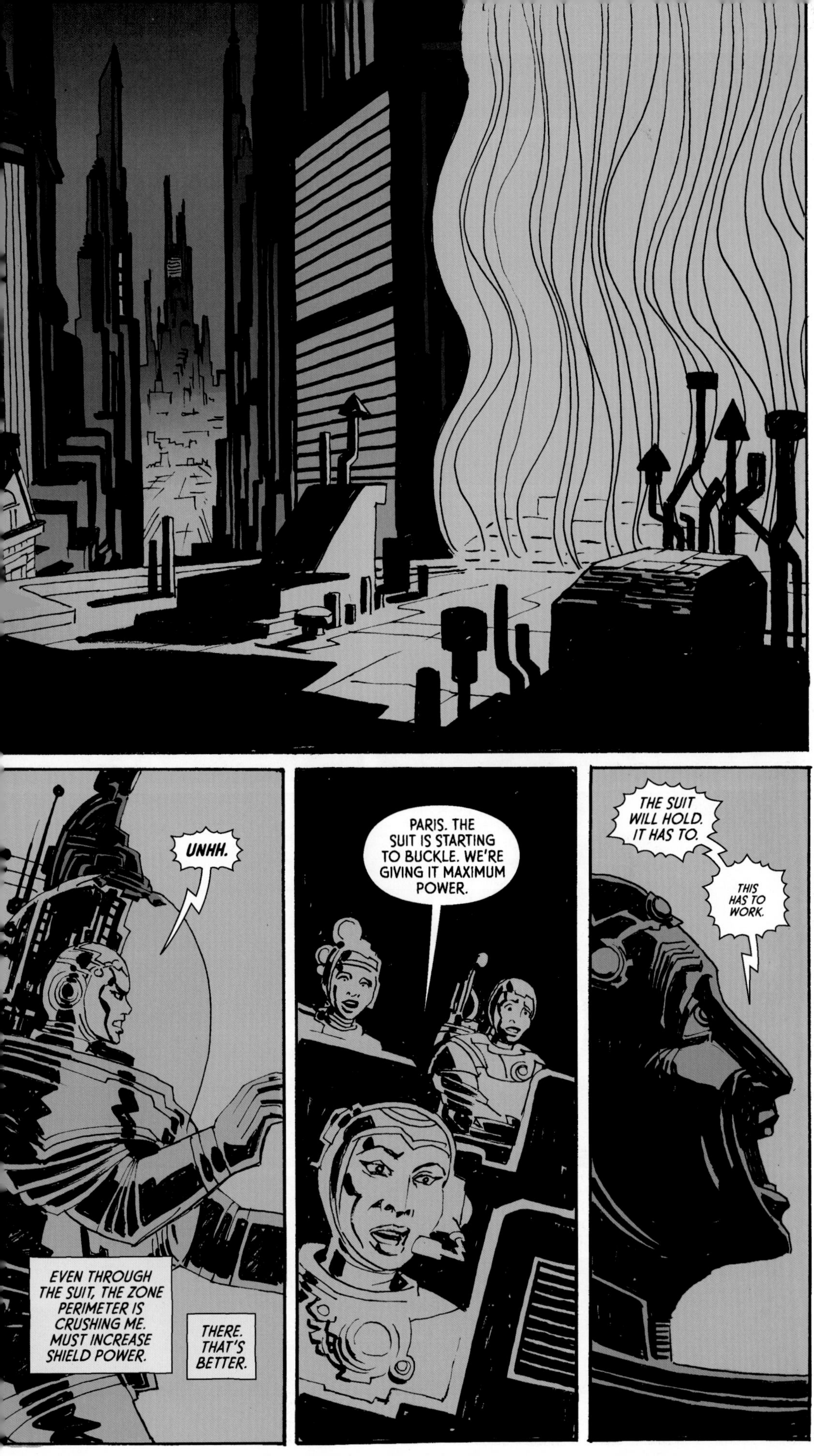
UNHH.
EVEN THROUGH THE SUIT, THE ZONE PERIMETER IS CRUSHING ME. MUST INCREASE SHIELD POWER.
THERE. THAT'S BETTER.
PARIS. THE SUIT IS STARTING TO BUCKLE. WE'RE GIVING IT MAXIMUM POWER.
THE SUIT WILL HOLD. IT HAS TO.
THIS HAS TO WORK.

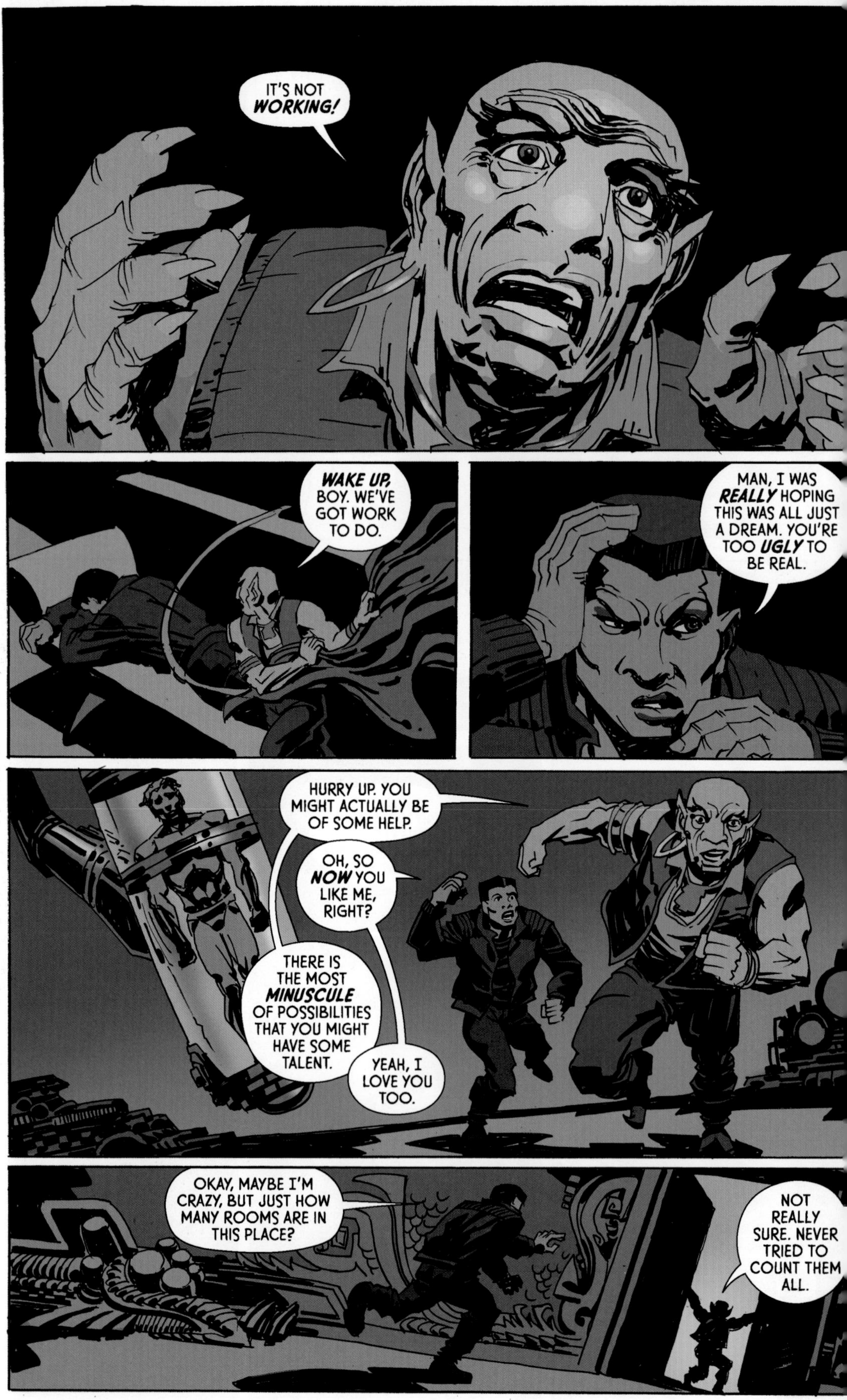
IT'S NOT ***WORKING!***
WAKE UP, BOY. WE'VE GOT WORK TO DO.
MAN, I WAS ***REALLY*** HOPING THIS WAS ALL JUST A DREAM. YOU'RE TOO ***UGLY*** TO BE REAL.
HURRY UP. YOU MIGHT ACTUALLY BE OF SOME HELP.
OH, SO ***NOW*** YOU LIKE ME, RIGHT?
THERE IS THE MOST ***MINUSCULE*** OF POSSIBILITIES THAT YOU MIGHT HAVE SOME TALENT.
YEAH, I LOVE YOU TOO.
OKAY, MAYBE I'M CRAZY, BUT JUST HOW MANY ROOMS ARE IN THIS PLACE?
NOT REALLY SURE. NEVER TRIED TO COUNT THEM ALL.

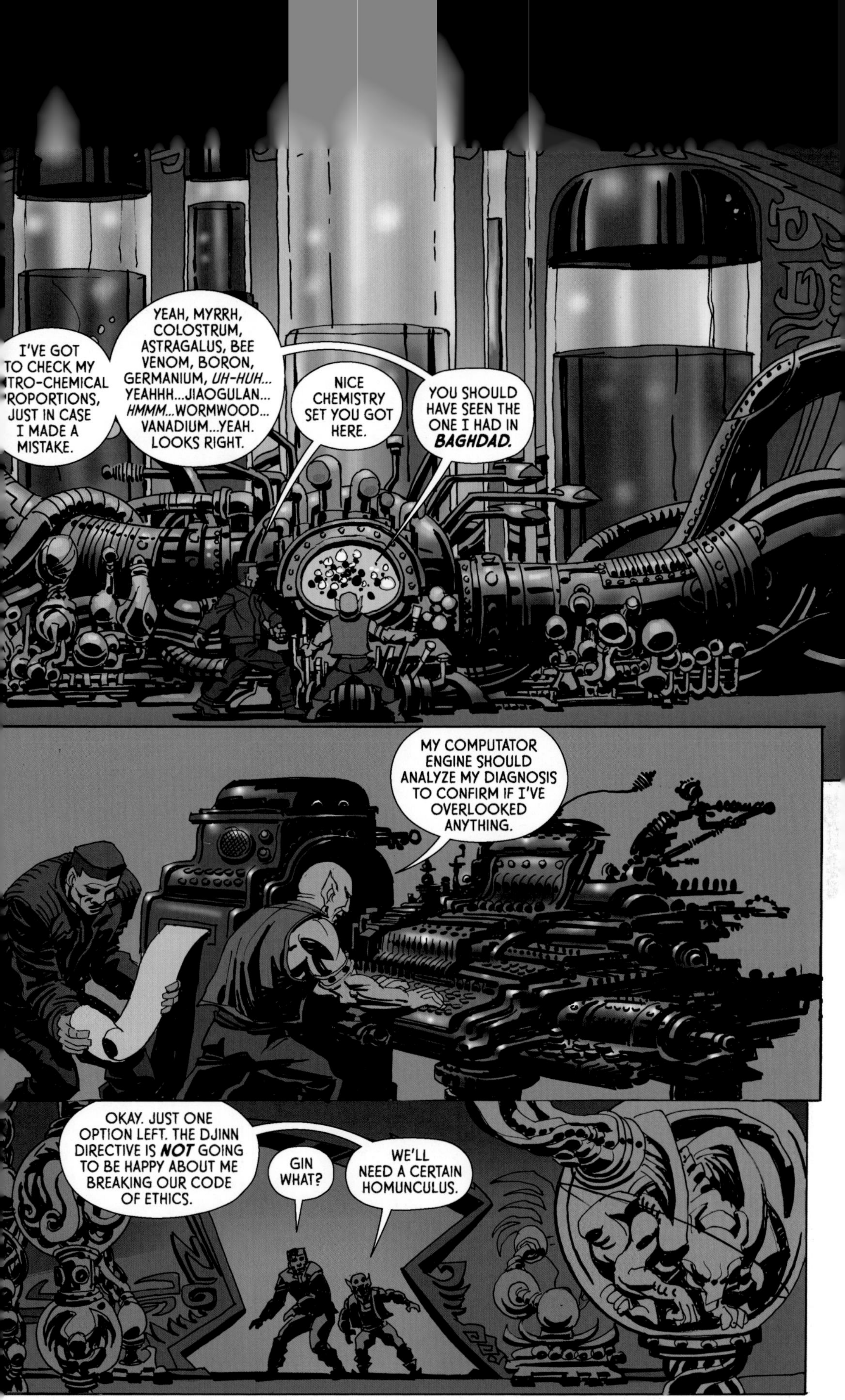
I'VE GOT TO CHECK MY
TRO-CHEMICAL
ROPORTIONS,
JUST IN CASE
I MADE A MISTAKE.
YEAH, MYRRH, COLOSTRUM, ASTRAGALUS, BEE VENOM, BORON, GERMANIUM, *UH-HUH...* YEAHHH...JIAOGULAN... *HMMM...*WORMWOOD... VANADIUM...YEAH. LOOKS RIGHT.
NICE CHEMISTRY SET YOU GOT HERE.
YOU SHOULD HAVE SEEN THE ONE I HAD IN ***BAGHDAD.***
MY COMPUTATOR ENGINE SHOULD ANALYZE MY DIAGNOSIS TO CONFIRM IF I'VE OVERLOOKED ANYTHING.
OKAY. JUST ONE OPTION LEFT. THE DJINN DIRECTIVE IS ***NOT*** GOING TO BE HAPPY ABOUT ME BREAKING OUR CODE OF ETHICS.
GIN WHAT?
WE'LL NEED A CERTAIN HOMUNCULUS.

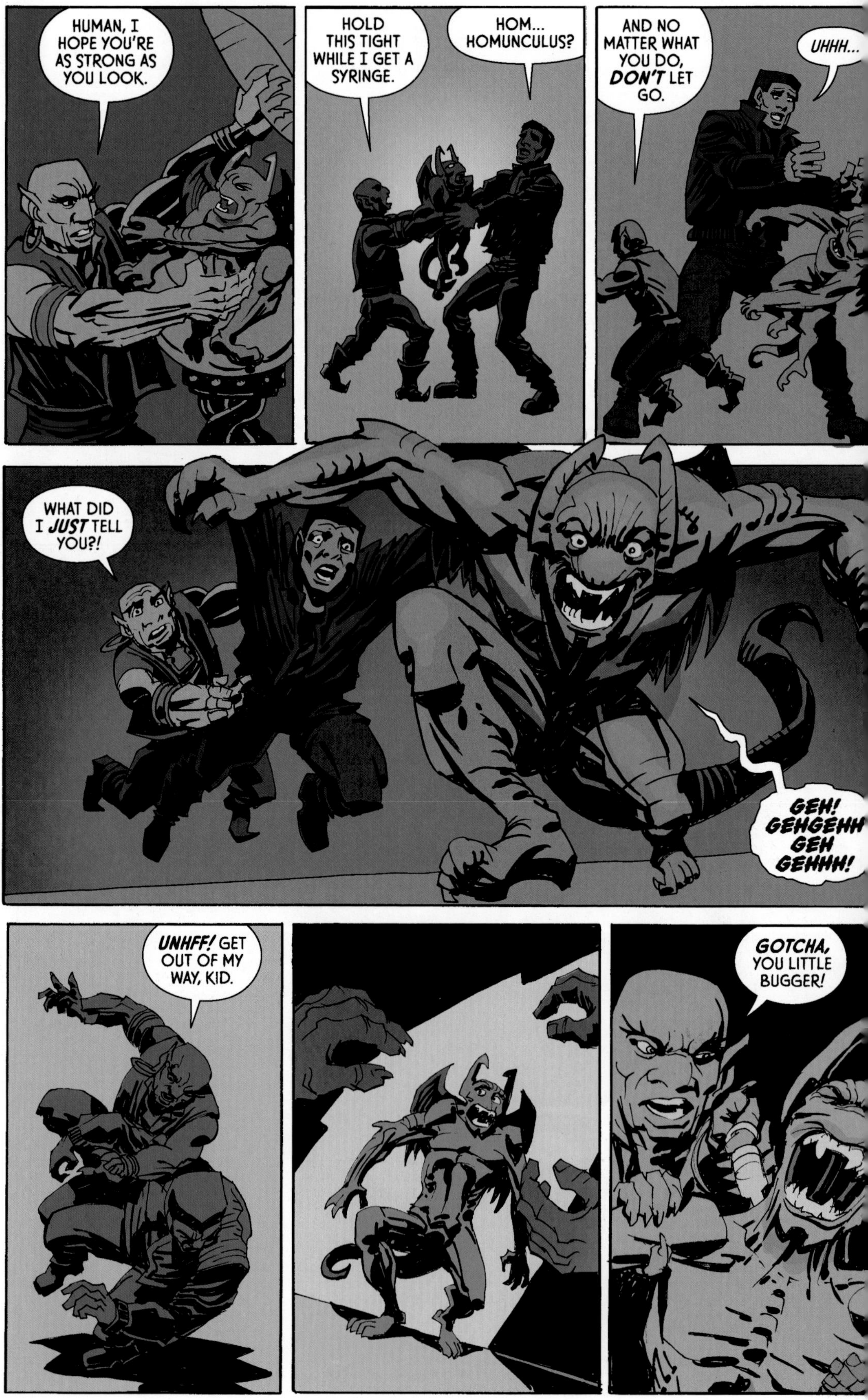
HUMAN, I HOPE YOU'RE AS STRONG AS YOU LOOK.
HOLD THIS TIGHT WHILE I GET A SYRINGE.
HOM... HOMUNCULUS?
AND NO MATTER WHAT YOU DO, DON'T LET GO.
UHHH...
WHAT DID I JUST TELL YOU?!
GEH! GEHGEHH GEH GEHHH!
UNHFF! GET OUT OF MY WAY, KID.
GOTCHA, YOU LITTLE BUGGER!

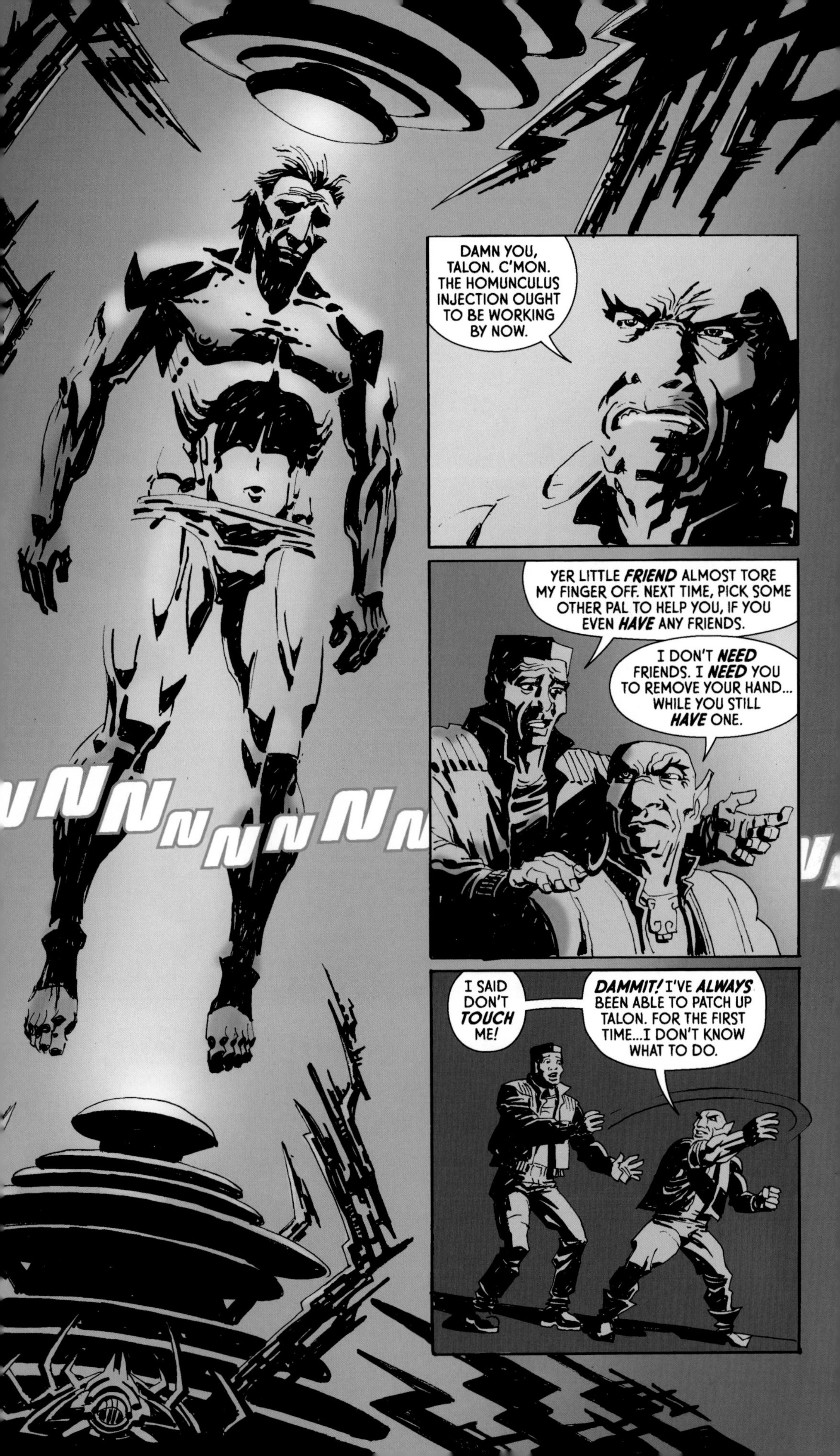

DAMN YOU, TALON. C'MON. THE HOMUNCULUS INJECTION OUGHT TO BE WORKING BY NOW.
YER LITTLE *FRIEND* ALMOST TORE MY FINGER OFF. NEXT TIME, PICK SOME OTHER PAL TO HELP YOU, IF YOU EVEN *HAVE* ANY FRIENDS.
I DON'T *NEED* FRIENDS. I *NEED* YOU TO REMOVE YOUR HAND... WHILE YOU STILL *HAVE* ONE.
NNNNNNNN
I SAID DON'T *TOUCH* ME!
DAMMIT! I'VE *ALWAYS* BEEN ABLE TO PATCH UP TALON. FOR THE FIRST TIME...I DON'T KNOW WHAT TO DO.

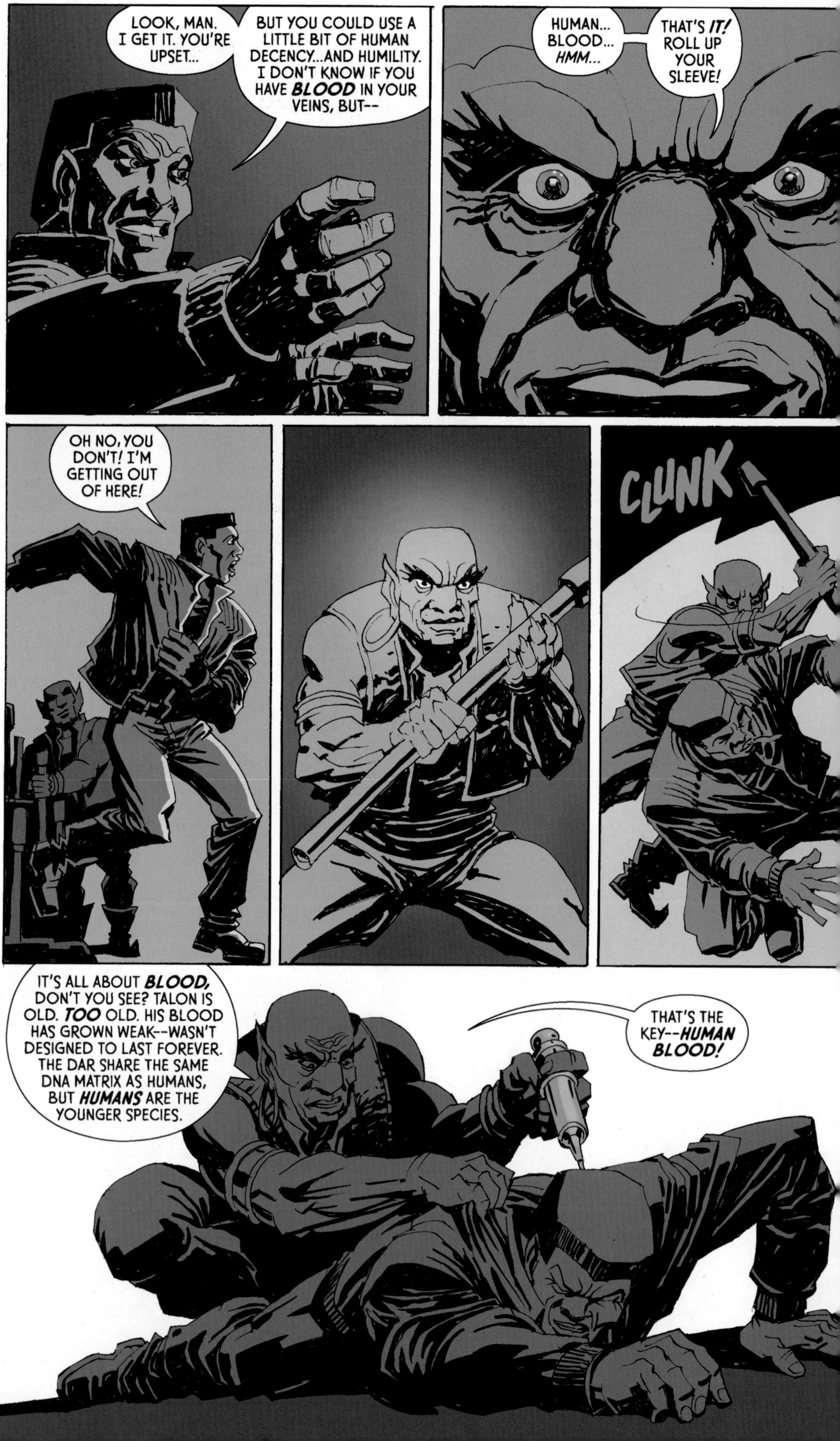
LOOK, MAN. I GET IT. YOU'RE UPSET...
BUT YOU COULD USE A LITTLE BIT OF HUMAN DECENCY...AND HUMILITY. I DON'T KNOW IF YOU HAVE *BLOOD* IN YOUR VEINS, BUT--
HUMAN... BLOOD... *HMM...*
THAT'S *IT!* ROLL UP YOUR SLEEVE!
OH NO, YOU DON'T! I'M GETTING OUT OF HERE!
CLUNK
IT'S ALL ABOUT *BLOOD,* DON'T YOU SEE? TALON IS OLD. *TOO* OLD. HIS BLOOD HAS GROWN WEAK--WASN'T DESIGNED TO LAST FOREVER. THE DAR SHARE THE SAME DNA MATRIX AS HUMANS, BUT *HUMANS* ARE THE YOUNGER SPECIES.
THAT'S THE KEY--*HUMAN BLOOD!*

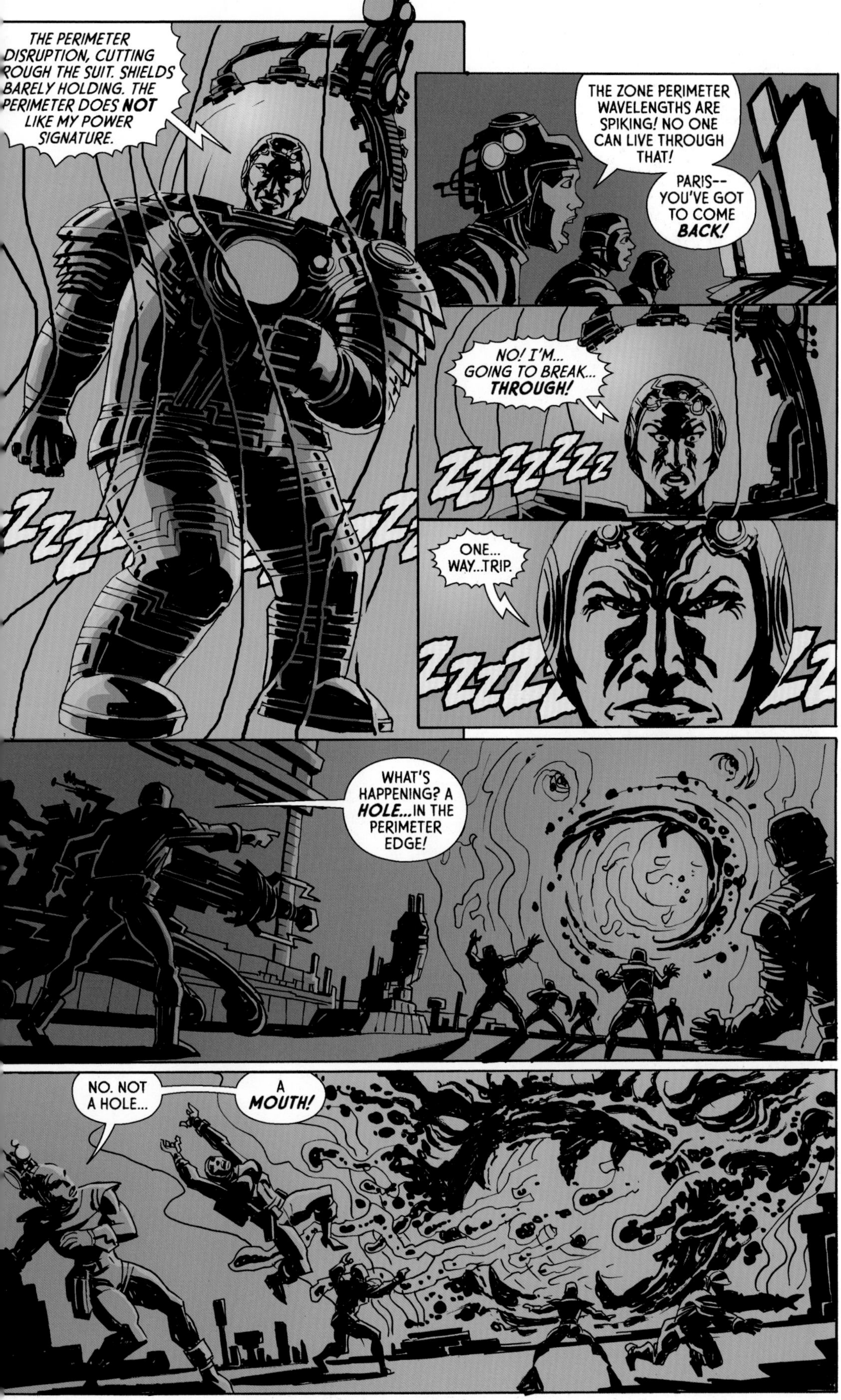

THE PERIMETER DISRUPTION, CUTTING ROUGH THE SUIT. SHIELDS BARELY HOLDING. THE PERIMETER DOES NOT LIKE MY POWER SIGNATURE.
THE ZONE PERIMETER WAVELENGTHS ARE SPIKING! NO ONE CAN LIVE THROUGH THAT!
PARIS-- YOU'VE GOT TO COME BACK!
NO! I'M... GOING TO BREAK... THROUGH!
ONE... WAY...TRIP.
WHAT'S HAPPENING? A HOLE...IN THE PERIMETER EDGE!
NO. NOT A HOLE...
A MOUTH!

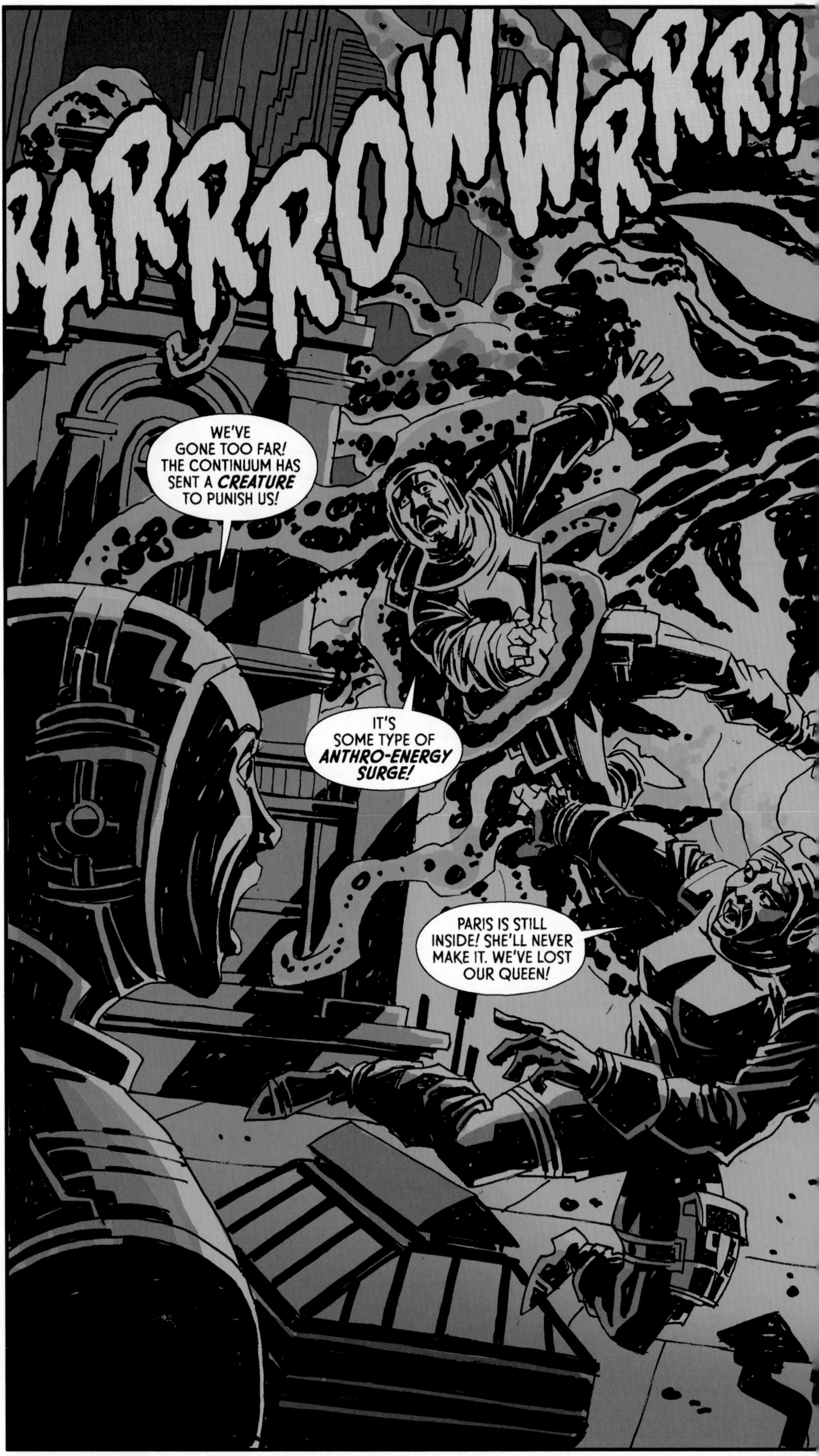
RARRROWWRRR!
WE'VE GONE TOO FAR! THE CONTINUUM HAS SENT A *CREATURE* TO PUNISH US!
IT'S SOME TYPE OF ***ANTHRO-ENERGY SURGE!***
PARIS IS STILL INSIDE! SHE'LL NEVER MAKE IT. WE'VE LOST OUR QUEEN!

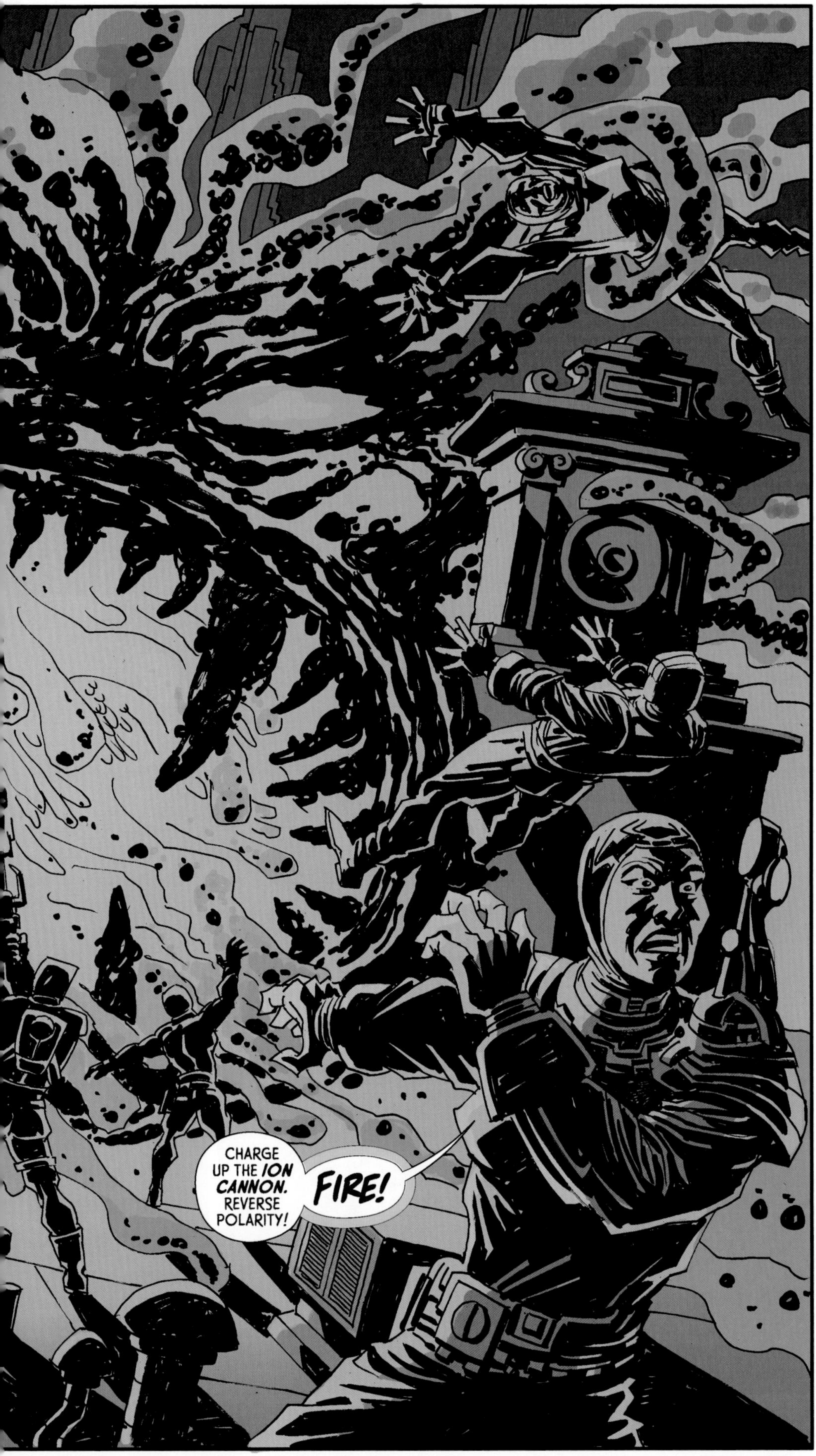
CHARGE UP THE ION CANNON. REVERSE POLARITY!
FIRE!

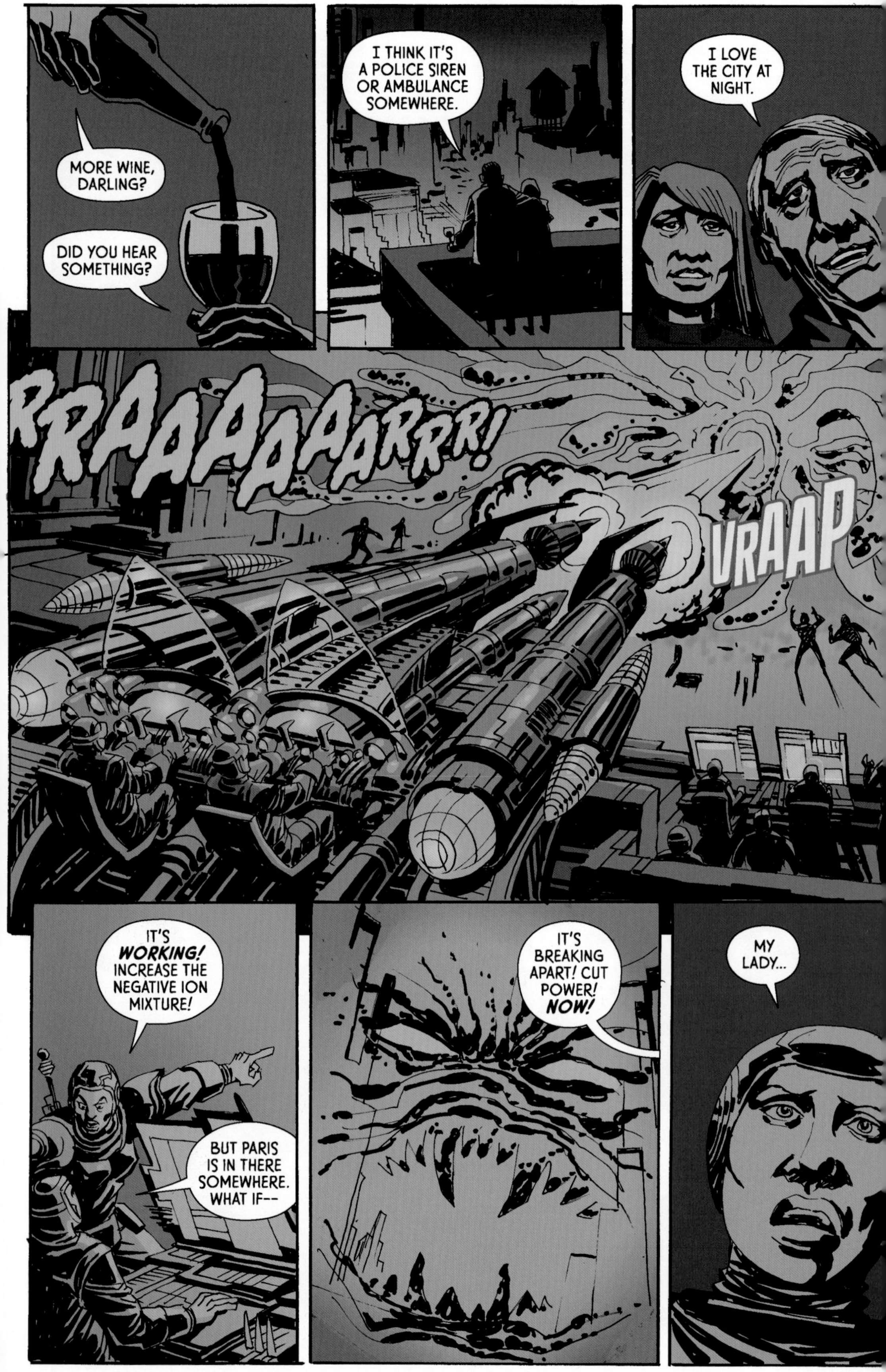

MORE WINE, DARLING?
DID YOU HEAR SOMETHING?
I THINK IT'S A POLICE SIREN OR AMBULANCE SOMEWHERE.
I LOVE THE CITY AT NIGHT.
RRAAAAAARRRR!
VRAAP
IT'S WORKING! INCREASE THE NEGATIVE ION MIXTURE!
BUT PARIS IS IN THERE SOMEWHERE. WHAT IF--
IT'S BREAKING APART! CUT POWER! NOW!
MY LADY...

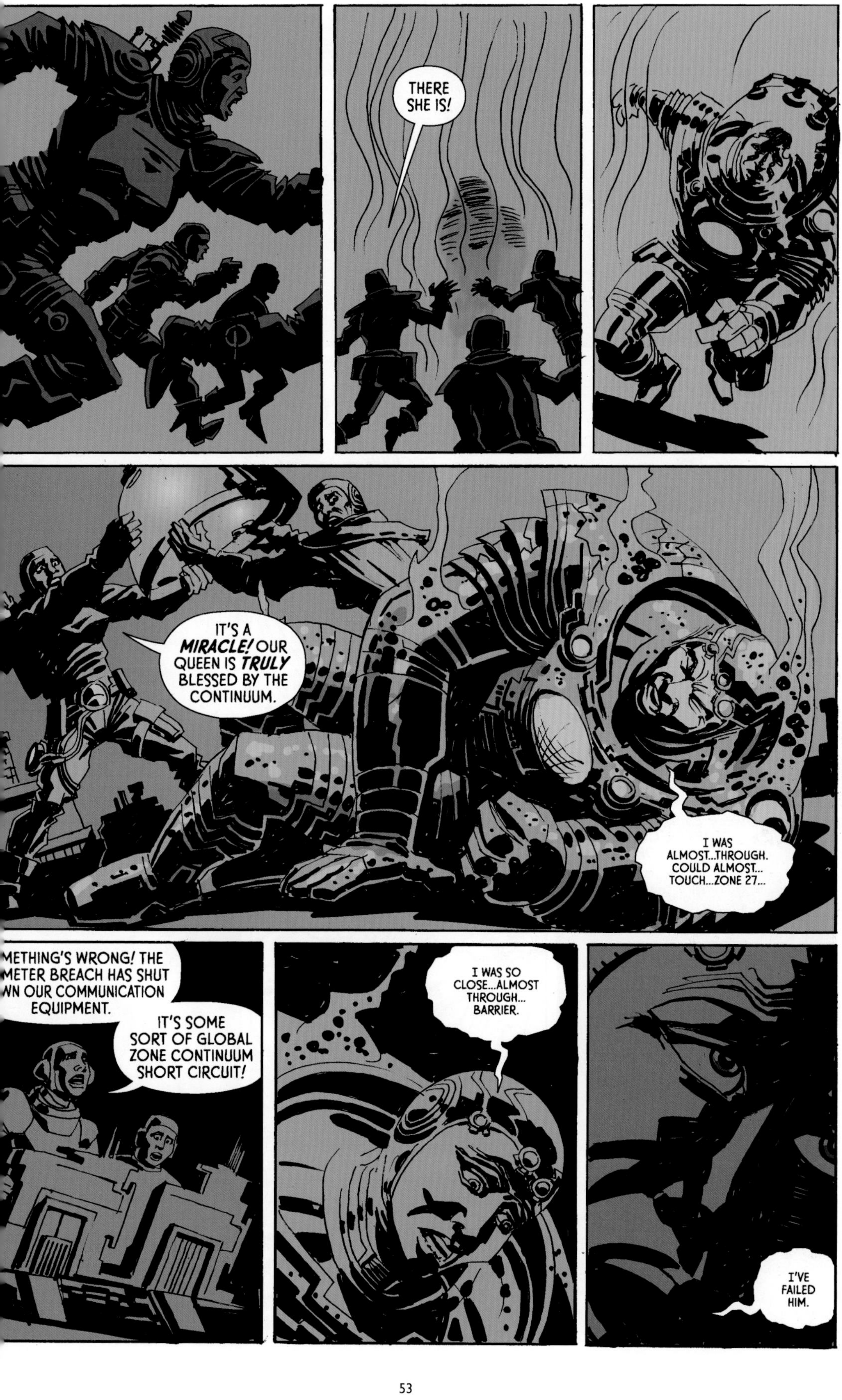
THERE SHE IS!
IT'S A *MIRACLE!* OUR QUEEN IS *TRULY* BLESSED BY THE CONTINUUM.
I WAS ALMOST...THROUGH. COULD ALMOST... TOUCH...ZONE 27...
METHING'S WRONG! THE METER BREACH HAS SHUT WN OUR COMMUNICATION EQUIPMENT.
IT'S SOME SORT OF GLOBAL ZONE CONTINUUM SHORT CIRCUIT!
I WAS SO CLOSE...ALMOST THROUGH... BARRIER.
I'VE FAILED HIM.

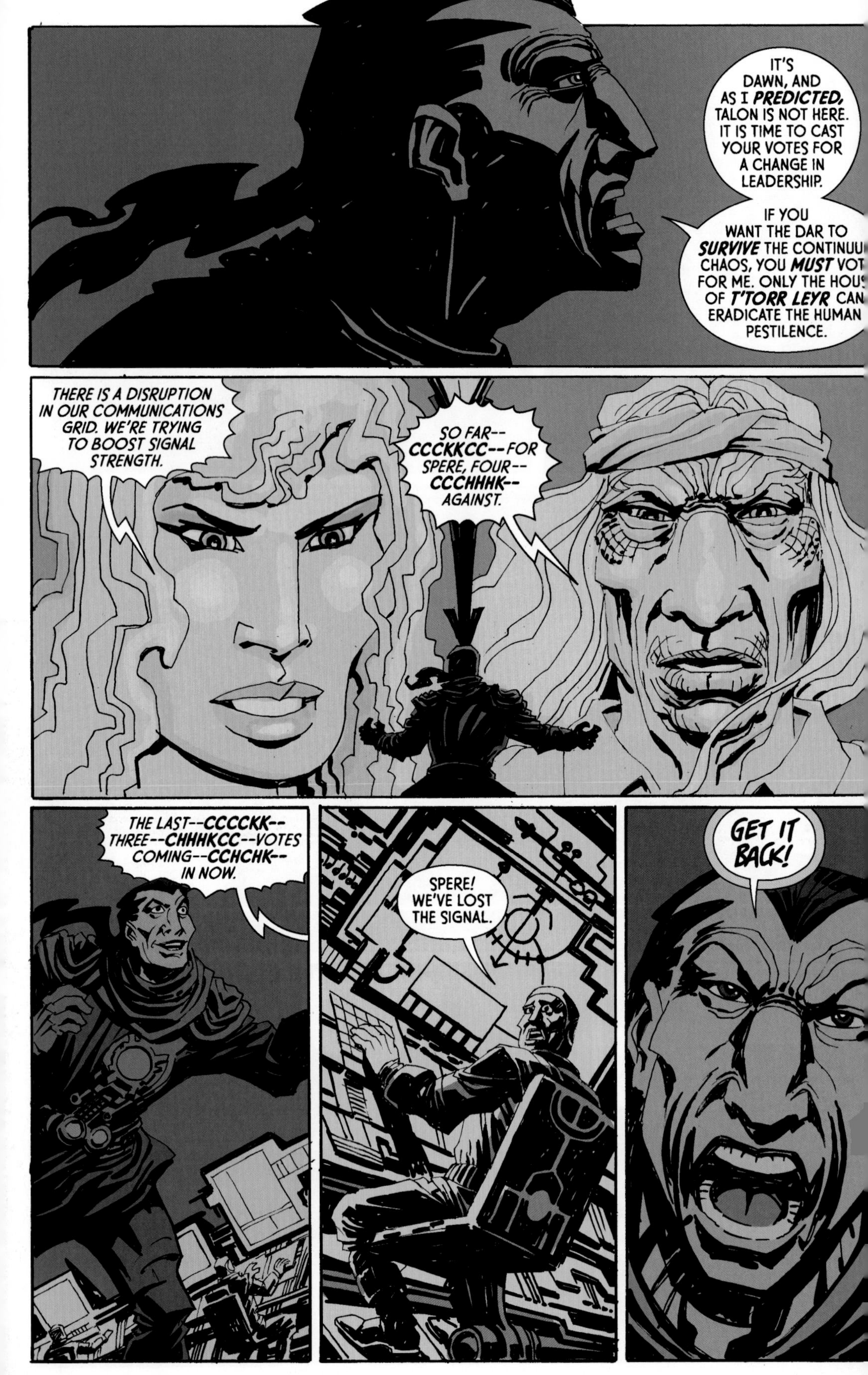
IT'S DAWN, AND AS I *PREDICTED,* TALON IS NOT HERE. IT IS TIME TO CAST YOUR VOTES FOR A CHANGE IN LEADERSHIP.
IF YOU WANT THE DAR TO *SURVIVE* THE CONTINUU CHAOS, YOU *MUST* VOT FOR ME. ONLY THE HOUS OF *T'TORR LEYR* CAN ERADICATE THE HUMAN PESTILENCE.
THERE IS A DISRUPTION IN OUR COMMUNICATIONS GRID. WE'RE TRYING TO BOOST SIGNAL STRENGTH.
SO FAR-- **CCCKKCC**--FOR SPERE, FOUR-- **CCCHHHK**-- AGAINST.
THE LAST--**CCCCKK**-- THREE--**CHHHKCC**--VOTES COMING--**CCHCHK**-- IN NOW.
SPERE! WE'VE LOST THE SIGNAL.
GET IT BACK!

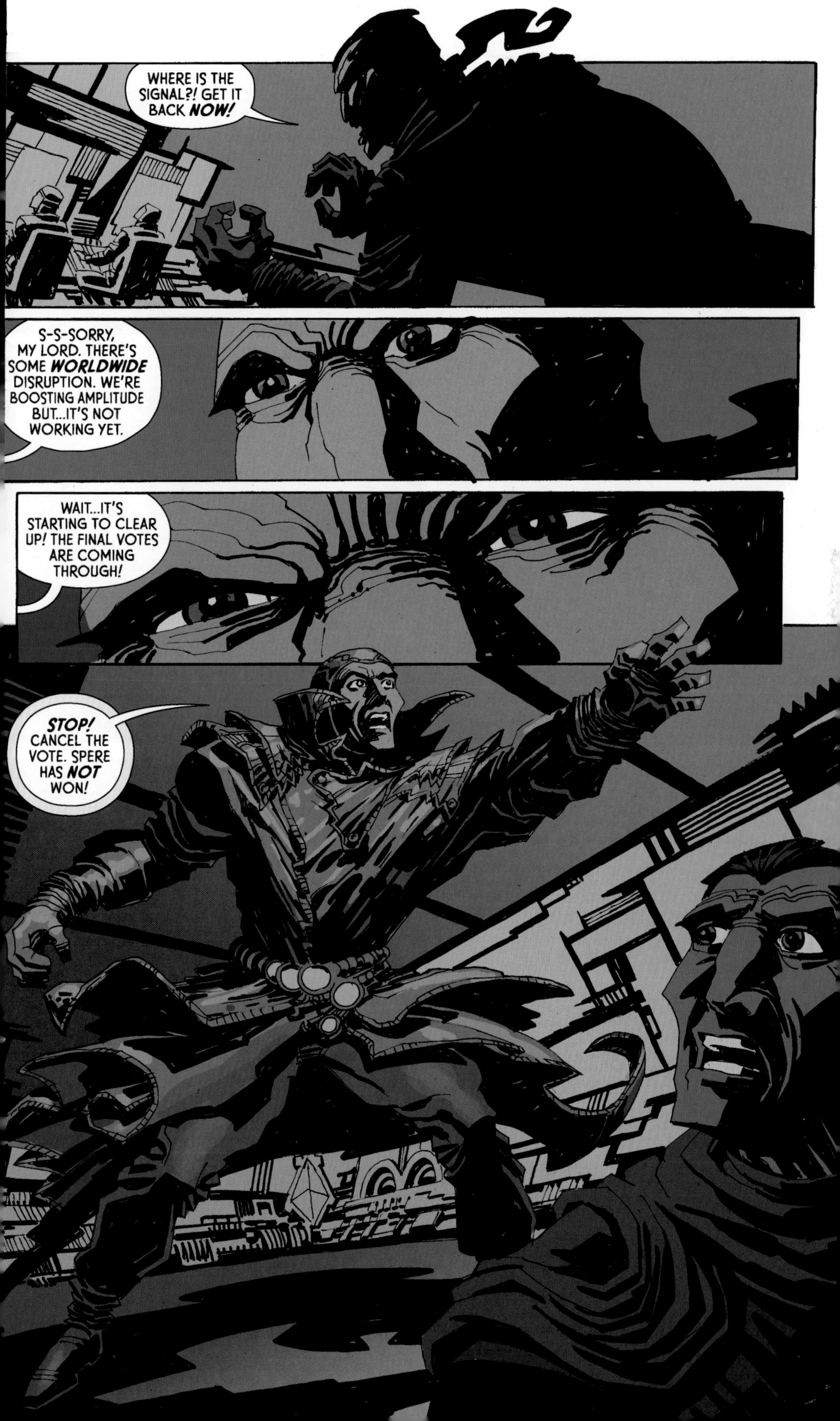
WHERE IS THE SIGNAL?! GET IT BACK NOW!
S-S-SORRY, MY LORD. THERE'S SOME WORLDWIDE DISRUPTION. WE'RE BOOSTING AMPLITUDE BUT...IT'S NOT WORKING YET.
WAIT...IT'S STARTING TO CLEAR UP! THE FINAL VOTES ARE COMING THROUGH!
STOP! CANCEL THE VOTE. SPERE HAS NOT WON!

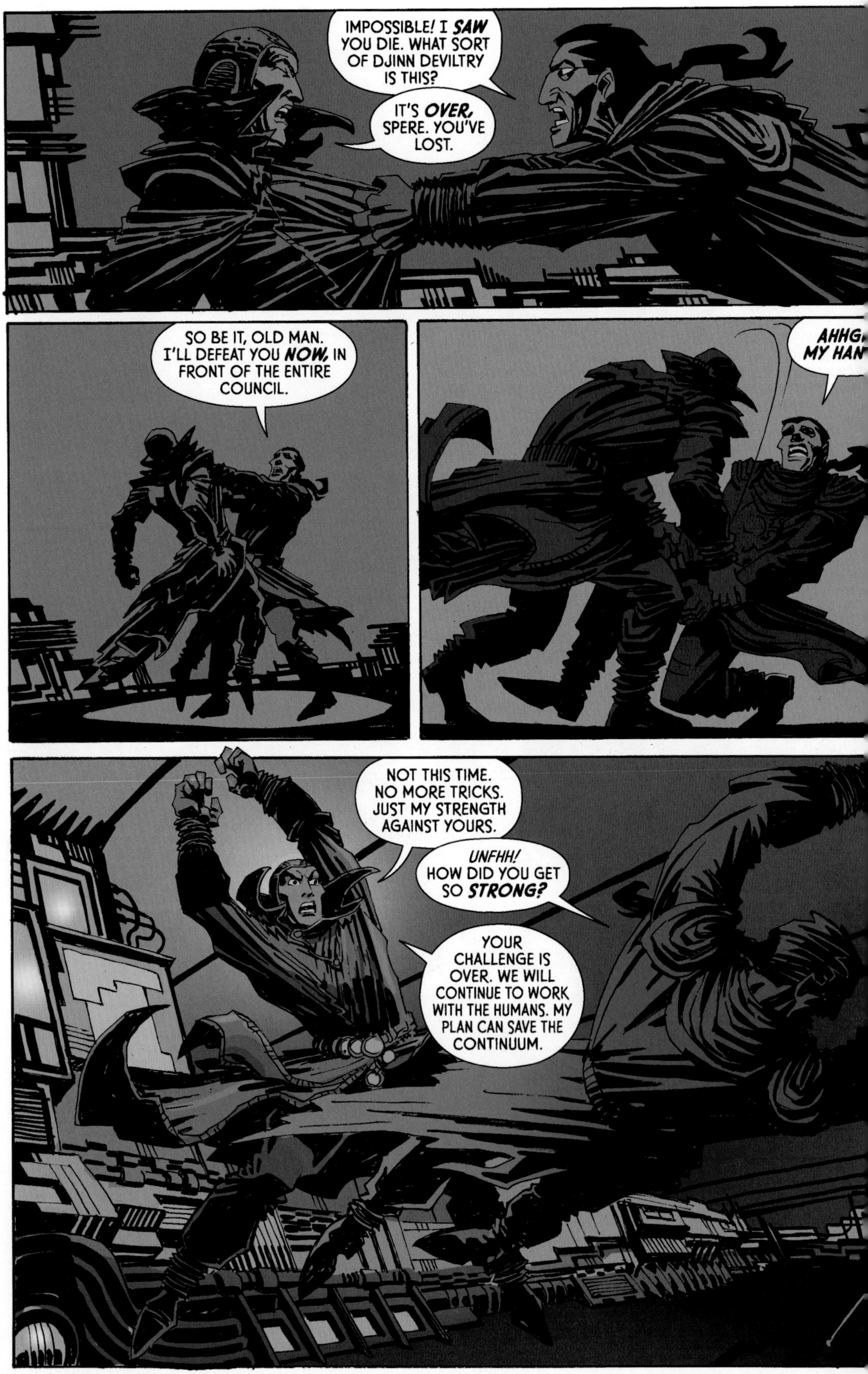
IMPOSSIBLE! I SAW YOU DIE. WHAT SORT OF DJINN DEVILTRY IS THIS?
IT'S OVER, SPERE. YOU'VE LOST.
SO BE IT, OLD MAN. I'LL DEFEAT YOU NOW, IN FRONT OF THE ENTIRE COUNCIL.
AHHG
MY HAN
NOT THIS TIME. NO MORE TRICKS. JUST MY STRENGTH AGAINST YOURS.
UNFHH! HOW DID YOU GET SO STRONG?
YOUR CHALLENGE IS OVER. WE WILL CONTINUE TO WORK WITH THE HUMANS. MY PLAN CAN SAVE THE CONTINUUM.

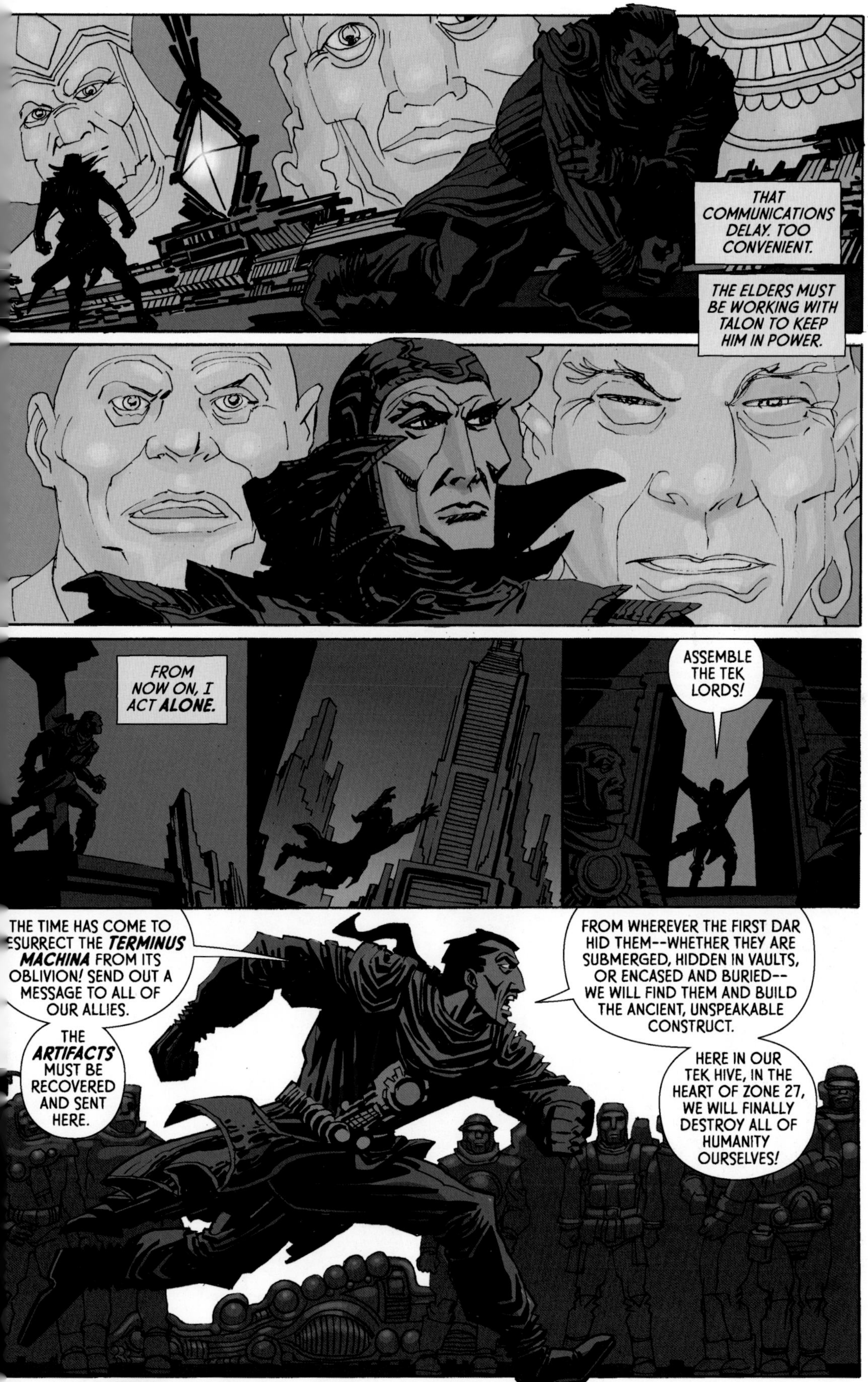
THAT COMMUNICATIONS DELAY. TOO CONVENIENT.
THE ELDERS MUST BE WORKING WITH TALON TO KEEP HIM IN POWER.
FROM NOW ON, I ACT **ALONE.**
ASSEMBLE THE TEK LORDS!
THE TIME HAS COME TO ESURRECT THE ***TERMINUS MACHINA*** FROM ITS OBLIVION! SEND OUT A MESSAGE TO ALL OF OUR ALLIES.
THE ***ARTIFACTS*** MUST BE RECOVERED AND SENT HERE.
FROM WHEREVER THE FIRST DAR HID THEM--WHETHER THEY ARE SUBMERGED, HIDDEN IN VAULTS, OR ENCASED AND BURIED--WE WILL FIND THEM AND BUILD THE ANCIENT, UNSPEAKABLE CONSTRUCT.
HERE IN OUR TEK HIVE, IN THE HEART OF ZONE 27, WE WILL FINALLY DESTROY ALL OF HUMANITY OURSELVES!

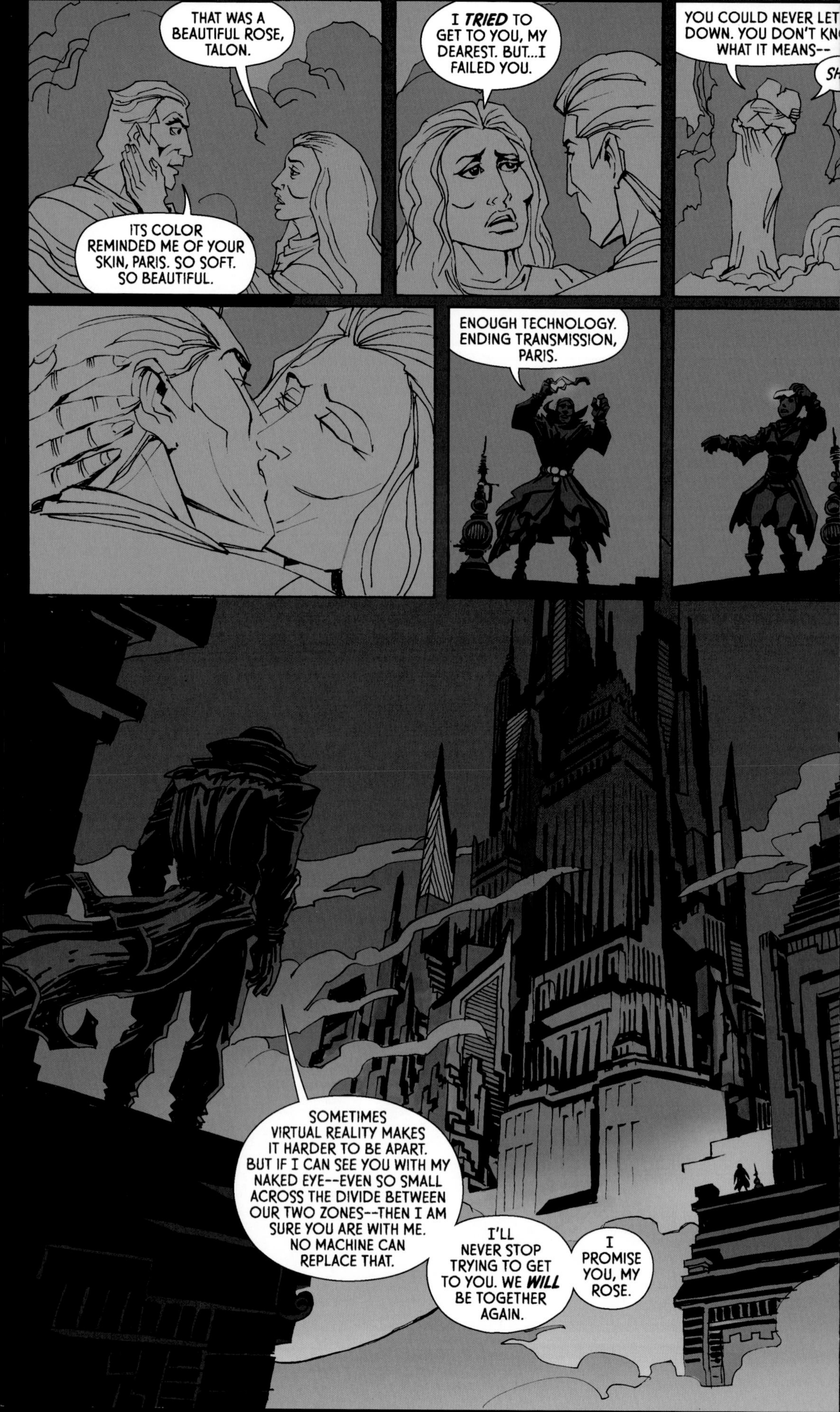
THAT WAS A BEAUTIFUL ROSE, TALON.
ITS COLOR REMINDED ME OF YOUR SKIN, PARIS. SO SOFT. SO BEAUTIFUL.
I *TRIED* TO GET TO YOU, MY DEAREST. BUT...I FAILED YOU.
YOU COULD NEVER LET DOWN. YOU DON'T KN WHAT IT MEANS--
ENOUGH TECHNOLOGY. ENDING TRANSMISSION, PARIS.
SOMETIMES VIRTUAL REALITY MAKES IT HARDER TO BE APART. BUT IF I CAN SEE YOU WITH MY NAKED EYE--EVEN SO SMALL ACROSS THE DIVIDE BETWEEN OUR TWO ZONES--THEN I AM SURE YOU ARE WITH ME. NO MACHINE CAN REPLACE THAT.
I'LL NEVER STOP TRYING TO GET TO YOU. WE *WILL* BE TOGETHER AGAIN.
I PROMISE YOU, MY ROSE.

CHAPTER THREE

TEST OF STRENGTH

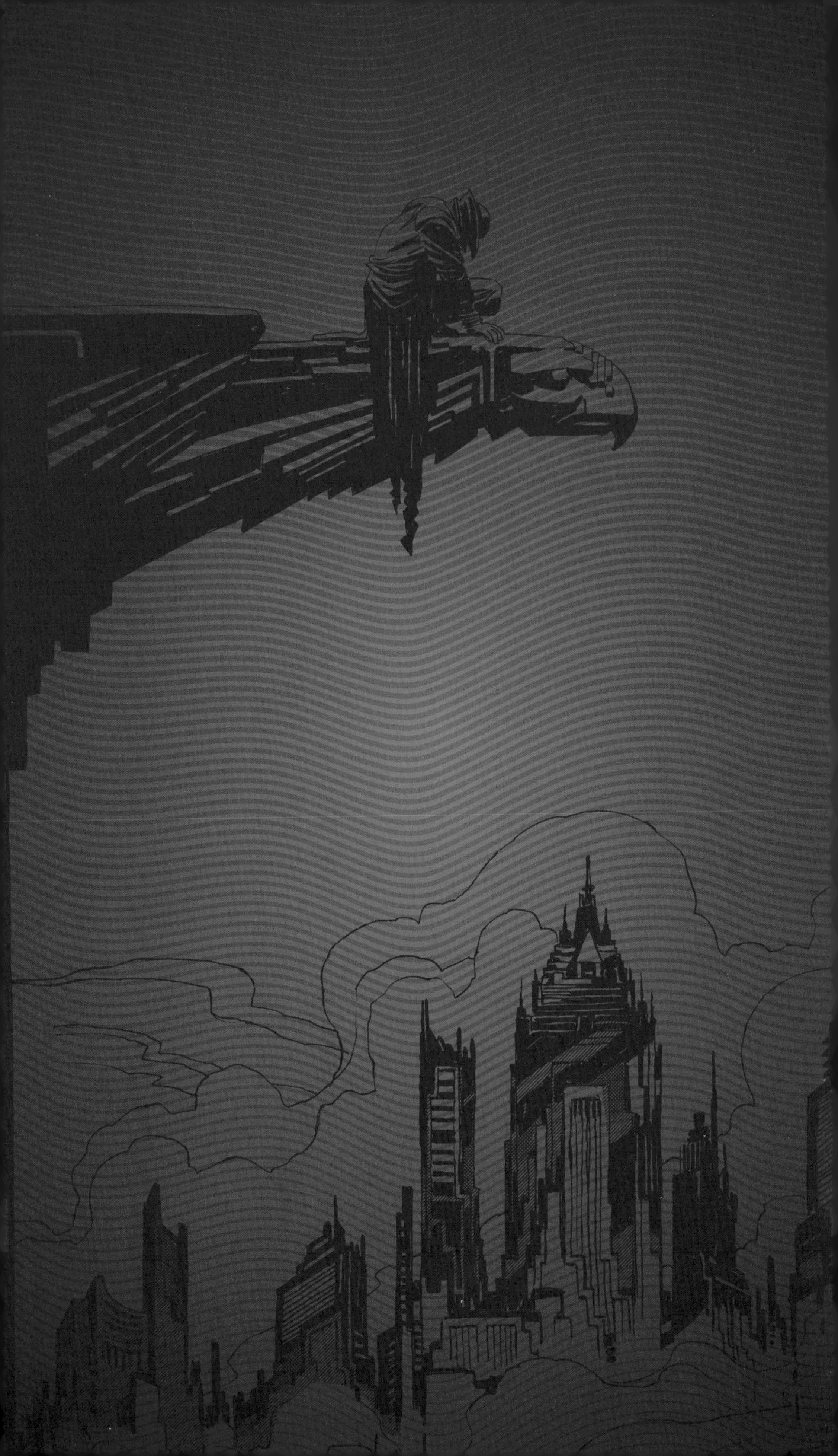

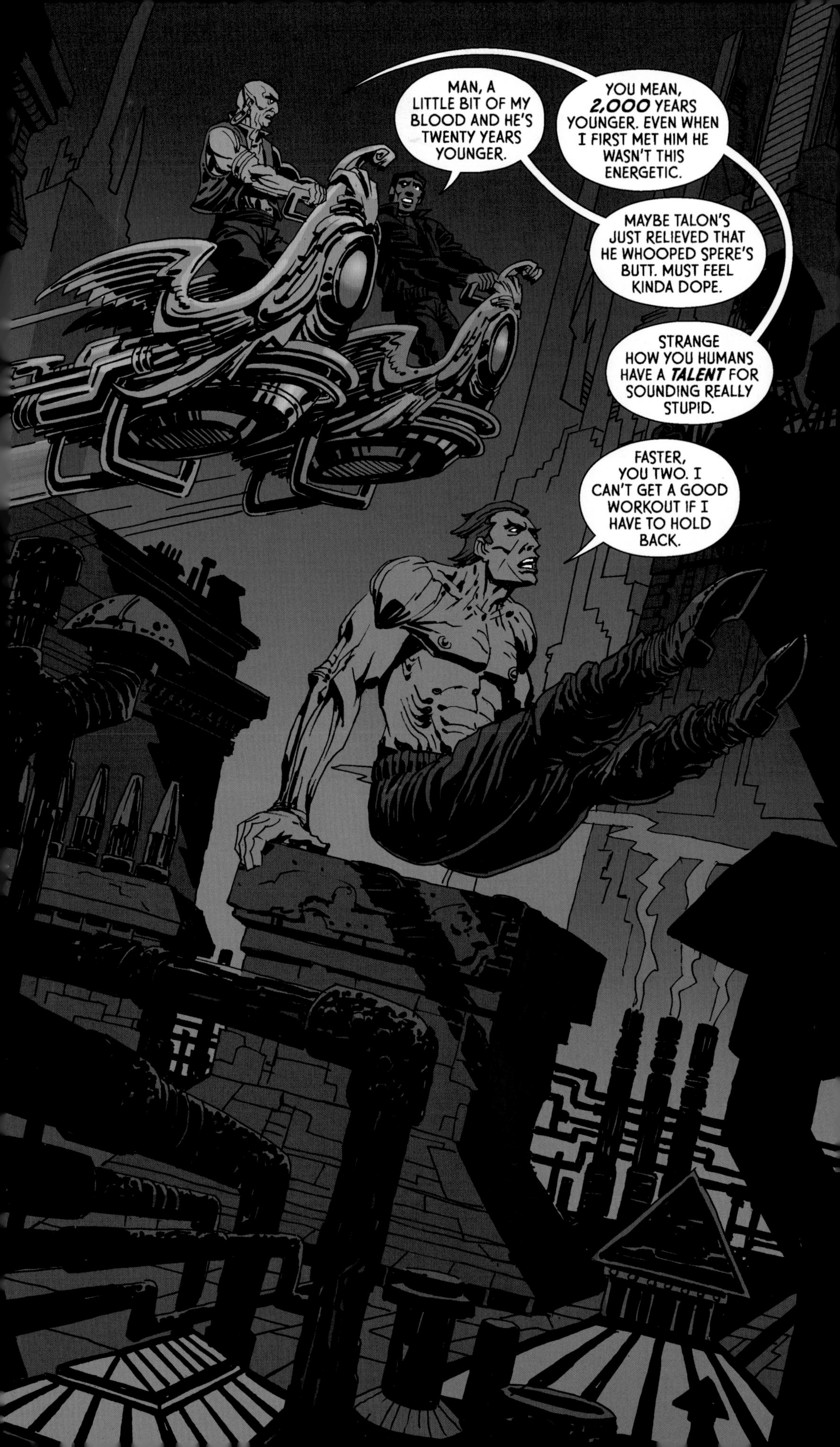
MAN, A LITTLE BIT OF MY BLOOD AND HE'S TWENTY YEARS YOUNGER.
YOU MEAN, 2,000 YEARS YOUNGER. EVEN WHEN I FIRST MET HIM HE WASN'T THIS ENERGETIC.
MAYBE TALON'S JUST RELIEVED THAT HE WHOOPED SPERE'S BUTT. MUST FEEL KINDA DOPE.
STRANGE HOW YOU HUMANS HAVE A TALENT FOR SOUNDING REALLY STUPID.
FASTER, YOU TWO. I CAN'T GET A GOOD WORKOUT IF I HAVE TO HOLD BACK.

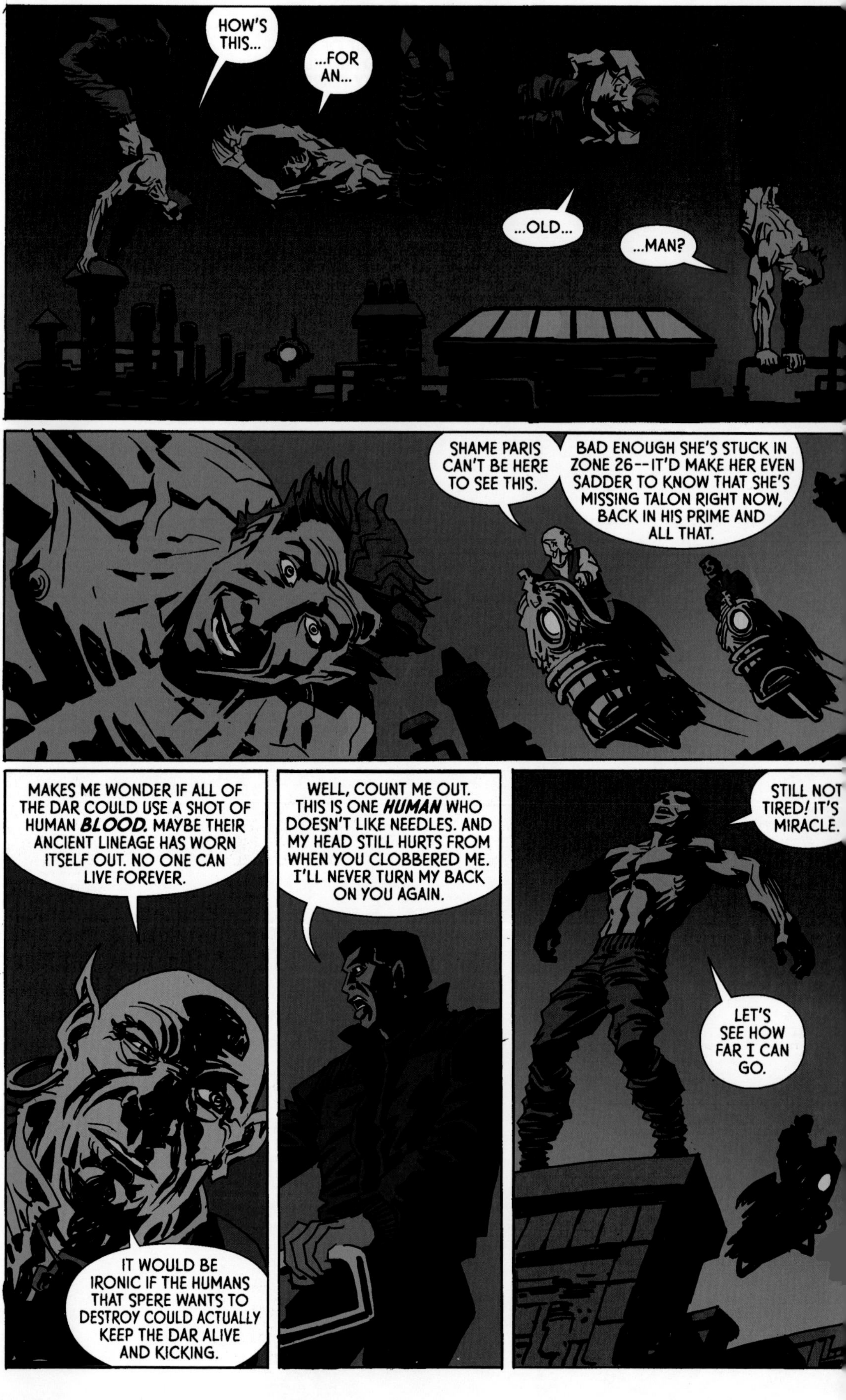
HOW'S THIS...
...FOR AN...
...OLD...
...MAN?
SHAME PARIS CAN'T BE HERE TO SEE THIS.
BAD ENOUGH SHE'S STUCK IN ZONE 26--IT'D MAKE HER EVEN SADDER TO KNOW THAT SHE'S MISSING TALON RIGHT NOW, BACK IN HIS PRIME AND ALL THAT.
MAKES ME WONDER IF ALL OF THE DAR COULD USE A SHOT OF HUMAN BLOOD. MAYBE THEIR ANCIENT LINEAGE HAS WORN ITSELF OUT. NO ONE CAN LIVE FOREVER.
IT WOULD BE IRONIC IF THE HUMANS THAT SPERE WANTS TO DESTROY COULD ACTUALLY KEEP THE DAR ALIVE AND KICKING.
WELL, COUNT ME OUT. THIS IS ONE HUMAN WHO DOESN'T LIKE NEEDLES. AND MY HEAD STILL HURTS FROM WHEN YOU CLOBBERED ME. I'LL NEVER TURN MY BACK ON YOU AGAIN.
STILL NOT TIRED! IT'S MIRACLE.
LET'S SEE HOW FAR I CAN GO.

HEY, LOOKS LIKE WE'VE GOT VISITORS.

'BOUT TIME THOSE TEKS SHOWED UP.

OHAILA, MEN OF ROC'S NEST.

SORRY WE'RE LATE. WE WANTED OUR WORK TO BE PERFECT.

THE *LEADER* OF THE DAR SHOULD HAVE ONLY THE VERY BEST.

WAIT A MINUTE. THOSE GUYS ONLY HAVE ONE...

...EYE!

OF COURSE. WHO EVER HEARD OF A TWO-EYED *SYKLOPS, EH, DAEMOS?* AND WHAT'S SO SPECIAL ABOUT TWO EYES, ANYWAY?

HA! VASTLY OVERRATED, *PHOBOS,* MY BROTHER. TWO EYES ARE REALLY QUITE REDUNDANT.

ANYWAY, DOWN TO BUSINESS.

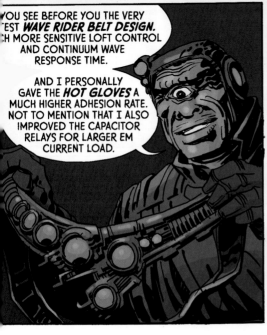

YOU SEE BEFORE YOU THE VERY ?EST *WAVE RIDER BELT DESIGN.* :H MORE SENSITIVE LOFT CONTROL AND CONTINUUM WAVE RESPONSE TIME.

AND I PERSONALLY GAVE THE *HOT GLOVES* A MUCH HIGHER ADHESION RATE. NOT TO MENTION THAT I ALSO IMPROVED THE CAPACITOR RELAYS FOR LARGER EM CURRENT LOAD.

SO TRUE, SO TRUE. AND *I* MINIATURIZED MANY OF THE *ZONE GOGGLES'* ACCESSORIES-- NOT QUITE SO BULKY. IMPRESSIVE, DON'T YOU THINK? I'VE REALLY OUTDONE MYSELF THIS TIME.

AND AS PROMISED, THE ZONE GOGGLES WILL ALSO PROVIDE A FASTER CAMOUFLAGE RESPONSE TIME TO THE ZONE SUIT BY .26 SECONDS.

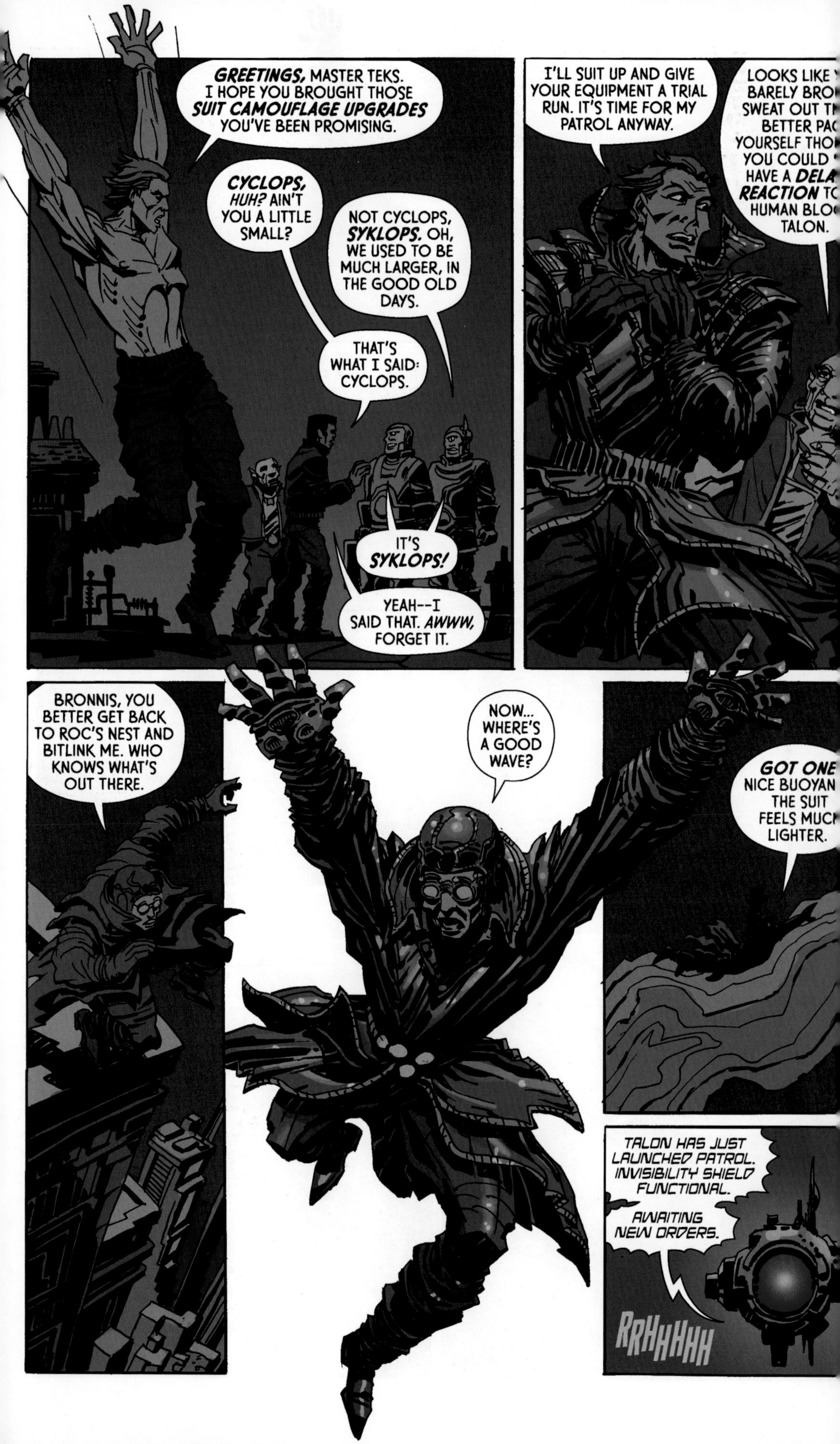

GREETINGS, MASTER TEKS. I HOPE YOU BROUGHT THOSE SUIT CAMOUFLAGE UPGRADES YOU'VE BEEN PROMISING.
CYCLOPS, HUH? AIN'T YOU A LITTLE SMALL?
NOT CYCLOPS, SYKLOPS. OH, WE USED TO BE MUCH LARGER, IN THE GOOD OLD DAYS.
THAT'S WHAT I SAID: CYCLOPS.
IT'S SYKLOPS!
YEAH--I SAID THAT. AWWW, FORGET IT.
I'LL SUIT UP AND GIVE YOUR EQUIPMENT A TRIAL RUN. IT'S TIME FOR MY PATROL ANYWAY.
LOOKS LIKE BARELY BRO SWEAT OUT T BETTER PA YOURSELF THO YOU COULD HAVE A DELA REACTION TO HUMAN BLO TALON.
BRONNIS, YOU BETTER GET BACK TO ROC'S NEST AND BITLINK ME. WHO KNOWS WHAT'S OUT THERE.
NOW... WHERE'S A GOOD WAVE?
GOT ONE NICE BUOYAN THE SUIT FEELS MUC LIGHTER.
TALON HAS JUST LAUNCHED PATROL. INVISIBILITY SHIELD FUNCTIONAL.
AWAITING NEW ORDERS.
RRHHHHH

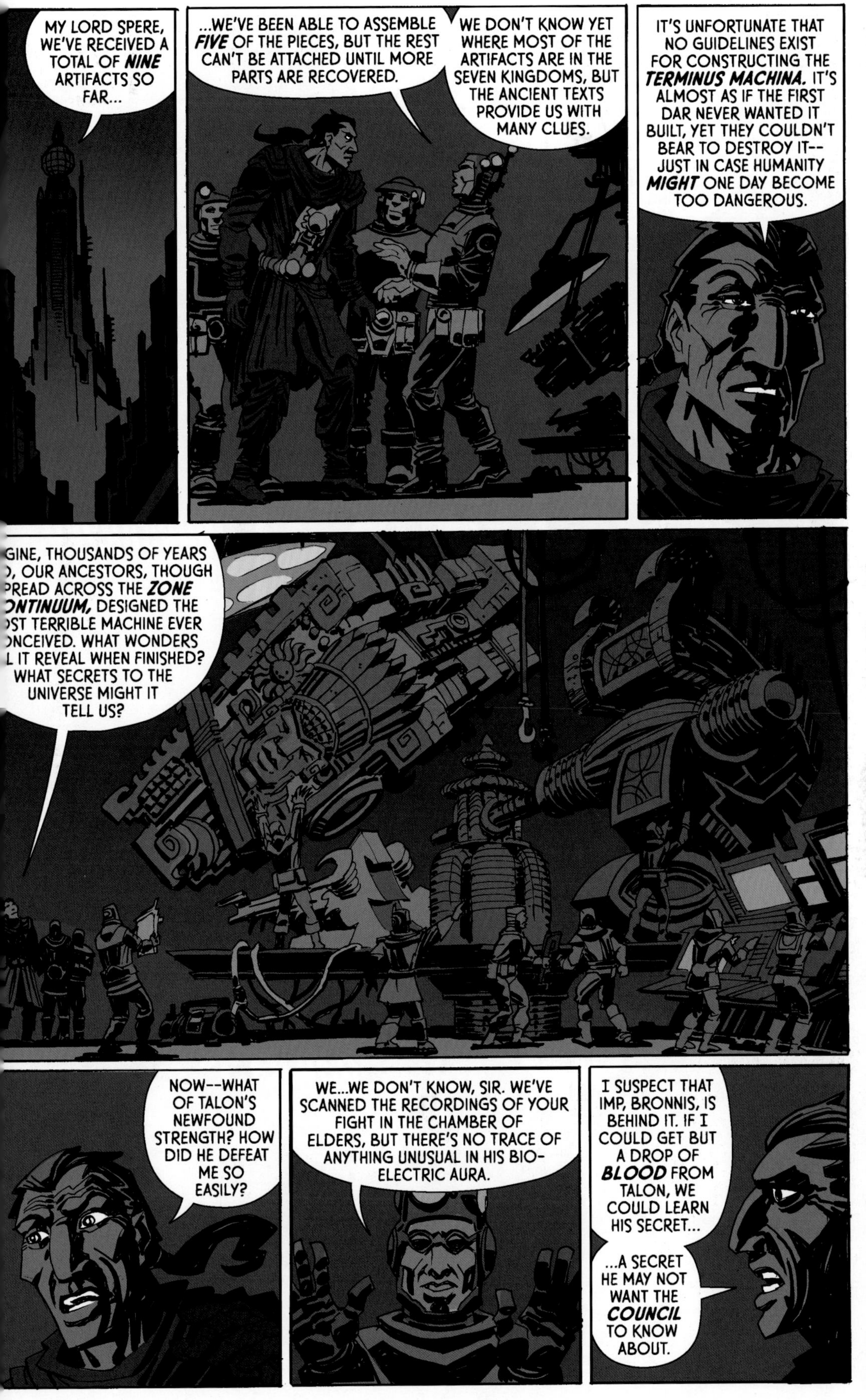
MY LORD SPERE, WE'VE RECEIVED A TOTAL OF NINE ARTIFACTS SO FAR...
...WE'VE BEEN ABLE TO ASSEMBLE FIVE OF THE PIECES, BUT THE REST CAN'T BE ATTACHED UNTIL MORE PARTS ARE RECOVERED.
WE DON'T KNOW YET WHERE MOST OF THE ARTIFACTS ARE IN THE SEVEN KINGDOMS, BUT THE ANCIENT TEXTS PROVIDE US WITH MANY CLUES.
IT'S UNFORTUNATE THAT NO GUIDELINES EXIST FOR CONSTRUCTING THE TERMINUS MACHINA. IT'S ALMOST AS IF THE FIRST DAR NEVER WANTED IT BUILT, YET THEY COULDN'T BEAR TO DESTROY IT--JUST IN CASE HUMANITY MIGHT ONE DAY BECOME TOO DANGEROUS.
GINE, THOUSANDS OF YEARS), OUR ANCESTORS, THOUGH PREAD ACROSS THE ZONE ONTINUUM, DESIGNED THE OST TERRIBLE MACHINE EVER ONCEIVED. WHAT WONDERS L IT REVEAL WHEN FINISHED? WHAT SECRETS TO THE UNIVERSE MIGHT IT TELL US?
NOW--WHAT OF TALON'S NEWFOUND STRENGTH? HOW DID HE DEFEAT ME SO EASILY?
WE...WE DON'T KNOW, SIR. WE'VE SCANNED THE RECORDINGS OF YOUR FIGHT IN THE CHAMBER OF ELDERS, BUT THERE'S NO TRACE OF ANYTHING UNUSUAL IN HIS BIO-ELECTRIC AURA.
I SUSPECT THAT IMP, BRONNIS, IS BEHIND IT. IF I COULD GET BUT A DROP OF BLOOD FROM TALON, WE COULD LEARN HIS SECRET...
...A SECRET HE MAY NOT WANT THE COUNCIL TO KNOW ABOUT.

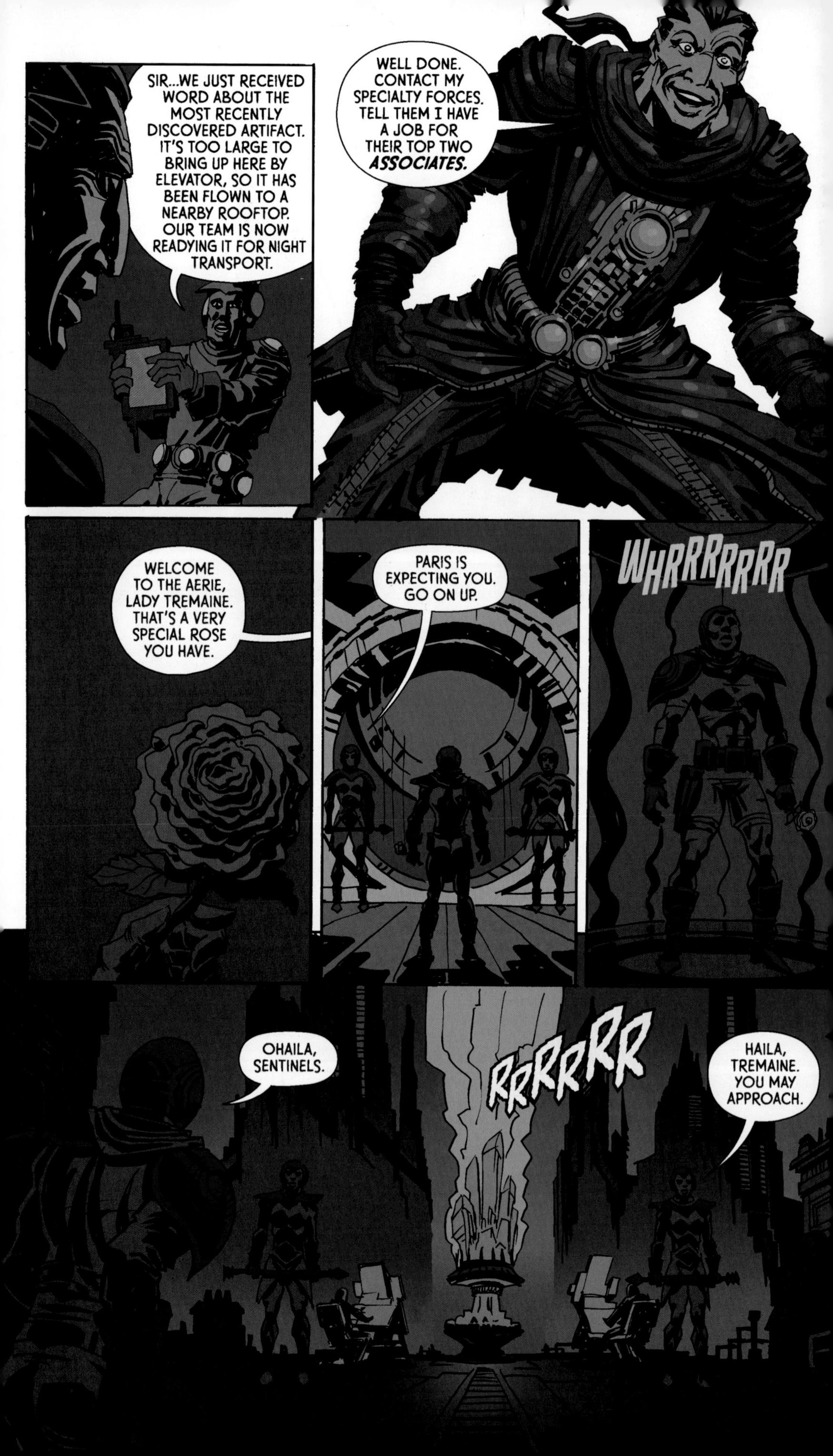
SIR...WE JUST RECEIVED WORD ABOUT THE MOST RECENTLY DISCOVERED ARTIFACT. IT'S TOO LARGE TO BRING UP HERE BY ELEVATOR, SO IT HAS BEEN FLOWN TO A NEARBY ROOFTOP. OUR TEAM IS NOW READYING IT FOR NIGHT TRANSPORT.
WELL DONE. CONTACT MY SPECIALTY FORCES. TELL THEM I HAVE A JOB FOR THEIR TOP TWO *ASSOCIATES.*
WELCOME TO THE AERIE, LADY TREMAINE. THAT'S A VERY SPECIAL ROSE YOU HAVE.
PARIS IS EXPECTING YOU. GO ON UP.
WHRRRRRRR
OHAILA, SENTINELS.
RRRRRR
HAILA, TREMAINE. YOU MAY APPROACH.

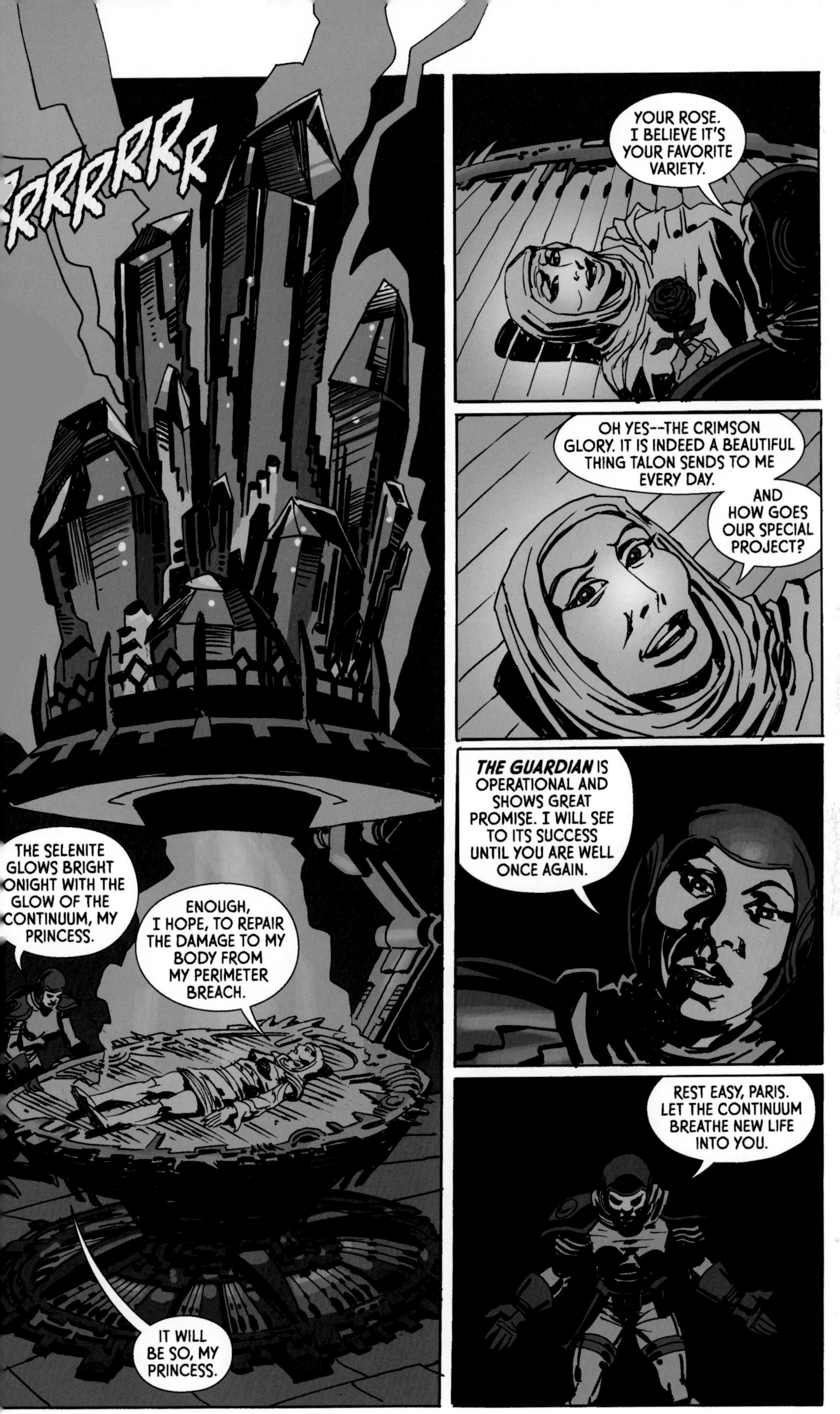
RRRRRRR
YOUR ROSE. I BELIEVE IT'S YOUR FAVORITE VARIETY.
OH YES--THE CRIMSON GLORY. IT IS INDEED A BEAUTIFUL THING TALON SENDS TO ME EVERY DAY.
AND HOW GOES OUR SPECIAL PROJECT?
THE GUARDIAN IS OPERATIONAL AND SHOWS GREAT PROMISE. I WILL SEE TO ITS SUCCESS UNTIL YOU ARE WELL ONCE AGAIN.
REST EASY, PARIS. LET THE CONTINUUM BREATHE NEW LIFE INTO YOU.
THE SELENITE GLOWS BRIGHT ONIGHT WITH THE GLOW OF THE CONTINUUM, MY PRINCESS.
ENOUGH, I HOPE, TO REPAIR THE DAMAGE TO MY BODY FROM MY PERIMETER BREACH.
IT WILL BE SO, MY PRINCESS.

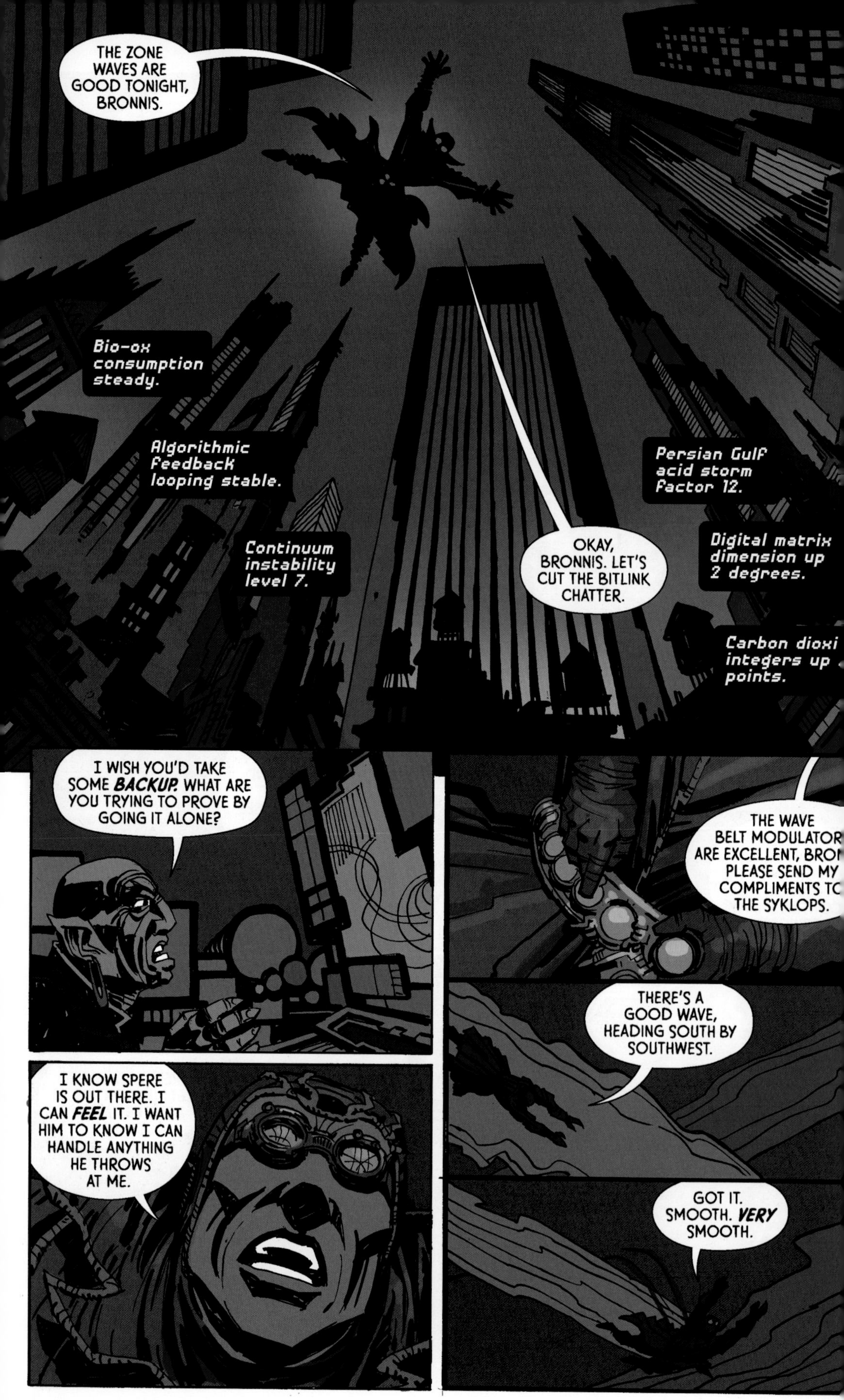
THE ZONE WAVES ARE GOOD TONIGHT, BRONNIS.
Bio-ox consumption steady.
Algorithmic feedback looping stable.
Continuum instability level 7.
Persian Gulf acid storm factor 12.
OKAY, BRONNIS. LET'S CUT THE BITLINK CHATTER.
Digital matrix dimension up 2 degrees.
Carbon dioxi integers up points.
I WISH YOU'D TAKE SOME BACKUP. WHAT ARE YOU TRYING TO PROVE BY GOING IT ALONE?
I KNOW SPERE IS OUT THERE. I CAN FEEL IT. I WANT HIM TO KNOW I CAN HANDLE ANYTHING HE THROWS AT ME.
THE WAVE BELT MODULATOR ARE EXCELLENT, BRO PLEASE SEND MY COMPLIMENTS TO THE SYKLOPS.
THERE'S A GOOD WAVE, HEADING SOUTH BY SOUTHWEST.
GOT IT. SMOOTH. VERY SMOOTH.

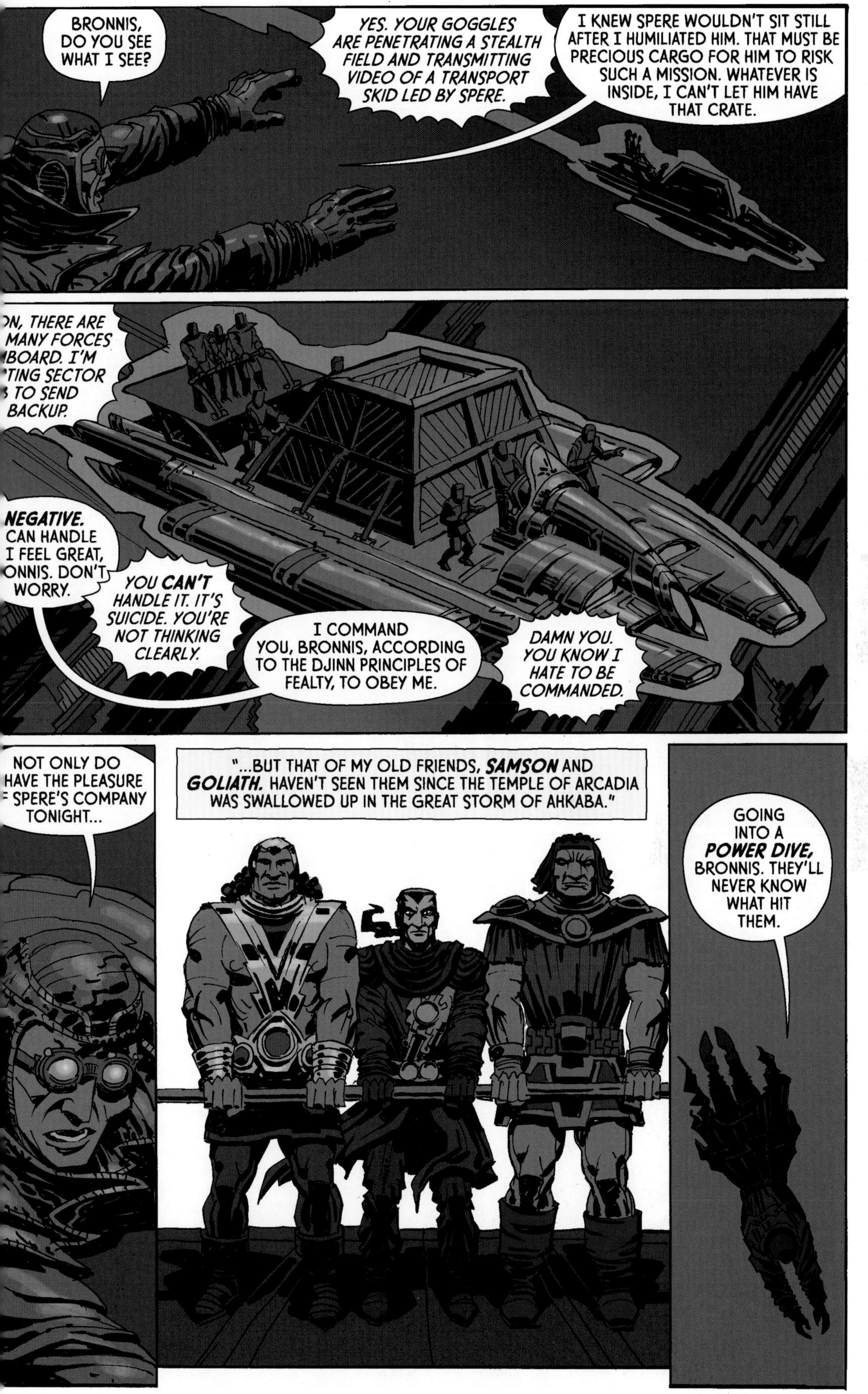

BRONNIS, DO YOU SEE WHAT I SEE?
YES. YOUR GOGGLES ARE PENETRATING A STEALTH FIELD AND TRANSMITTING VIDEO OF A TRANSPORT SKID LED BY SPERE.
I KNEW SPERE WOULDN'T SIT STILL AFTER I HUMILIATED HIM. THAT MUST BE PRECIOUS CARGO FOR HIM TO RISK SUCH A MISSION. WHATEVER IS INSIDE, I CAN'T LET HIM HAVE THAT CRATE.
N, THERE ARE MANY FORCES BOARD. I'M TING SECTOR TO SEND BACKUP.
NEGATIVE. CAN HANDLE I FEEL GREAT, ONNIS. DON'T WORRY.
YOU CAN'T HANDLE IT. IT'S SUICIDE. YOU'RE NOT THINKING CLEARLY.
I COMMAND YOU, BRONNIS, ACCORDING TO THE DJINN PRINCIPLES OF FEALTY, TO OBEY ME.
DAMN YOU. YOU KNOW I HATE TO BE COMMANDED.
NOT ONLY DO HAVE THE PLEASURE SPERE'S COMPANY TONIGHT...
"...BUT THAT OF MY OLD FRIENDS, SAMSON AND GOLIATH. HAVEN'T SEEN THEM SINCE THE TEMPLE OF ARCADIA WAS SWALLOWED UP IN THE GREAT STORM OF AHKABA."
GOING INTO A POWER DIVE, BRONNIS. THEY'LL NEVER KNOW WHAT HIT THEM.

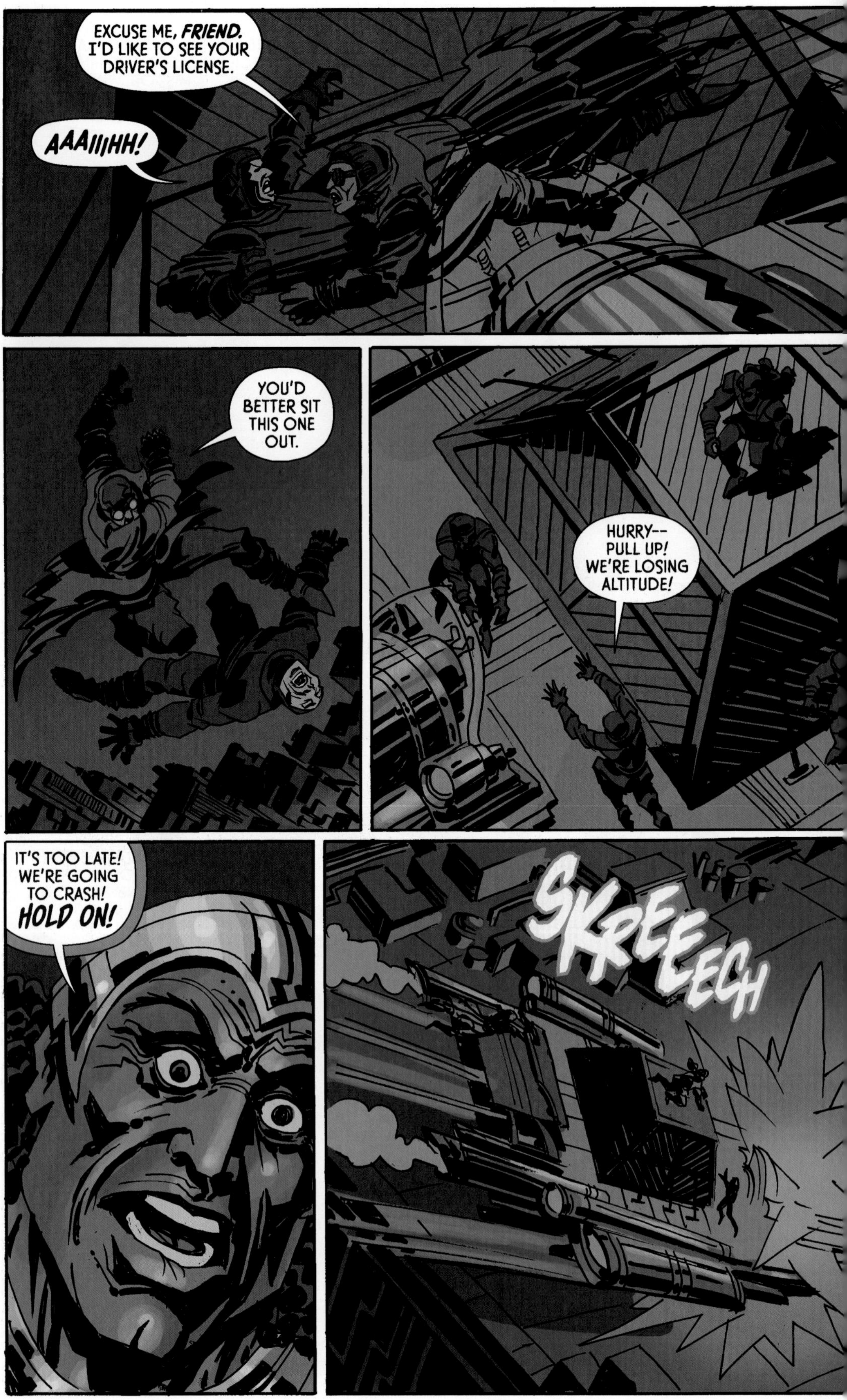
EXCUSE ME, ***FRIEND.*** I'D LIKE TO SEE YOUR DRIVER'S LICENSE.
AAAIIIHH!
YOU'D BETTER SIT THIS ONE OUT.
HURRY-- PULL UP! WE'RE LOSING ALTITUDE!
IT'S TOO LATE! WE'RE GOING TO CRASH! ***HOLD ON!***
SKREEEECH

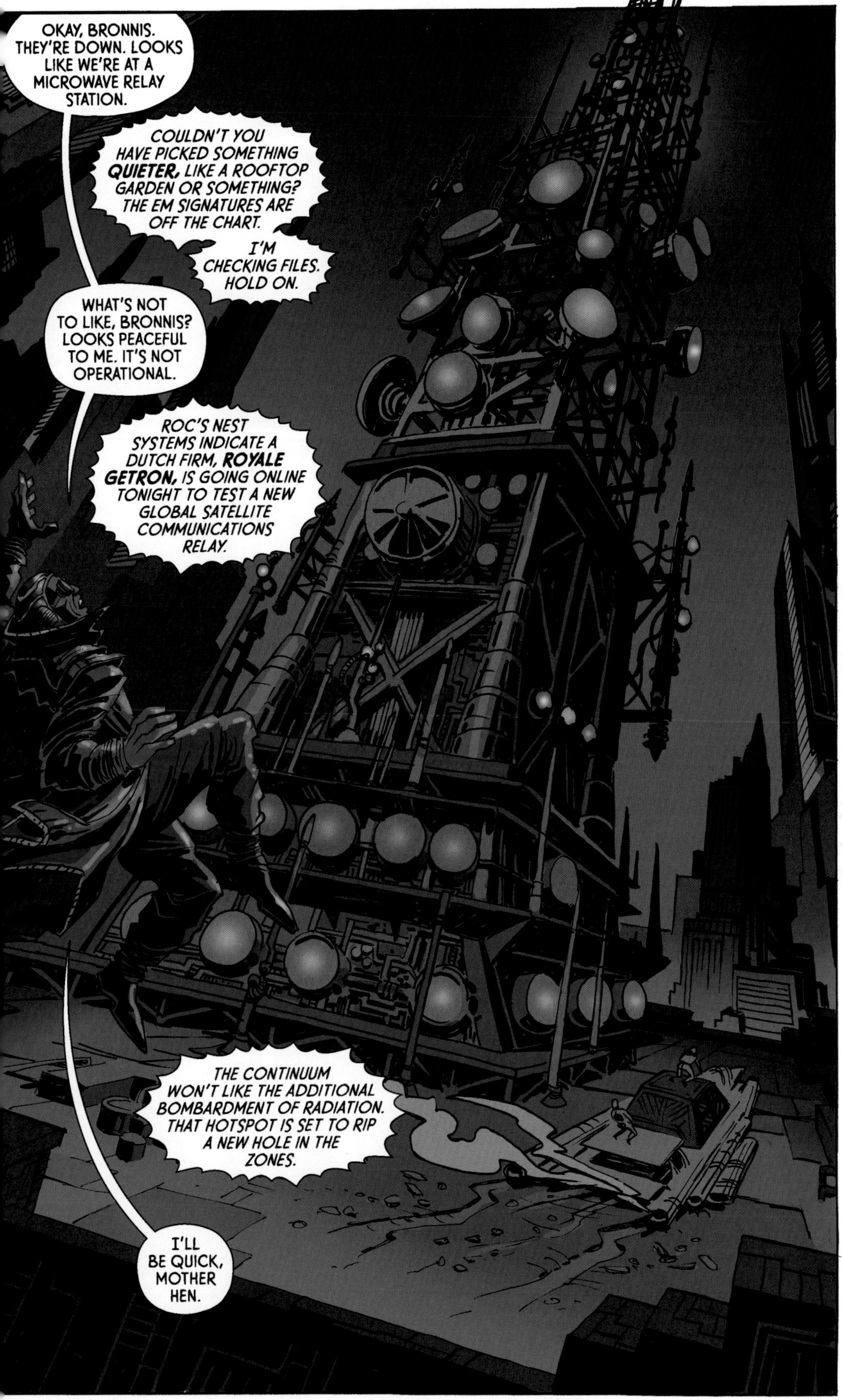
OKAY, BRONNIS. THEY'RE DOWN. LOOKS LIKE WE'RE AT A MICROWAVE RELAY STATION.
COULDN'T YOU HAVE PICKED SOMETHING QUIETER, LIKE A ROOFTOP GARDEN OR SOMETHING? THE EM SIGNATURES ARE OFF THE CHART.
I'M CHECKING FILES. HOLD ON.
WHAT'S NOT TO LIKE, BRONNIS? LOOKS PEACEFUL TO ME. IT'S NOT OPERATIONAL.
ROC'S NEST SYSTEMS INDICATE A DUTCH FIRM, ROYALE GETRON, IS GOING ONLINE TONIGHT TO TEST A NEW GLOBAL SATELLITE COMMUNICATIONS RELAY.
THE CONTINUUM WON'T LIKE THE ADDITIONAL BOMBARDMENT OF RADIATION. THAT HOTSPOT IS SET TO RIP A NEW HOLE IN THE ZONES.
I'LL BE QUICK, MOTHER HEN.

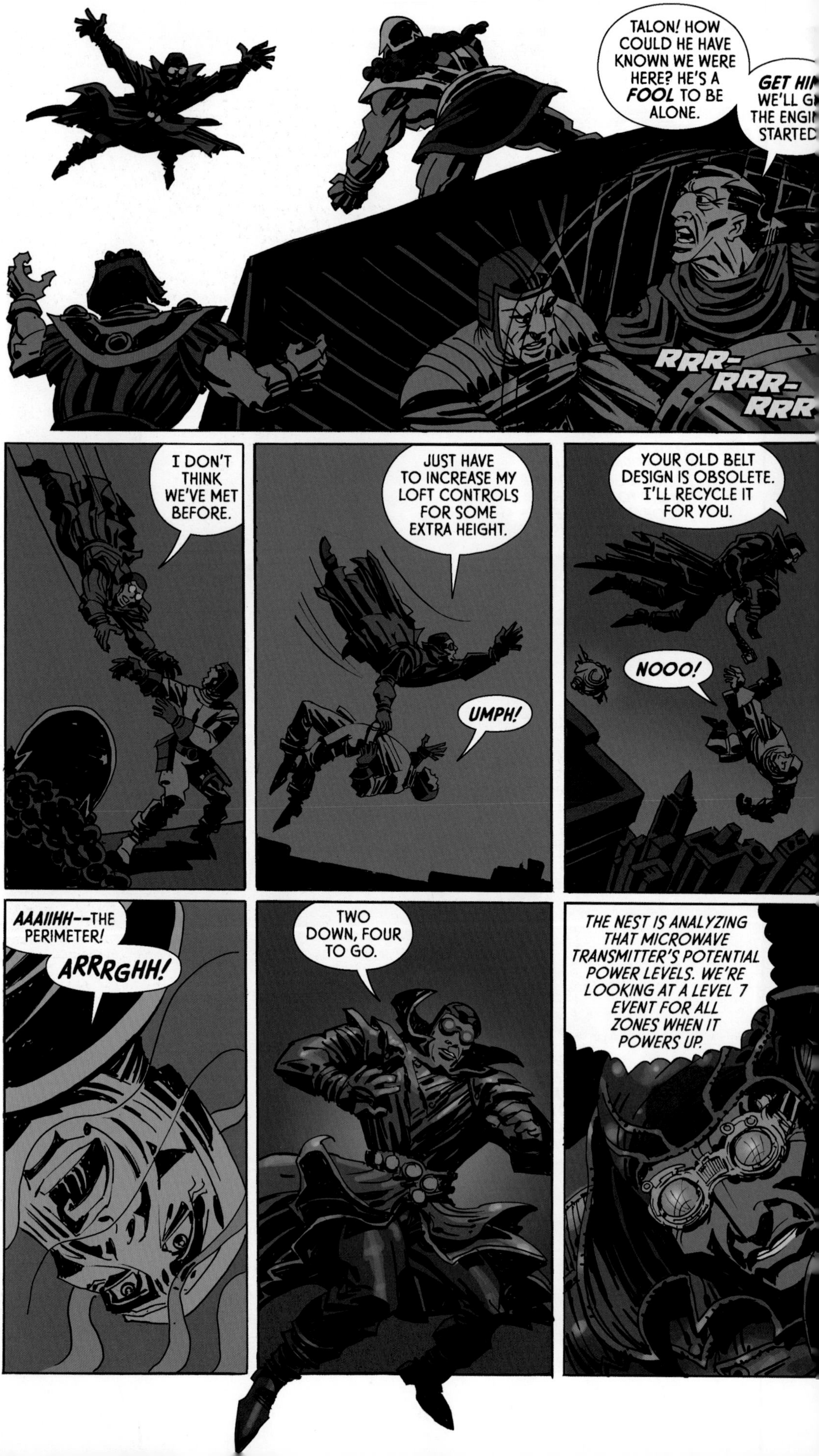

TALON! HOW COULD HE HAVE KNOWN WE WERE HERE? HE'S A FOOL TO BE ALONE.
RRR-RRR-RRR
I DON'T THINK WE'VE MET BEFORE.
JUST HAVE TO INCREASE MY LOFT CONTROLS FOR SOME EXTRA HEIGHT.
UMPH!
YOUR OLD BELT DESIGN IS OBSOLETE. I'LL RECYCLE IT FOR YOU.
NOOO!
AAAIIHH--THE PERIMETER!
ARRRGHH!
TWO DOWN, FOUR TO GO.
THE NEST IS ANALYZING THAT MICROWAVE TRANSMITTER'S POTENTIAL POWER LEVELS. WE'RE LOOKING AT A LEVEL 7 EVENT FOR ALL ZONES WHEN IT POWERS UP.

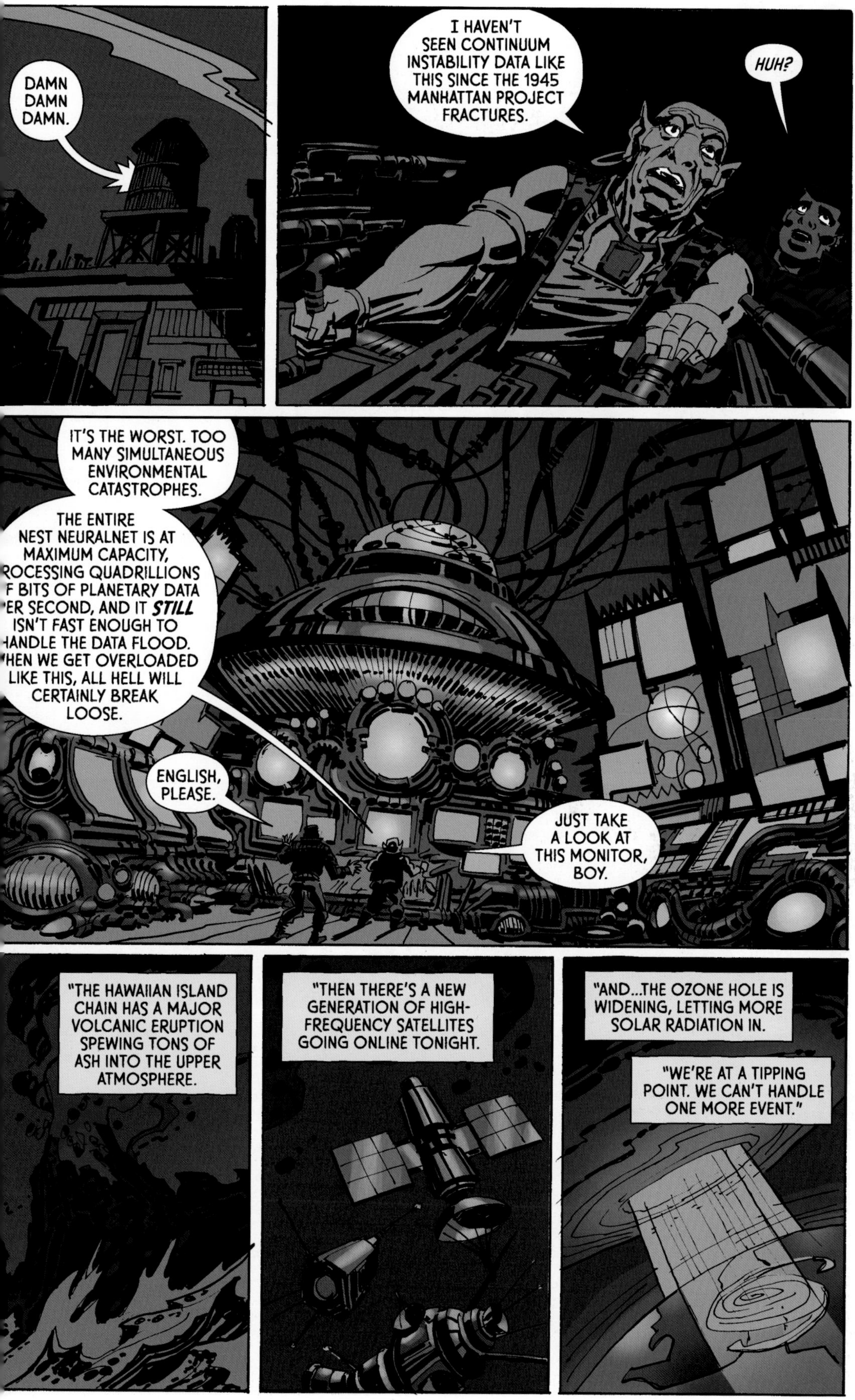

DAMN DAMN DAMN.
I HAVEN'T SEEN CONTINUUM INSTABILITY DATA LIKE THIS SINCE THE 1945 MANHATTAN PROJECT FRACTURES.
HUH?
IT'S THE WORST. TOO MANY SIMULTANEOUS ENVIRONMENTAL CATASTROPHES.
THE ENTIRE NEST NEURALNET IS AT MAXIMUM CAPACITY, ROCESSING QUADRILLIONS F BITS OF PLANETARY DATA ER SECOND, AND IT STILL ISN'T FAST ENOUGH TO HANDLE THE DATA FLOOD. HEN WE GET OVERLOADED LIKE THIS, ALL HELL WILL CERTAINLY BREAK LOOSE.
ENGLISH, PLEASE.
JUST TAKE A LOOK AT THIS MONITOR, BOY.
"THE HAWAIIAN ISLAND CHAIN HAS A MAJOR VOLCANIC ERUPTION SPEWING TONS OF ASH INTO THE UPPER ATMOSPHERE.
"THEN THERE'S A NEW GENERATION OF HIGH-FREQUENCY SATELLITES GOING ONLINE TONIGHT.
"AND...THE OZONE HOLE IS WIDENING, LETTING MORE SOLAR RADIATION IN.
"WE'RE AT A TIPPING POINT. WE CAN'T HANDLE ONE MORE EVENT."

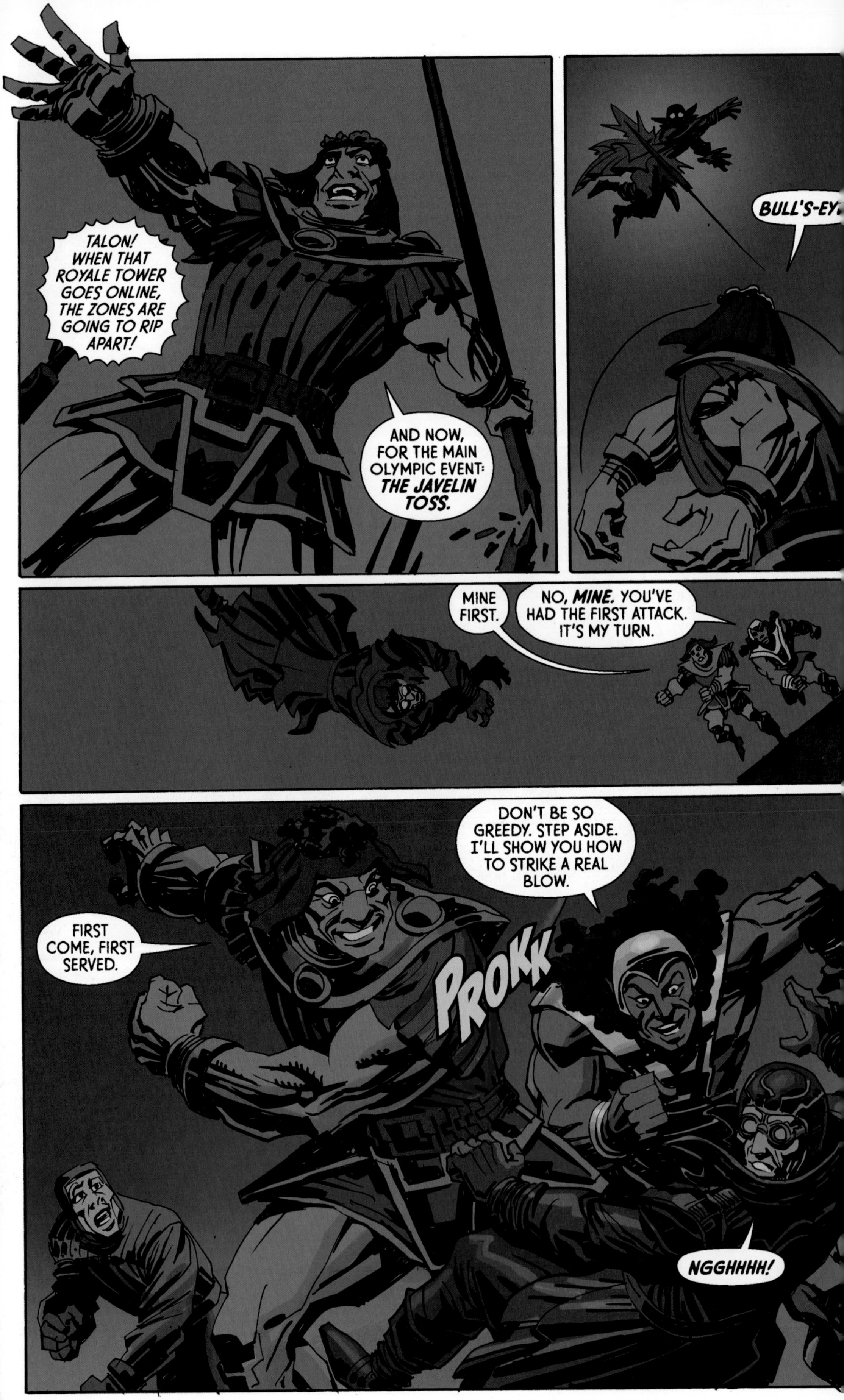
TALON! WHEN THAT ROYALE TOWER GOES ONLINE, THE ZONES ARE GOING TO RIP APART!
AND NOW, FOR THE MAIN OLYMPIC EVENT: THE JAVELIN TOSS.
MINE FIRST.
NO, MINE. YOU'VE HAD THE FIRST ATTACK. IT'S MY TURN.
DON'T BE SO GREEDY. STEP ASIDE. I'LL SHOW YOU HOW TO STRIKE A REAL BLOW.
FIRST COME, FIRST SERVED.
PROKK
NGGHHHH!

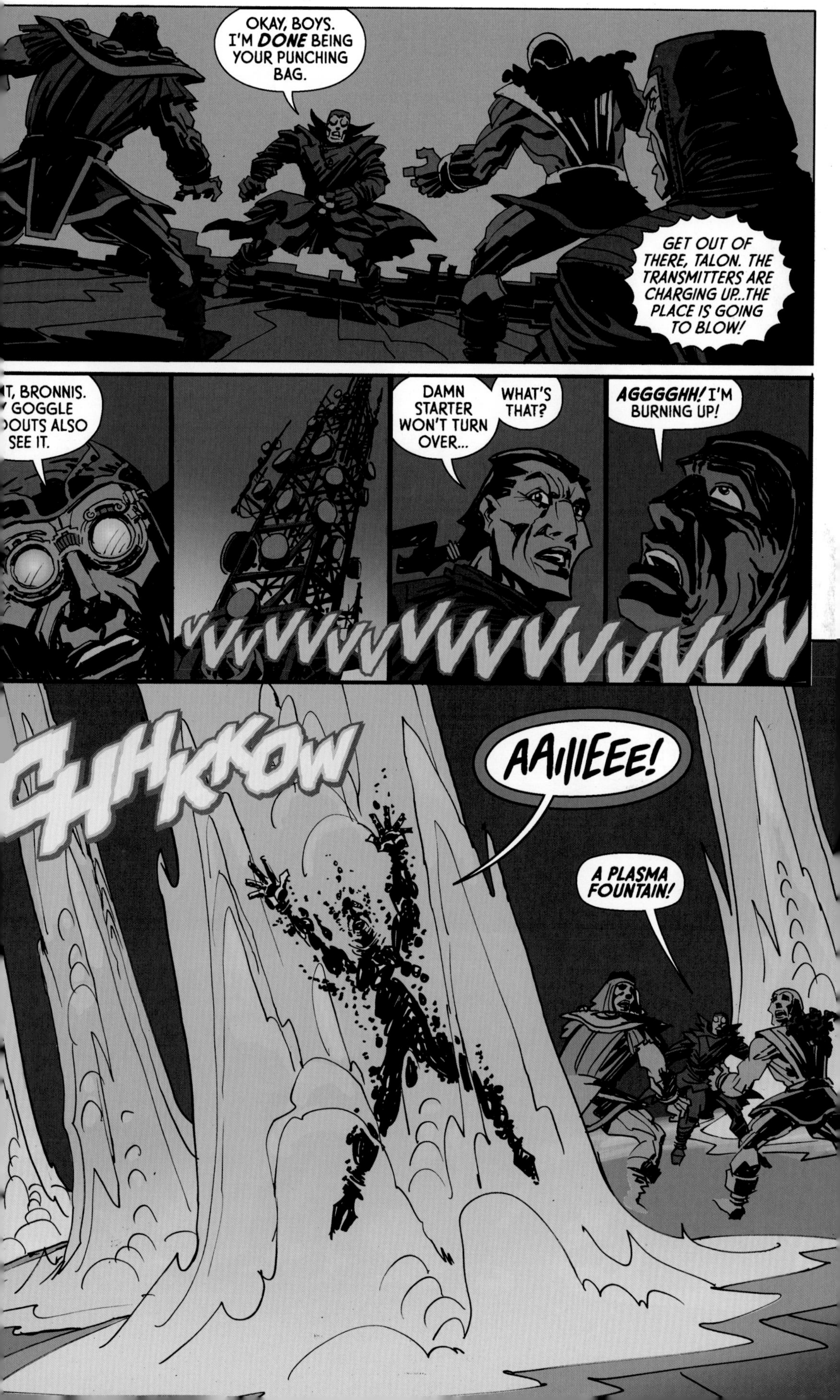
OKAY, BOYS. I'M **DONE** BEING YOUR PUNCHING BAG.
GET OUT OF THERE, TALON. THE TRANSMITTERS ARE CHARGING UP...THE PLACE IS GOING TO BLOW!
T, BRONNIS. GOGGLE OUTS ALSO SEE IT.
DAMN STARTER WON'T TURN OVER...
WHAT'S THAT?
AGGGGH! I'M BURNING UP!
VVVVVVVVVVVVVVVVVVVVVVV
CHHKKOW
AAIIIIEEE!
A PLASMA FOUNTAIN!

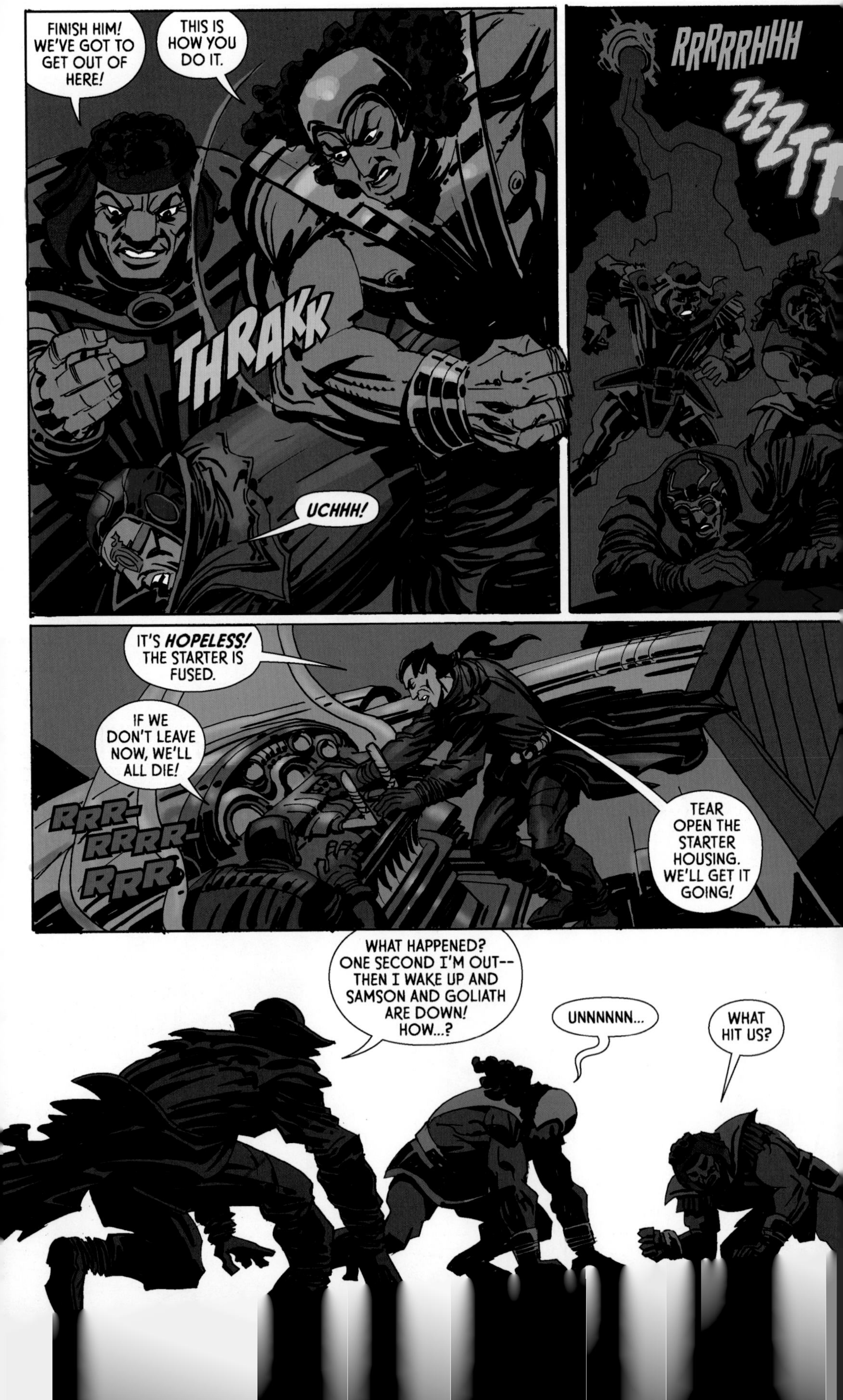
FINISH HIM! WE'VE GOT TO GET OUT OF HERE!
THIS IS HOW YOU DO IT.
THRAKK
UCHHH!
RRRRRHHH
ZZZTT
IT'S *HOPELESS!* THE STARTER IS FUSED.
IF WE DON'T LEAVE NOW, WE'LL ALL DIE!
RRR-RRRR-RRR
TEAR OPEN THE STARTER HOUSING. WE'LL GET IT GOING!
WHAT HAPPENED? ONE SECOND I'M OUT-- THEN I WAKE UP AND SAMSON AND GOLIATH ARE DOWN! HOW...?
UNNNNNN...
WHAT HIT US?

N'T BE S. WE'VE O WORK THER OR WON'T KE IT.

TALON-- DESTROY THE TOWER! ANOTHER POWER SURGE IS BUILDING...

I'VE GOT YOU NOW, LITTLE MAN. NO ONE CAN ESCAPE *SAMSON'S RIB CRUSHER.* I ONCE DEFEATED A RAGING MINOTAUR WITH THIS HOLD.

ACCKKGG...

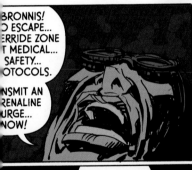

BRONNIS! O ESCAPE... ERRIDE ZONE T MEDICAL... SAFETY... OTOCOLS. NSMIT AN RENALINE URGE... NOW!

NO! I WON'T. YOU CAN'T SURVIVE IT.

DAMMIT-- I'M DEAD IF YOU DON'T.

NOW!

NOW, YOU POINTY- EARED DEVIL!

BOKK

WUCCCHH!

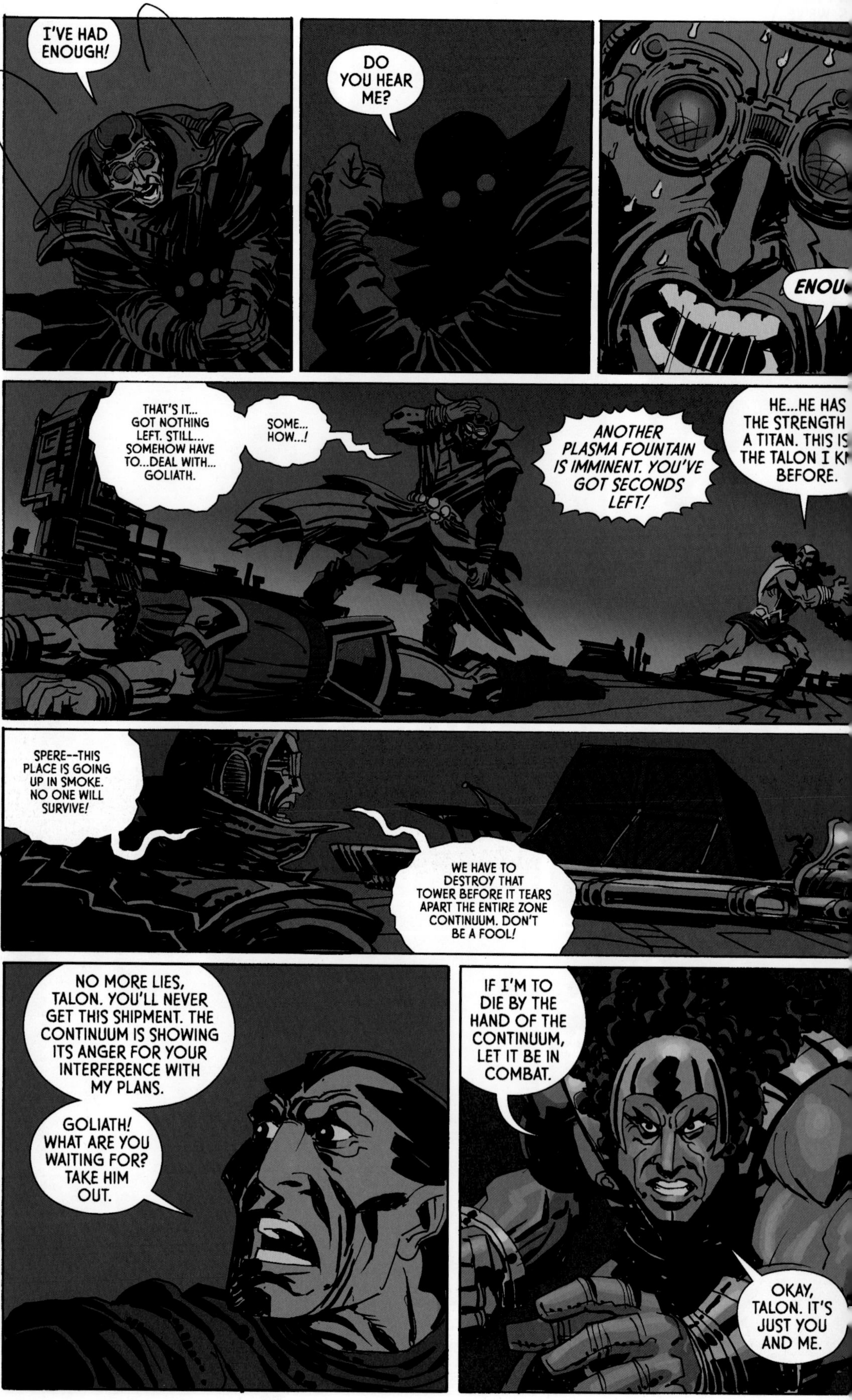

I'VE HAD ENOUGH!
DO YOU HEAR ME?
ENOU
THAT'S IT... GOT NOTHING LEFT. STILL... SOMEHOW HAVE TO...DEAL WITH... GOLIATH.
SOME... HOW...!
ANOTHER PLASMA FOUNTAIN IS IMMINENT. YOU'VE GOT SECONDS LEFT!
HE...HE HAS THE STRENGTH A TITAN. THIS IS THE TALON I K BEFORE.
SPERE--THIS PLACE IS GOING UP IN SMOKE. NO ONE WILL SURVIVE!
WE HAVE TO DESTROY THAT TOWER BEFORE IT TEARS APART THE ENTIRE ZONE CONTINUUM. DON'T BE A FOOL!
NO MORE LIES, TALON. YOU'LL NEVER GET THIS SHIPMENT. THE CONTINUUM IS SHOWING ITS ANGER FOR YOUR INTERFERENCE WITH MY PLANS.
GOLIATH! WHAT ARE YOU WAITING FOR? TAKE HIM OUT.
IF I'M TO DIE BY THE HAND OF THE CONTINUUM, LET IT BE IN COMBAT.
OKAY, TALON. IT'S JUST YOU AND ME.

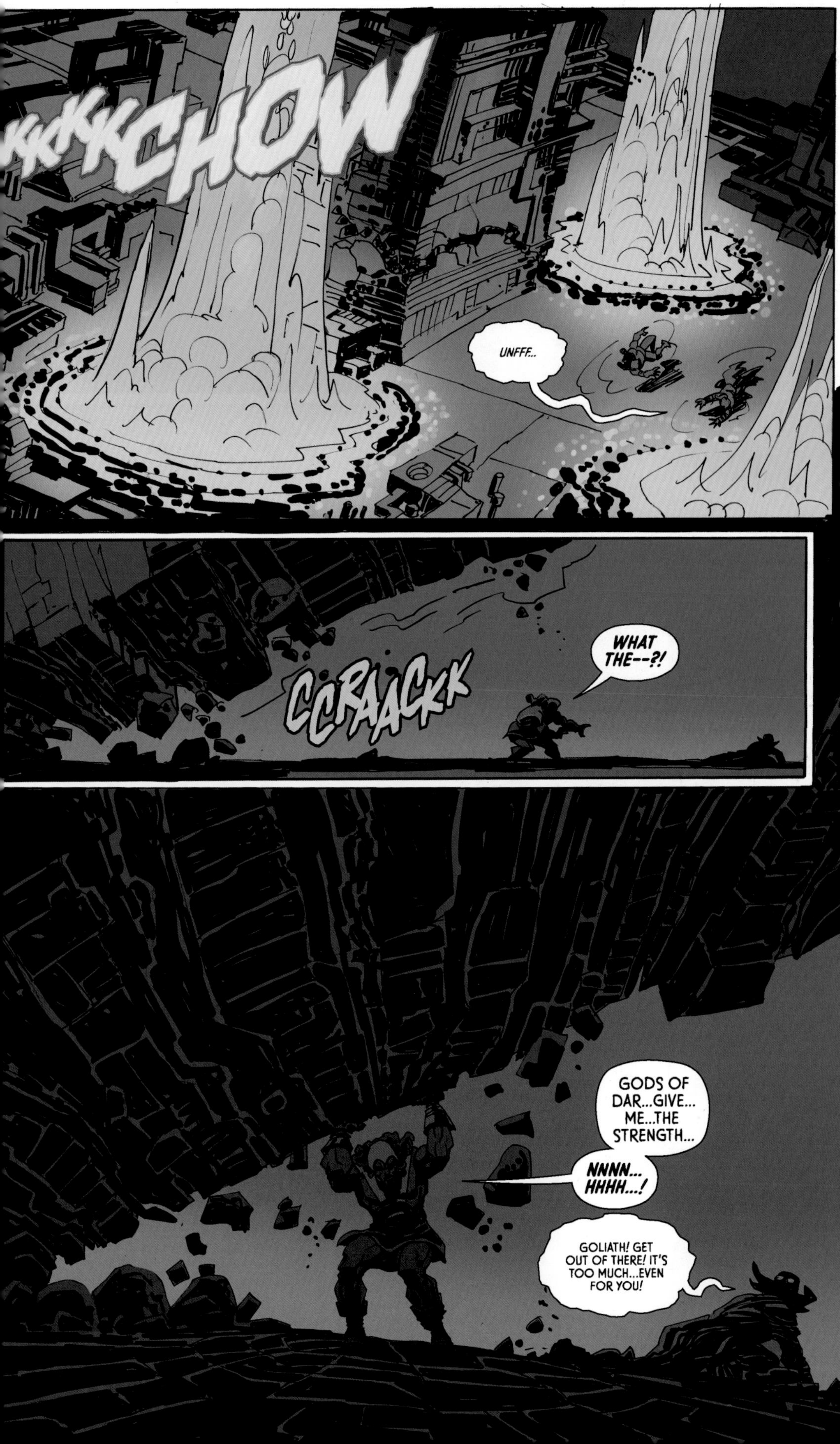
KKKKKCHOW
UNFFF...
CCRAACKK
WHAT THE--?!
GODS OF DAR...GIVE... ME...THE STRENGTH...
NNNN... HHHH...!
GOLIATH! GET OUT OF THERE! IT'S TOO MUCH...EVEN FOR YOU!

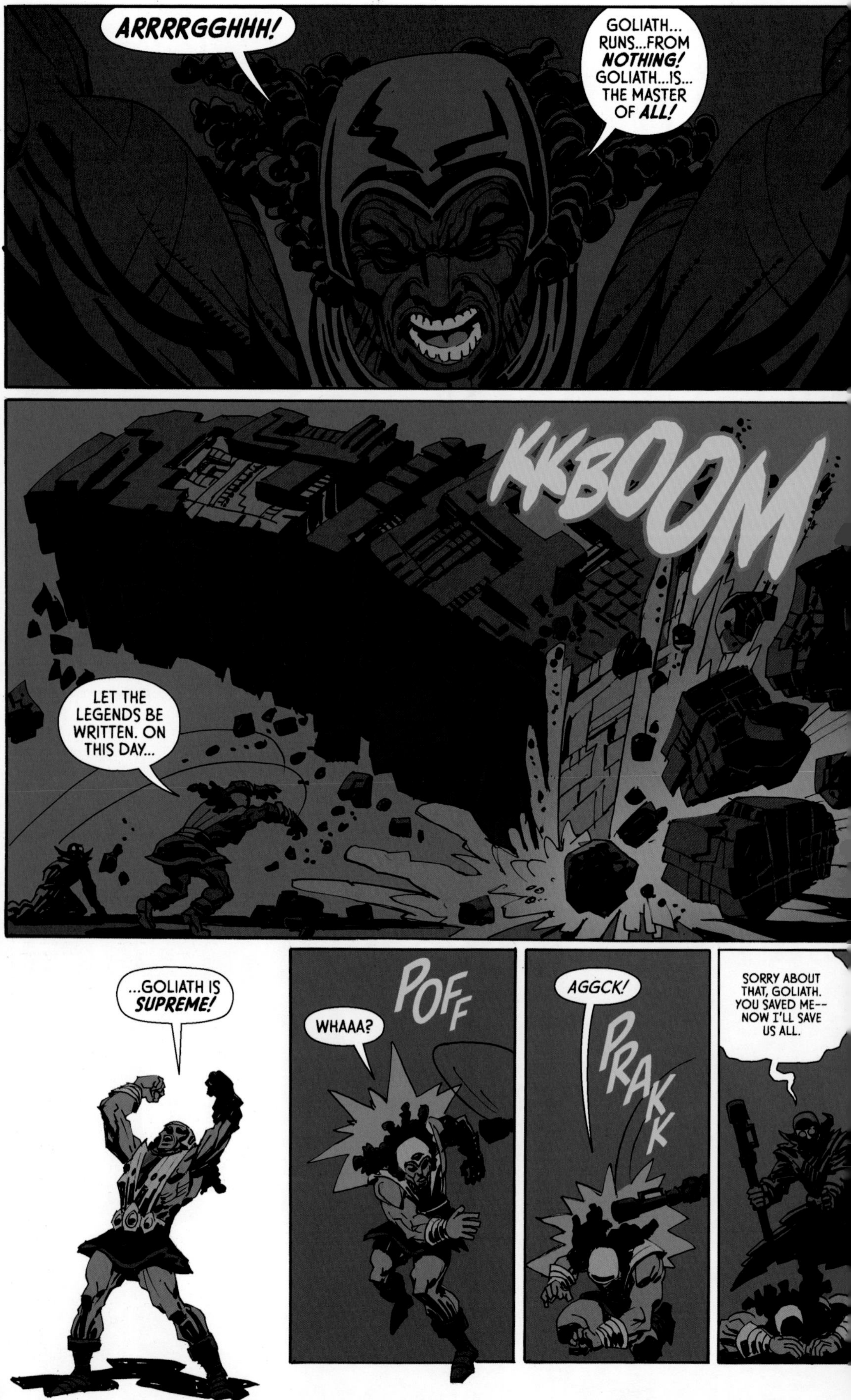
ARRRRGGHHH!
GOLIATH... RUNS...FROM NOTHING! GOLIATH...IS... THE MASTER OF ALL!
KKBOOM
LET THE LEGENDS BE WRITTEN. ON THIS DAY...
...GOLIATH IS SUPREME!
POFF
WHAAA?
AGGCK!
PRAKK
SORRY ABOUT THAT, GOLIATH. YOU SAVED ME-- NOW I'LL SAVE US ALL.

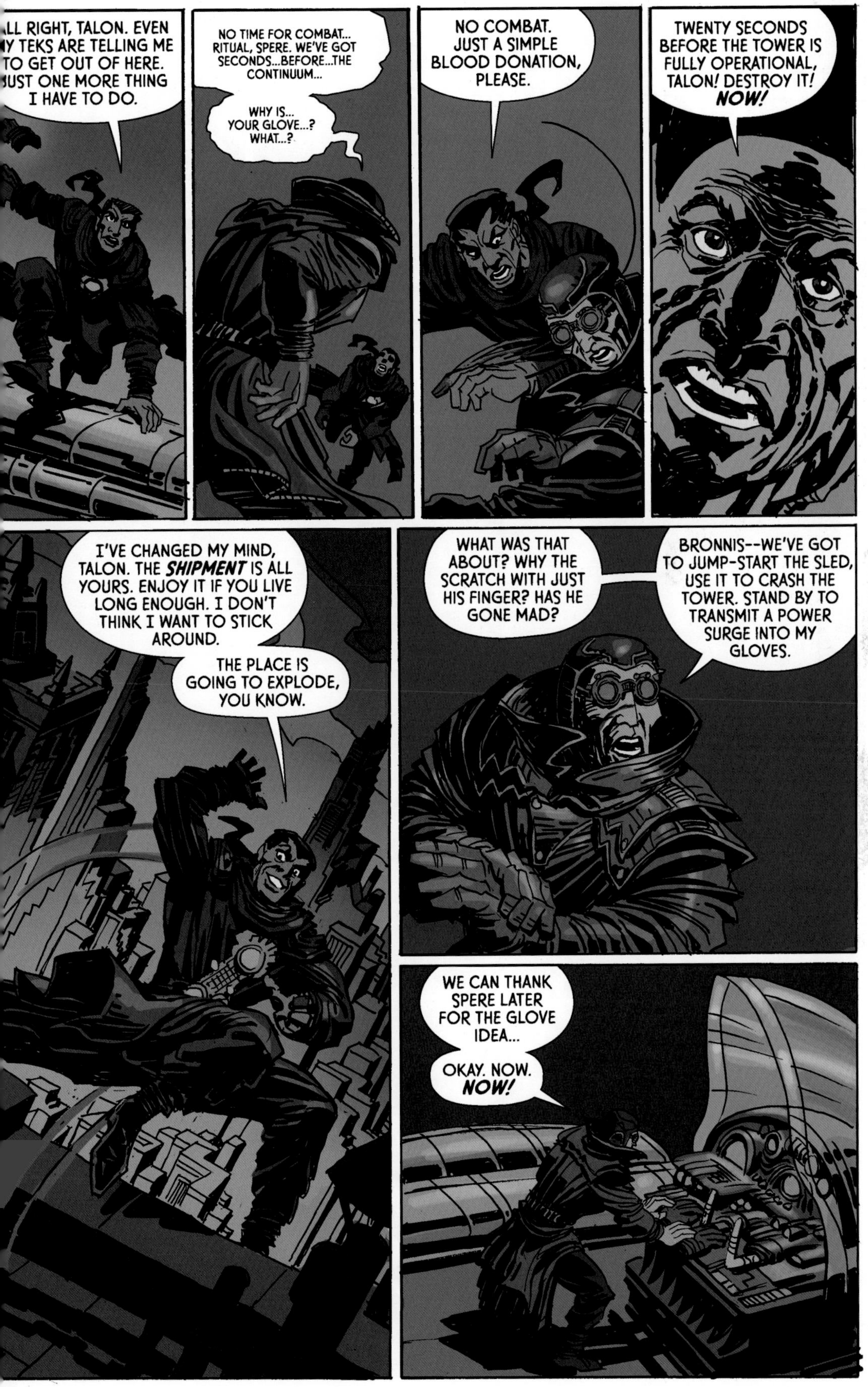

LL RIGHT, TALON. EVEN Y TEKS ARE TELLING ME TO GET OUT OF HERE. JUST ONE MORE THING I HAVE TO DO.
NO TIME FOR COMBAT... RITUAL, SPERE. WE'VE GOT SECONDS...BEFORE...THE CONTINUUM...
WHY IS... YOUR GLOVE...? WHAT...?
NO COMBAT. JUST A SIMPLE BLOOD DONATION, PLEASE.
TWENTY SECONDS BEFORE THE TOWER IS FULLY OPERATIONAL, TALON! DESTROY IT! NOW!
I'VE CHANGED MY MIND, TALON. THE SHIPMENT IS ALL YOURS. ENJOY IT IF YOU LIVE LONG ENOUGH. I DON'T THINK I WANT TO STICK AROUND.
THE PLACE IS GOING TO EXPLODE, YOU KNOW.
WHAT WAS THAT ABOUT? WHY THE SCRATCH WITH JUST HIS FINGER? HAS HE GONE MAD?
BRONNIS--WE'VE GOT TO JUMP-START THE SLED, USE IT TO CRASH THE TOWER. STAND BY TO TRANSMIT A POWER SURGE INTO MY GLOVES.
WE CAN THANK SPERE LATER FOR THE GLOVE IDEA...
OKAY. NOW. NOW!

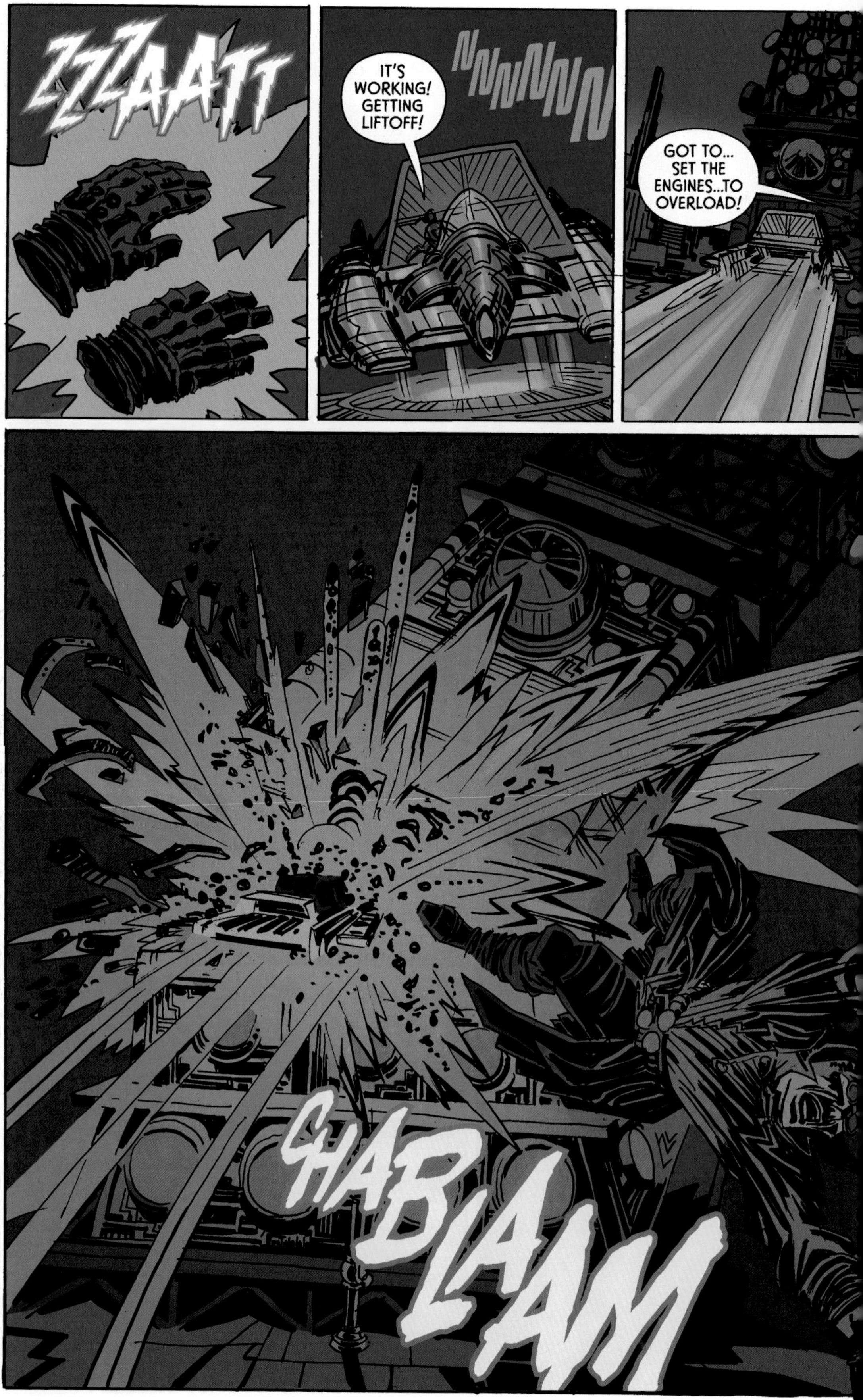
ZZZAATT
IT'S WORKING! GETTING LIFTOFF!
NNNNNN
GOT TO... SET THE ENGINES...TO OVERLOAD!
CHABLAAM

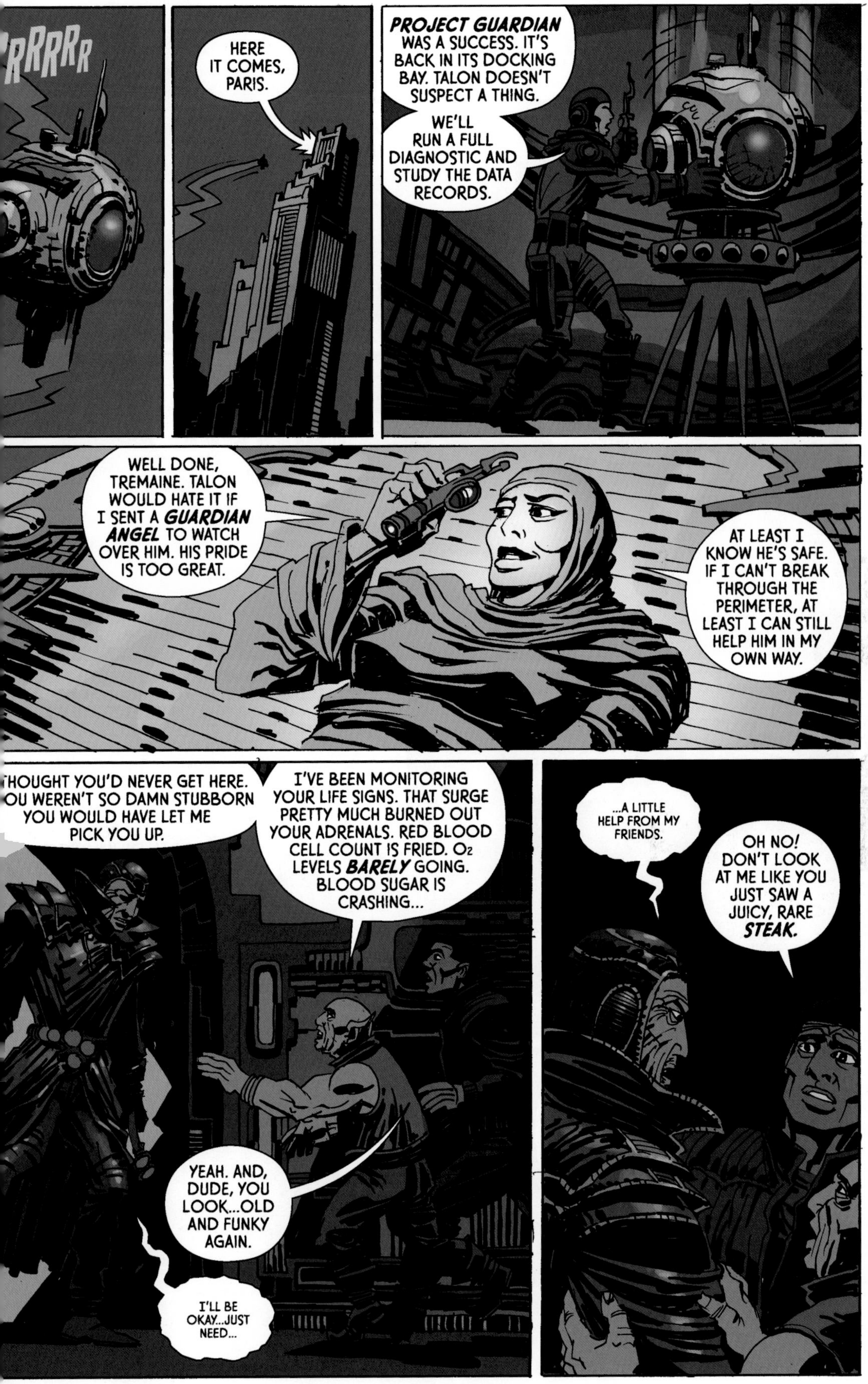
RRRRR
HERE IT COMES, PARIS.
PROJECT GUARDIAN WAS A SUCCESS. IT'S BACK IN ITS DOCKING BAY. TALON DOESN'T SUSPECT A THING.
WE'LL RUN A FULL DIAGNOSTIC AND STUDY THE DATA RECORDS.
WELL DONE, TREMAINE. TALON WOULD HATE IT IF I SENT A GUARDIAN ANGEL TO WATCH OVER HIM. HIS PRIDE IS TOO GREAT.
AT LEAST I KNOW HE'S SAFE. IF I CAN'T BREAK THROUGH THE PERIMETER, AT LEAST I CAN STILL HELP HIM IN MY OWN WAY.
THOUGHT YOU'D NEVER GET HERE. OU WEREN'T SO DAMN STUBBORN YOU WOULD HAVE LET ME PICK YOU UP.
I'VE BEEN MONITORING YOUR LIFE SIGNS. THAT SURGE PRETTY MUCH BURNED OUT YOUR ADRENALS. RED BLOOD CELL COUNT IS FRIED. O2 LEVELS BARELY GOING. BLOOD SUGAR IS CRASHING...
YEAH. AND, DUDE, YOU LOOK...OLD AND FUNKY AGAIN.
I'LL BE OKAY...JUST NEED...
...A LITTLE HELP FROM MY FRIENDS.
OH NO! DON'T LOOK AT ME LIKE YOU JUST SAW A JUICY, RARE STEAK.

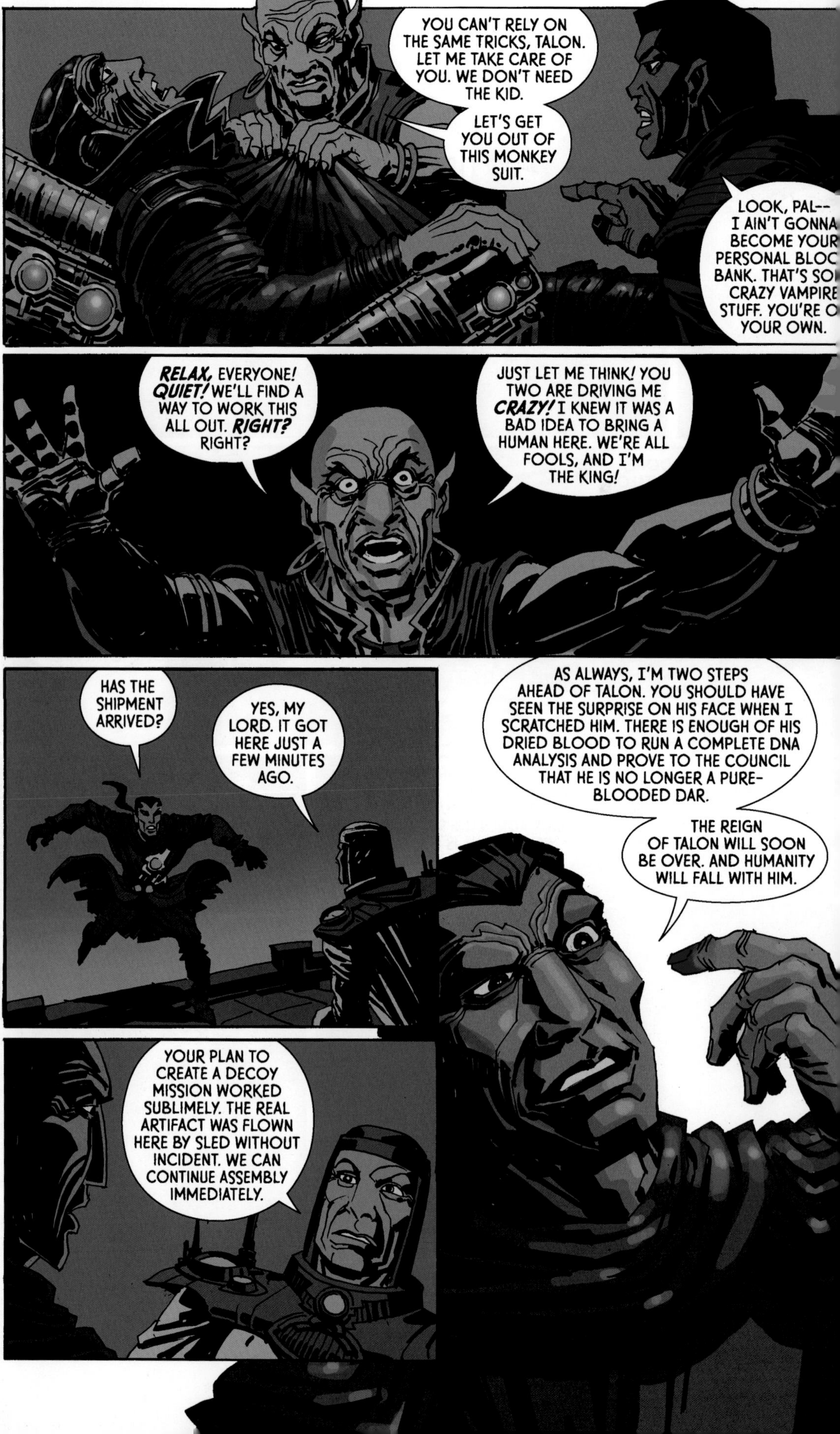
YOU CAN'T RELY ON THE SAME TRICKS, TALON. LET ME TAKE CARE OF YOU. WE DON'T NEED THE KID.
LET'S GET YOU OUT OF THIS MONKEY SUIT.
LOOK, PAL-- I AIN'T GONNA BECOME YOUR PERSONAL BLOO BANK. THAT'S SO CRAZY VAMPIRE STUFF. YOU'RE O YOUR OWN.
RELAX, EVERYONE! QUIET! WE'LL FIND A WAY TO WORK THIS ALL OUT. RIGHT? RIGHT?
JUST LET ME THINK! YOU TWO ARE DRIVING ME CRAZY! I KNEW IT WAS A BAD IDEA TO BRING A HUMAN HERE. WE'RE ALL FOOLS, AND I'M THE KING!
HAS THE SHIPMENT ARRIVED?
YES, MY LORD. IT GOT HERE JUST A FEW MINUTES AGO.
AS ALWAYS, I'M TWO STEPS AHEAD OF TALON. YOU SHOULD HAVE SEEN THE SURPRISE ON HIS FACE WHEN I SCRATCHED HIM. THERE IS ENOUGH OF HIS DRIED BLOOD TO RUN A COMPLETE DNA ANALYSIS AND PROVE TO THE COUNCIL THAT HE IS NO LONGER A PURE-BLOODED DAR.
THE REIGN OF TALON WILL SOON BE OVER. AND HUMANITY WILL FALL WITH HIM.
YOUR PLAN TO CREATE A DECOY MISSION WORKED SUBLIMELY. THE REAL ARTIFACT WAS FLOWN HERE BY SLED WITHOUT INCIDENT. WE CAN CONTINUE ASSEMBLY IMMEDIATELY.

CHAPTER FOUR

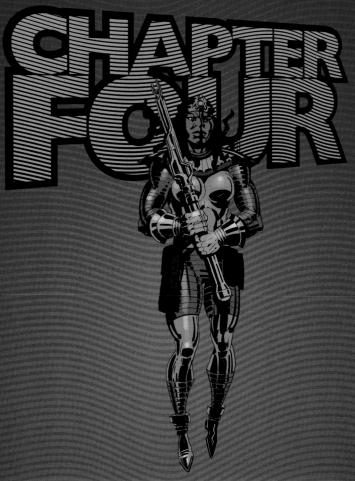

BATTLE FOR HUMANITY

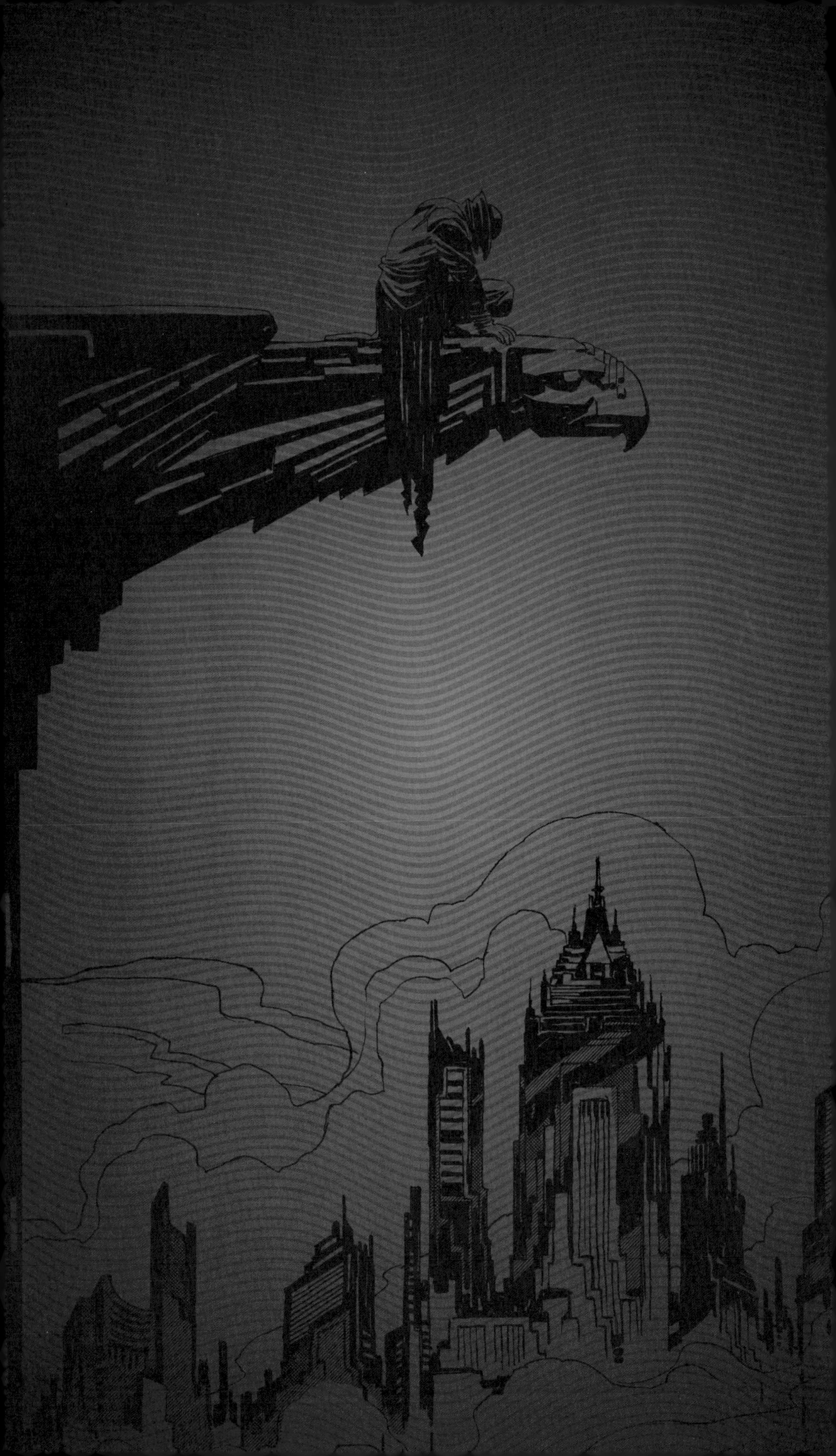

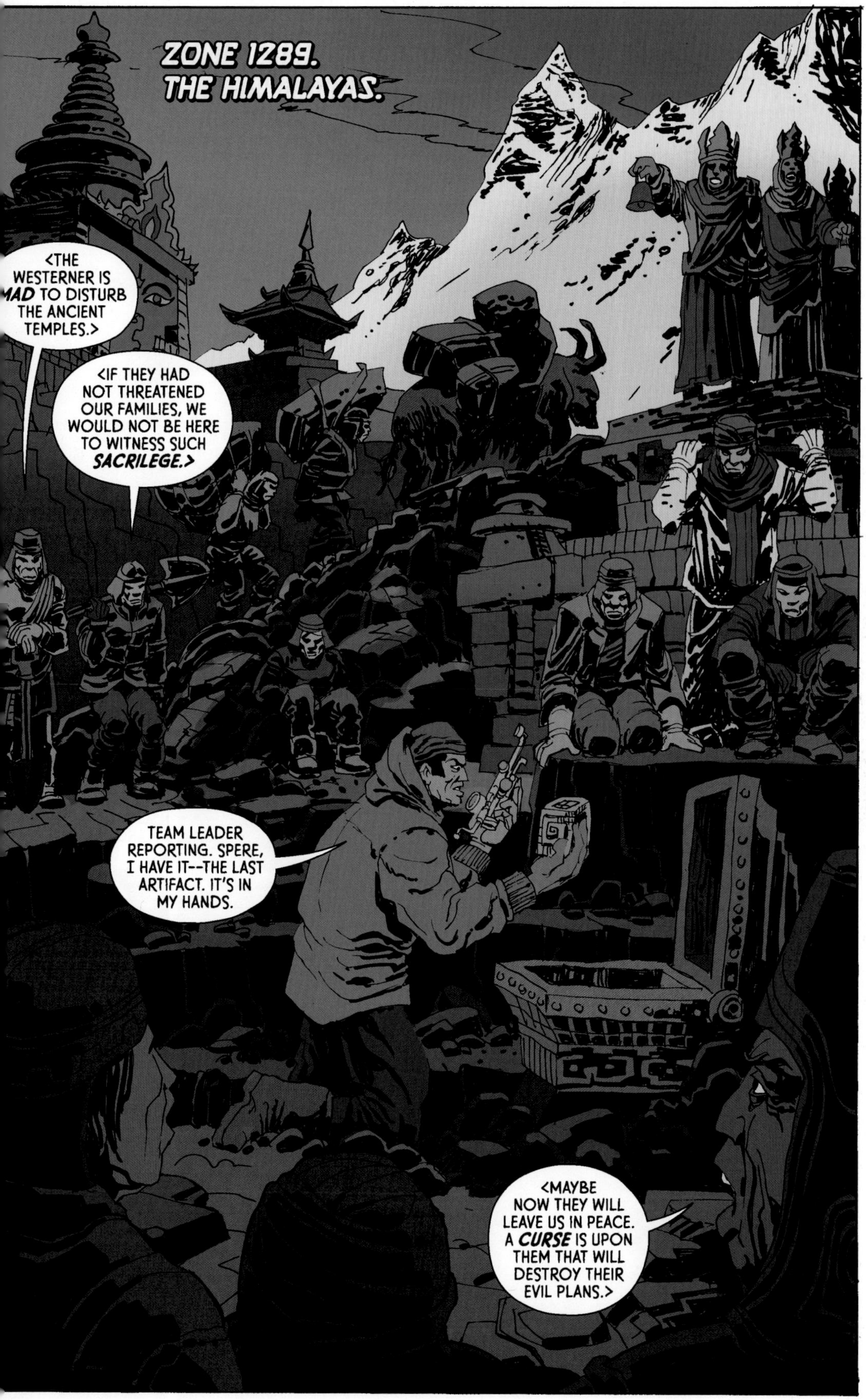
ZONE 1289. THE HIMALAYAS.
<THE WESTERNER IS MAD TO DISTURB THE ANCIENT TEMPLES.>
<IF THEY HAD NOT THREATENED OUR FAMILIES, WE WOULD NOT BE HERE TO WITNESS SUCH SACRILEGE.>
TEAM LEADER REPORTING. SPERE, I HAVE IT--THE LAST ARTIFACT. IT'S IN MY HANDS.
<MAYBE NOW THEY WILL LEAVE US IN PEACE. A CURSE IS UPON THEM THAT WILL DESTROY THEIR EVIL PLANS.>

EXCELLENT! MAKE SURE IT GETS TO US IN THE NEXT EIGHT HOURS. TERMINATE ALL OTHER DIG OPERATIONS.

BEGIN FINAL PHASE. SUMMON THE *GORGONNS.* MOVE THE TERMINUS MACHINA TO THE ROOFTOP ASSEMBLY.

DAMN, I CAN FEEL THE CHILL IN MY BONES ALREADY.

I COMMAND YOU TO FINISH THE SUB-ZONE MACHINE. AS AGREED, ONCE HUMANITY IS *DESTROYED,* YOU SHALL HAVE CONTROL OF THE ENTIRE MEDITERRANEAN REGION.

YOU *COMMAND?* TAKE CAUTION, DAR FLEA. NO ONE COMMANDS THE GORGONNS. WE ARE HERE BASED ONLY ON MUTUAL BENEFIT. WE MUST BE FREE OF THE STENCH OF MORTAL DECAY THAT ENVELOPS THE PLANET.

EVEN THE SMELL OF YOUR ROTTING DAR FLESH IS TOO MUCH FOR US. THE SOONER WE FINISH AND LEAVE, THE BETTER.

DON'T THINK FOR A MOMEN THAT YOU ARE C SUPERIOR. LO AFTER THE DAR GONE, WE GORG SHALL STILL WA THIS WORLD

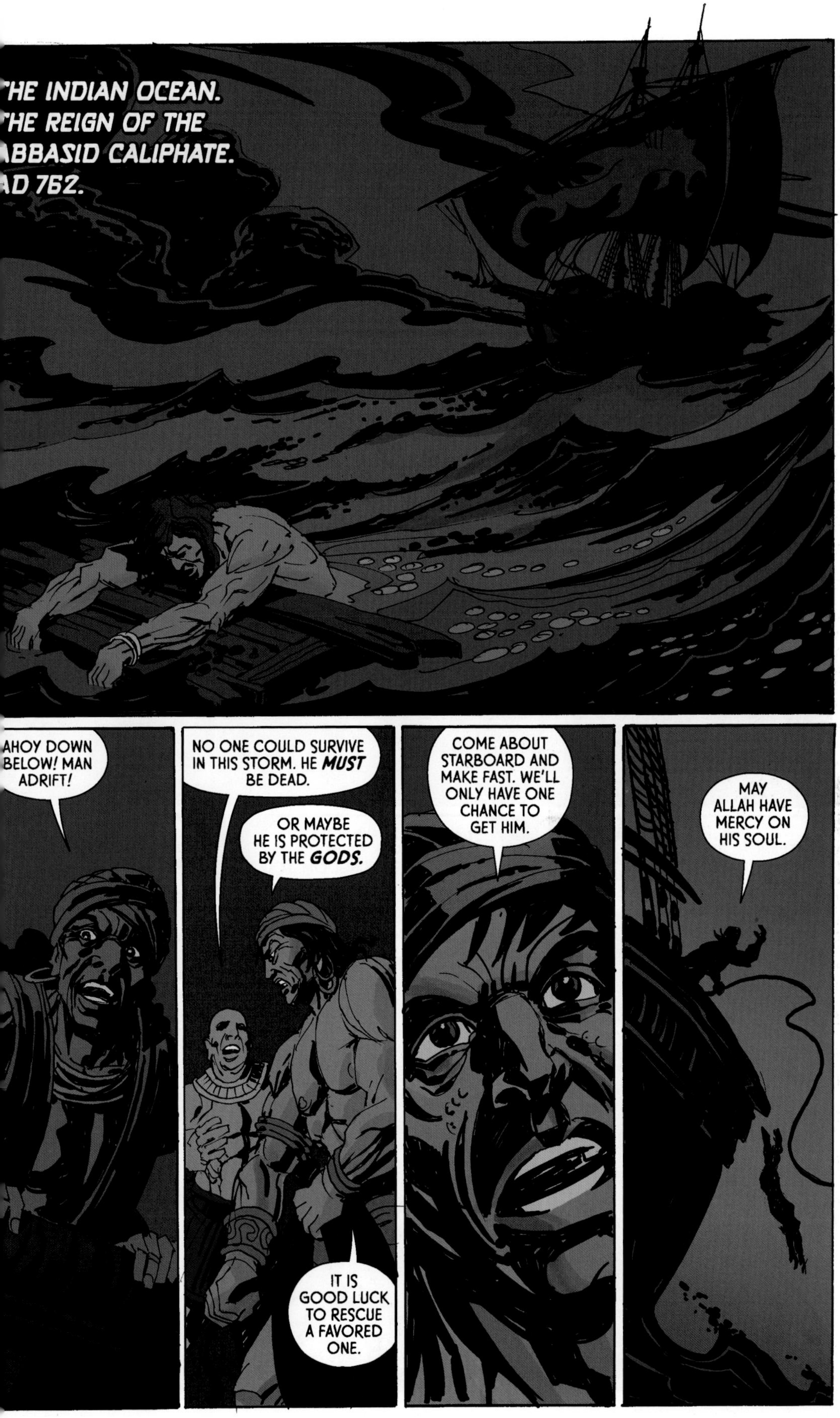
HE INDIAN OCEAN.
HE REIGN OF THE
BBASID CALIPHATE.
D 762.
AHOY DOWN BELOW! MAN ADRIFT!
NO ONE COULD SURVIVE IN THIS STORM. HE *MUST* BE DEAD.
OR MAYBE HE IS PROTECTED BY THE *GODS.*
IT IS GOOD LUCK TO RESCUE A FAVORED ONE.
COME ABOUT STARBOARD AND MAKE FAST. WE'LL ONLY HAVE ONE CHANCE TO GET HIM.
MAY ALLAH HAVE MERCY ON HIS SOUL.

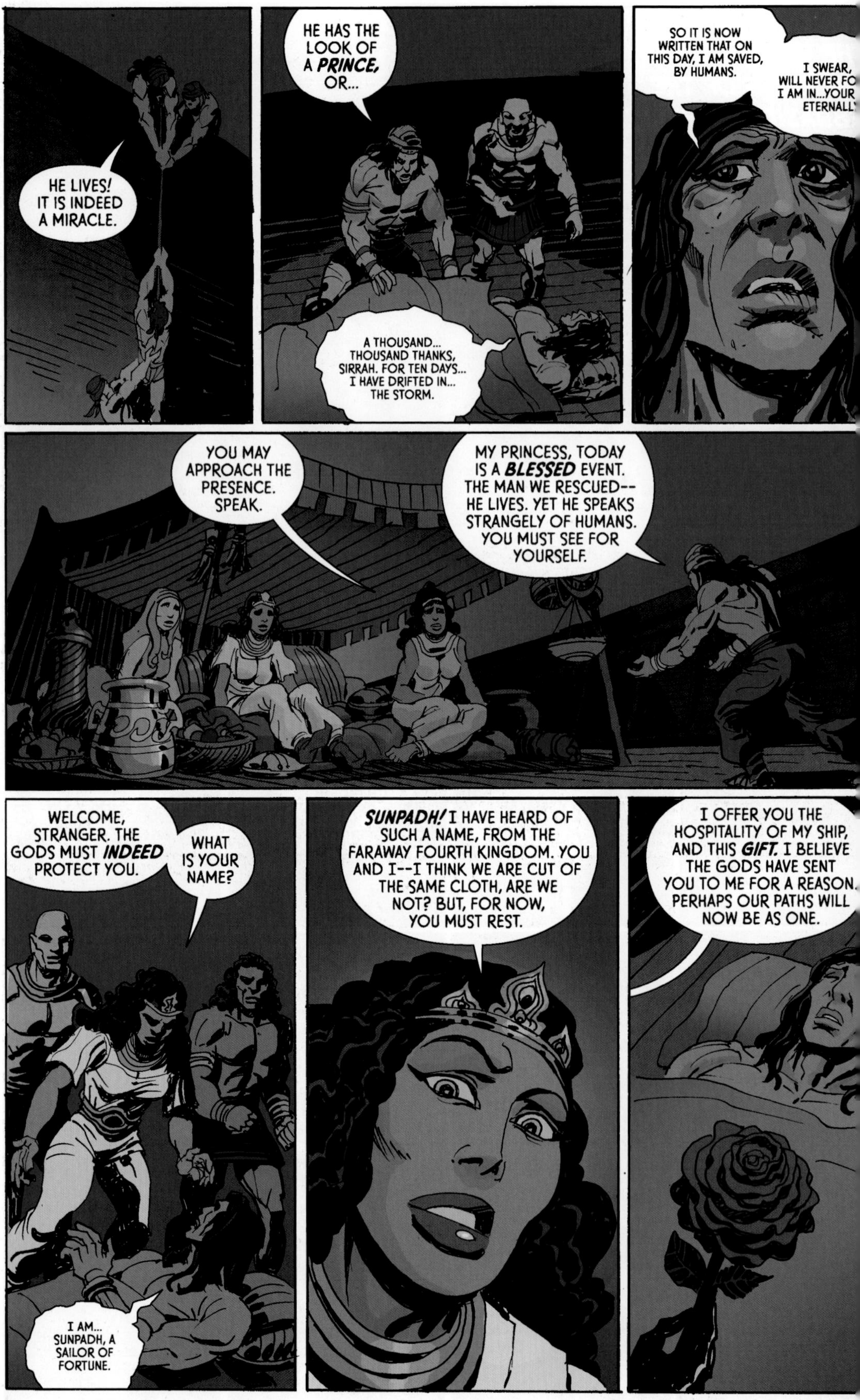
HE LIVES! IT IS INDEED A MIRACLE.
HE HAS THE LOOK OF A PRINCE, OR...
A THOUSAND... THOUSAND THANKS, SIRRAH. FOR TEN DAYS... I HAVE DRIFTED IN... THE STORM.
SO IT IS NOW WRITTEN THAT ON THIS DAY, I AM SAVED, BY HUMANS.
I SWEAR, WILL NEVER FO I AM IN...YOUR ETERNALL
YOU MAY APPROACH THE PRESENCE. SPEAK.
MY PRINCESS, TODAY IS A BLESSED EVENT. THE MAN WE RESCUED-- HE LIVES. YET HE SPEAKS STRANGELY OF HUMANS. YOU MUST SEE FOR YOURSELF.
WELCOME, STRANGER. THE GODS MUST INDEED PROTECT YOU.
WHAT IS YOUR NAME?
I AM... SUNPADH, A SAILOR OF FORTUNE.
SUNPADH! I HAVE HEARD OF SUCH A NAME, FROM THE FARAWAY FOURTH KINGDOM. YOU AND I--I THINK WE ARE CUT OF THE SAME CLOTH, ARE WE NOT? BUT, FOR NOW, YOU MUST REST.
I OFFER YOU THE HOSPITALITY OF MY SHIP, AND THIS GIFT. I BELIEVE THE GODS HAVE SENT YOU TO ME FOR A REASON. PERHAPS OUR PATHS WILL NOW BE AS ONE.

ROSES? YOU GOTTA BE KIDDING ME. NOT VERY MANLY, YA KNOW?

I GUESS EVERY GUY NEEDS A HOBBY.

MAKE SURE THIS GETS DELIVERED ON TIME.

SURE, SURE. JUST LIKE I DO EVERY DAMN DAY.

I'LL BRING ANOTHER ONE ALONG WITH ME TODAY...FOR GOOD LUCK.

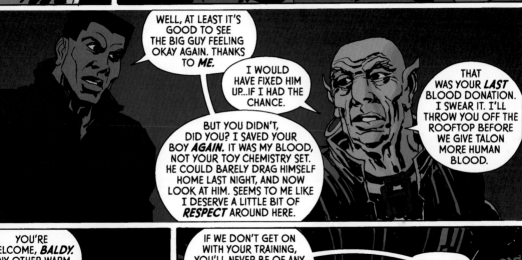

WELL, AT LEAST IT'S GOOD TO SEE THE BIG GUY FEELING OKAY AGAIN. THANKS TO ME.

I WOULD HAVE FIXED HIM UP...IF I HAD THE CHANCE.

BUT YOU DIDN'T, DID YOU? I SAVED YOUR BOY AGAIN. IT WAS MY BLOOD, NOT YOUR TOY CHEMISTRY SET. HE COULD BARELY DRAG HIMSELF HOME LAST NIGHT, AND NOW LOOK AT HIM. SEEMS TO ME LIKE I DESERVE A LITTLE BIT OF RESPECT AROUND HERE.

THAT WAS YOUR LAST BLOOD DONATION. I SWEAR IT. I'LL THROW YOU OFF THE ROOFTOP BEFORE WE GIVE TALON MORE HUMAN BLOOD.

YOU'RE WELCOME, BALDY. ANY OTHER WARM WORDS OF GRATITUDE?

IF WE DON'T GET ON WITH YOUR TRAINING, YOU'LL NEVER BE OF ANY REAL HELP AROUND HERE. I'VE GOT TO TEACH YOU HOW TO OPERATE ROC'S NEST.

WHAT'S THE RUSH? ARE YOU GOING SOMEWHERE?

ONE NEVER KNOWS.

NOW PAY ATTENTION. YOUR PRIMARY FUNCTION IS TO FEED TALON WITH ALL OF THE LATEST CALCULATIONS FROM THE NEST NEURALNET ON BIT-LINK. HIS LIFE *DEPENDS* ON MOMENT-TO-MOMENT PREDICTIONS OF CONTINUUM INSTABILITY.

YOU CAN TAKE CONTROL WITH A SIMPLE PASSWORD, AND AN AUTOMATED PROGRAM THAT I'VE CREATED WILL GIVE YOU VOICE COMMAND OVER THE AI INTERFACE. A SIMPLE QUESTION WILL GIVE YOU A SIMPLE ANSWER AND TEACH YOU ALONG THE WAY.

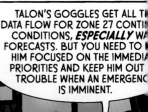

TALON'S GOGGLES GET ALL TH DATA FLOW FOR ZONE 27 CONTIN CONDITIONS, *ESPECIALLY* WA FORECASTS. BUT YOU NEED TO HIM FOCUSED ON THE IMMEDIA PRIORITIES AND KEEP HIM OUT TROUBLE WHEN AN EMERGENC IS IMMINENT.

OKAY, NOW THAT YOU'VE BLOWN MY MIND, WOULD YOU HELP PICK UP THE LITTLE PIECES?

WHAT ABOUT THAT BANK OF COMPUTERS OVER THERE?

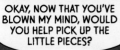

THAT'S A FULLY QUARANTINED AND AUTOMATED SECTOR DEALING WITH ALL OF THOMAS ALLEN'S *PRIVATE* ENTERPR DEDICATED TO POLLUTION CLEANUP AND DEVELOPMENT ALTERNATIVE ENERGIES. HE'S HELPED FUND OVER HALF O ALL GLOBAL ENERGY INNOVATIONS.

SINCE TALON IS COMMITTED TO SAVING HUMANITY, HE'S ALSO RESPONSIBLE FOR ENSURING THAT HUMAN DEGRADATION OF THE ZONE CONTINUUM ENDS AS QUICKLY AS POSSIBLE. OTHERWISE THE COUNCIL OF ELDERS WOULD *NEVER* VOTE FOR HIS LEADERSHIP.

THOMAS ALLEN? T. ALLEN...OR TALON, *HUH?* VERY CUTE.

YOU'RE SMARTER THAN YOU LOOK.

WISH I COULD SAY THE SAME OF YOU. YOU AIN'T SO BRIGHT IF YOU THINK I'M GOING TO BE ABLE TO RUN THINGS AROUND HERE ANYTIME SOON.

AND YOU'RE A *FOOL* IF YOU DON'T THINK I'M SERIOUS. TIME IS RUNNING OUT.

WHY DO YOU KEEP SAYING THAT? YOU GOING TO AN ELF CONVENTION OR SOMETHING?

IF YOU TWO LOVEBIRDS DON'T MIND, WE'VE GOT WORK TO DO AROUND HERE. I WANT A STATUS REPORT FROM THE FOUR CORNERS.

HUH?

MONITORING STATIONS IN THE FOUR CORNERS OF ZONE 27.

BRONNIS, I'LL TAKE THEIR REPORT THROUGH BITLINK. I'M SUITING UP AND HEADING OUT. SPERE IS UP TO SOMETHING.

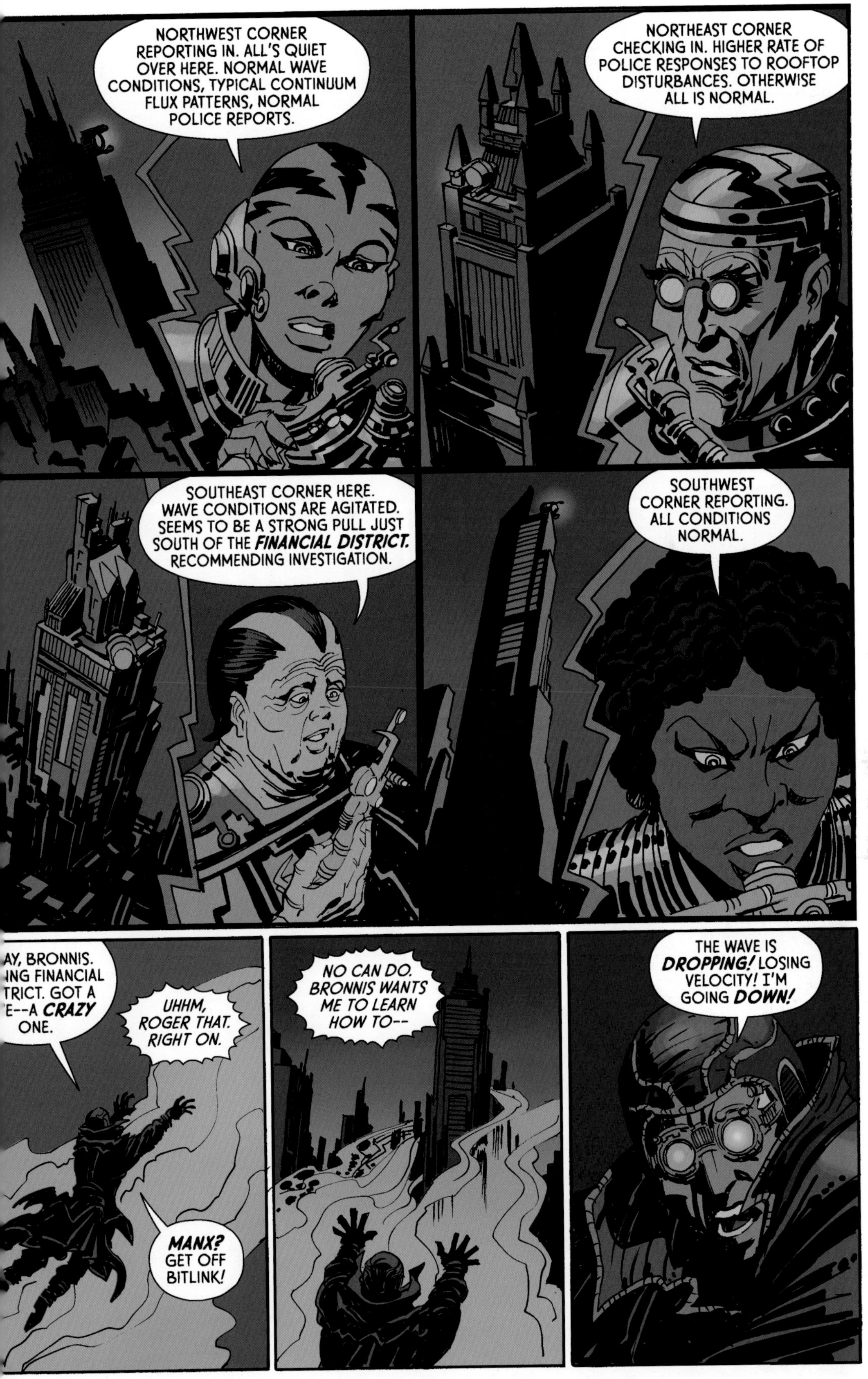
NORTHWEST CORNER REPORTING IN. ALL'S QUIET OVER HERE. NORMAL WAVE CONDITIONS, TYPICAL CONTINUUM FLUX PATTERNS, NORMAL POLICE REPORTS.
NORTHEAST CORNER CHECKING IN. HIGHER RATE OF POLICE RESPONSES TO ROOFTOP DISTURBANCES. OTHERWISE ALL IS NORMAL.
SOUTHEAST CORNER HERE. WAVE CONDITIONS ARE AGITATED. SEEMS TO BE A STRONG PULL JUST SOUTH OF THE *FINANCIAL DISTRICT.* RECOMMENDING INVESTIGATION.
SOUTHWEST CORNER REPORTING. ALL CONDITIONS NORMAL.
AY, BRONNIS. ING FINANCIAL TRICT. GOT A E--A *CRAZY* ONE.
UHHM, ROGER THAT. RIGHT ON.
MANX? GET OFF BITLINK!
NO CAN DO. BRONNIS WANTS ME TO LEARN HOW TO--
THE WAVE IS *DROPPING!* LOSING VELOCITY! I'M GOING *DOWN!*

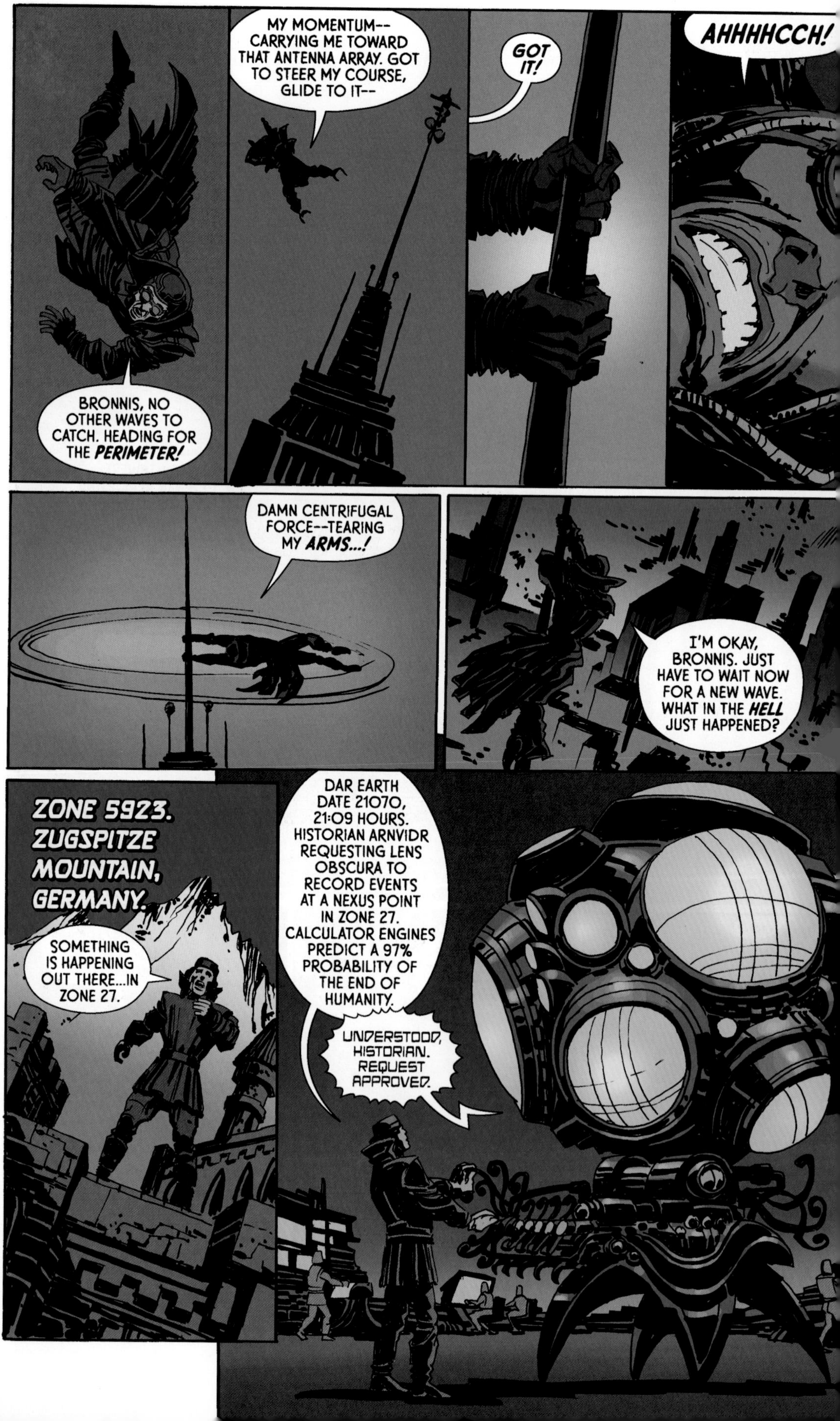
BRONNIS, NO OTHER WAVES TO CATCH. HEADING FOR THE PERIMETER!
MY MOMENTUM-- CARRYING ME TOWARD THAT ANTENNA ARRAY. GOT TO STEER MY COURSE, GLIDE TO IT--
GOT IT!
AHHHHCCH!
DAMN CENTRIFUGAL FORCE--TEARING MY ARMS...!
I'M OKAY, BRONNIS. JUST HAVE TO WAIT NOW FOR A NEW WAVE. WHAT IN THE HELL JUST HAPPENED?
ZONE 5923. ZUGSPITZE MOUNTAIN, GERMANY.
SOMETHING IS HAPPENING OUT THERE...IN ZONE 27.
DAR EARTH DATE 21070, 21:09 HOURS. HISTORIAN ARNVIDR REQUESTING LENS OBSCURA TO RECORD EVENTS AT A NEXUS POINT IN ZONE 27. CALCULATOR ENGINES PREDICT A 97% PROBABILITY OF THE END OF HUMANITY.
UNDERSTOOD, HISTORIAN. REQUEST APPROVED.

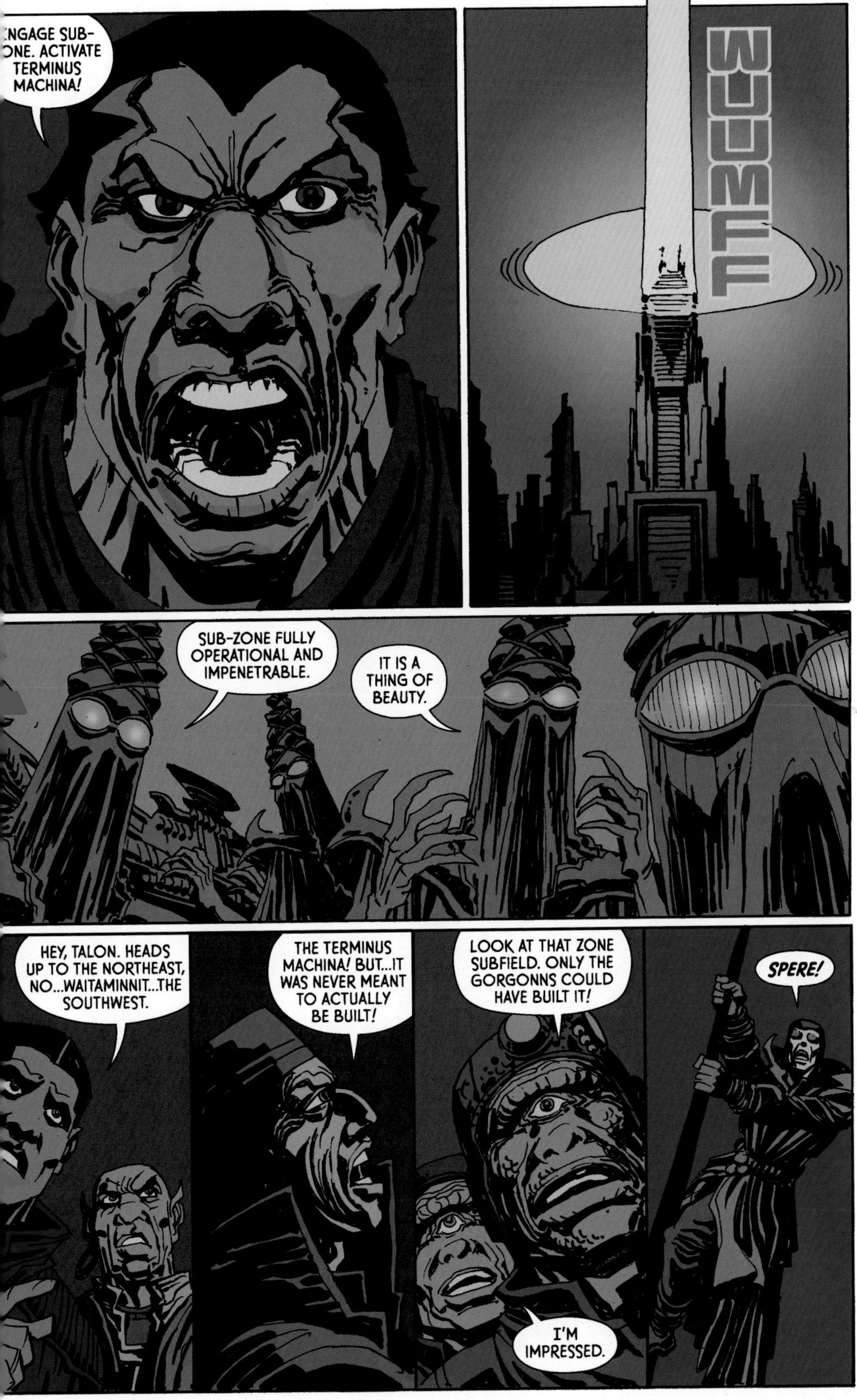

ENGAGE SUB-ZONE. ACTIVATE TERMINUS MACHINA!
WUUMFF
SUB-ZONE FULLY OPERATIONAL AND IMPENETRABLE.
IT IS A THING OF BEAUTY.
HEY, TALON. HEADS UP TO THE NORTHEAST, NO...WAITAMINNIT...THE SOUTHWEST.
THE TERMINUS MACHINA! BUT...IT WAS NEVER MEANT TO ACTUALLY BE BUILT!
LOOK AT THAT ZONE SUBFIELD. ONLY THE GORGONNS COULD HAVE BUILT IT!
I'M IMPRESSED.
SPERE!

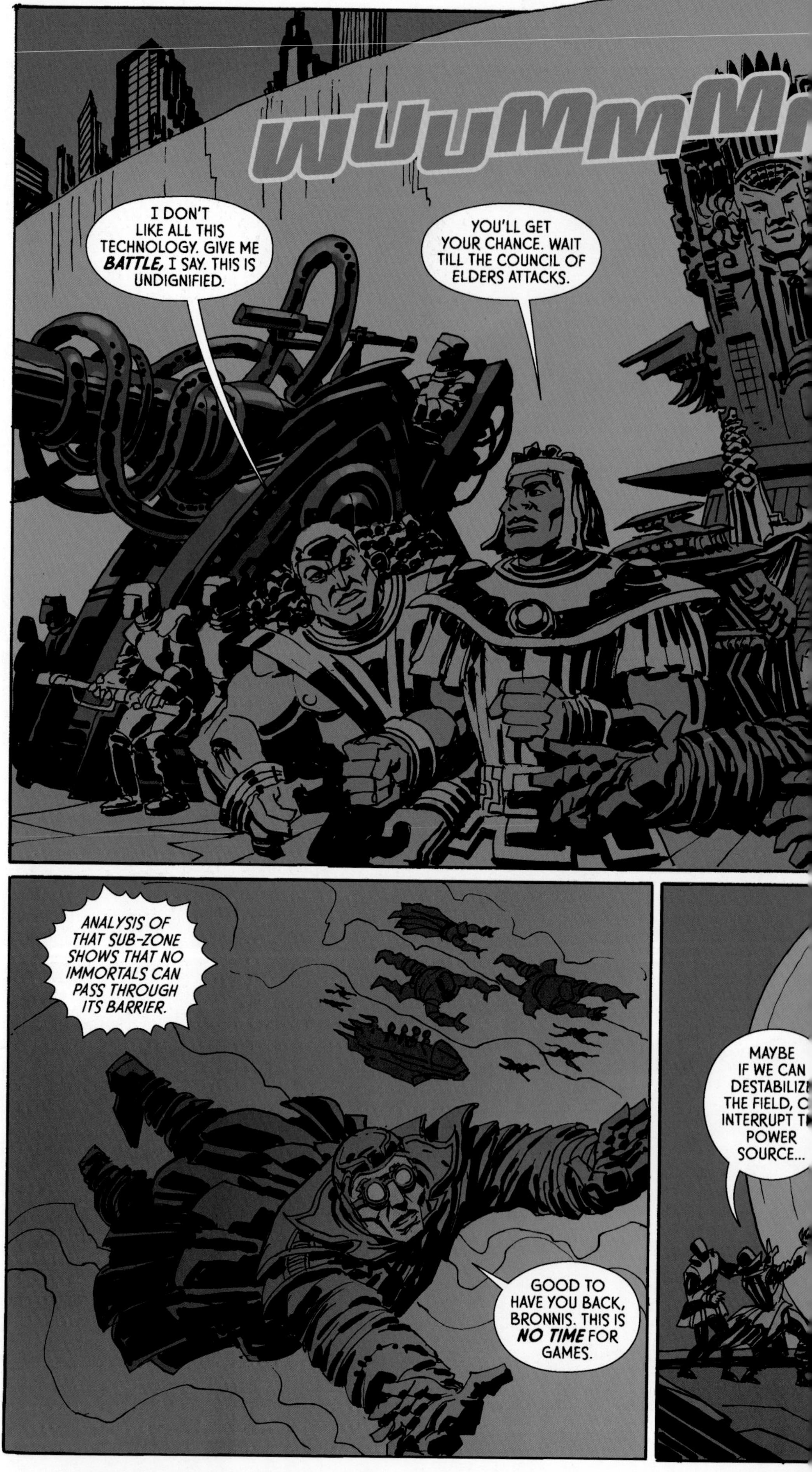
WUUMMM
I DON'T LIKE ALL THIS TECHNOLOGY. GIVE ME **BATTLE,** I SAY. THIS IS UNDIGNIFIED.
YOU'LL GET YOUR CHANCE. WAIT TILL THE COUNCIL OF ELDERS ATTACKS.
ANALYSIS OF THAT SUB-ZONE SHOWS THAT NO IMMORTALS CAN PASS THROUGH ITS BARRIER.
GOOD TO HAVE YOU BACK, BRONNIS. THIS IS ***NO TIME*** FOR GAMES.
MAYBE IF WE CAN DESTABILIZ THE FIELD, O INTERRUPT T POWER SOURCE...

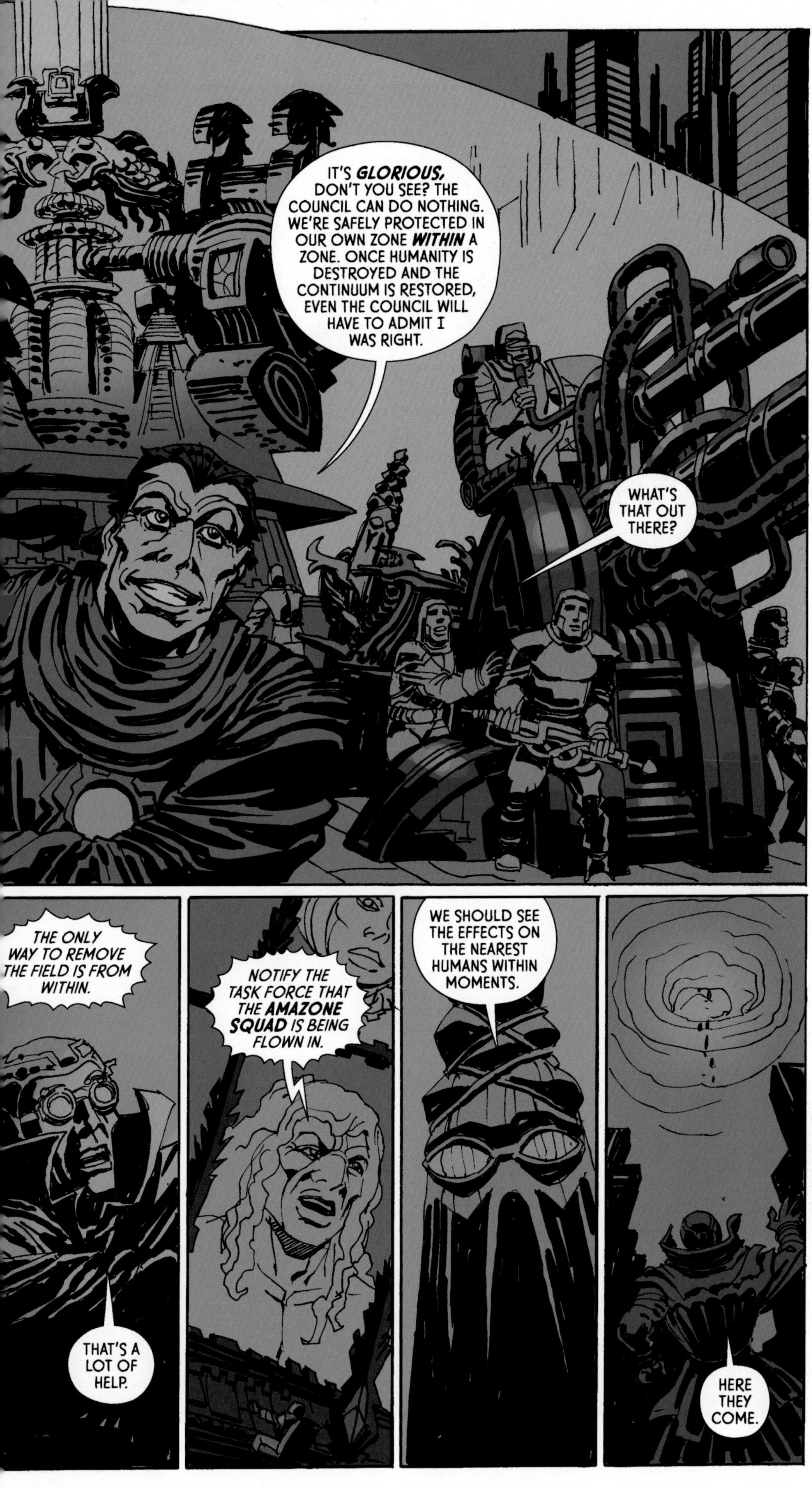
IT'S GLORIOUS, DON'T YOU SEE? THE COUNCIL CAN DO NOTHING. WE'RE SAFELY PROTECTED IN OUR OWN ZONE WITHIN A ZONE. ONCE HUMANITY IS DESTROYED AND THE CONTINUUM IS RESTORED, EVEN THE COUNCIL WILL HAVE TO ADMIT I WAS RIGHT.
WHAT'S THAT OUT THERE?
THE ONLY WAY TO REMOVE THE FIELD IS FROM WITHIN.
THAT'S A LOT OF HELP.
NOTIFY THE TASK FORCE THAT THE AMAZONE SQUAD IS BEING FLOWN IN.
WE SHOULD SEE THE EFFECTS ON THE NEAREST HUMANS WITHIN MOMENTS.
HERE THEY COME.

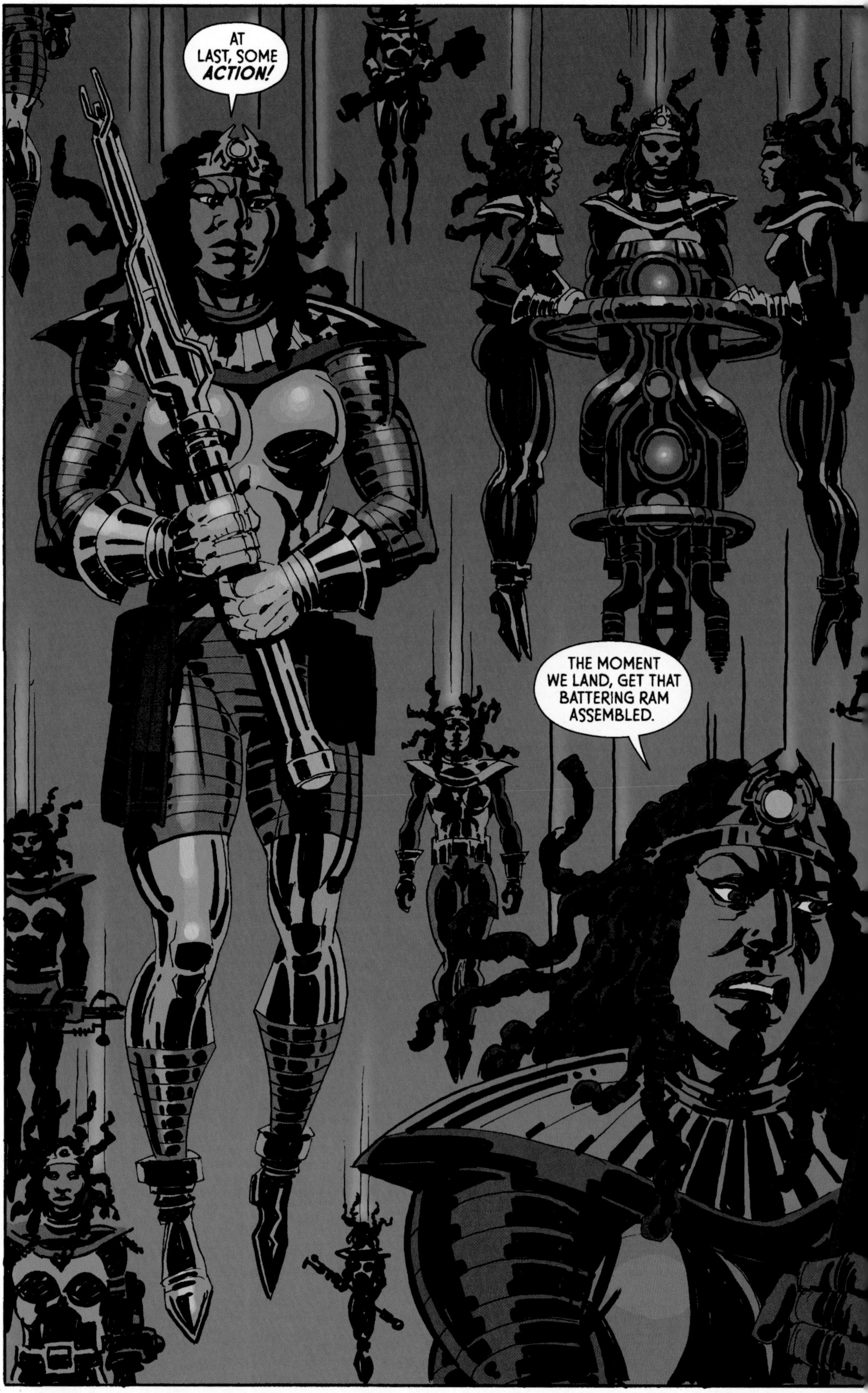
AT LAST, SOME ACTION!
THE MOMENT WE LAND, GET THAT BATTERING RAM ASSEMBLED.

IT'S NO GOOD. SHEER FORCE WON'T GET US IN THERE.

NICE TO SEE YOU LADIES AGAIN. I'M AFRAID WE CAN'T SHARE A HORN OF ALE RIGHT NOW.

VRRRRRRR

WHAT'S *HAPPENING* TO US? I CAN BARELY STAND.

VRRRRRRRRRRRRR

THAT *AWFUL* SOUND...CAN'T TAKE IT.

MY LORD. I HAVE GOOD NEWS.

SPEAK THEN. WE ARE AT THE CRITICAL POINT OF SUCCESS.

YOU WERE RIGHT. TALON'S BLOOD SAMPLE SHOWS OTHER DNA STRANDS-- *HUMAN* DNA. THERE'S NO DOUBT THAT THE THERAPEUTIC BENEFITS OF THE CROSS GAVE TALON GREAT STRENGTH. WE'RE CONTINUING TO RUN TESTS, BUT THIS COULD BE A *BREAKTHROUGH* IN DAR EVOLUTION.

THEN WE SHALL ENJOY THE IRONY. FOR IN MERE MOMENTS, THERE WILL BE NO HUMANS LEFT ON THE PLANET TO ENHANCE OUR GENETICS. THE DAR LINEAGE MUST REMAIN PURE. THIS BLOOD SAMPLE WILL BE TALON'S *FINAL* HUMILIATION TO THE COUNCIL.

NEWS NETWORKS ARE REPORTING THAT HUMANS ARE DROPPING IN THE STREETS, TALON. THE SICKNESS WILL BE *FATAL* IN A FEW MINUTES. IT'S NOW OR NEVER.

THERE *MUST* BE A WAY IN!

HAVE TO *THINK!* THERE'S ALWAYS A WAY! *ALWAYS!*

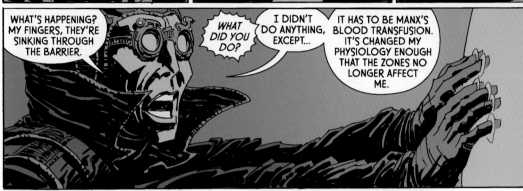

WHAT'S HAPPENING? MY FINGERS, THEY'RE SINKING THROUGH THE BARRIER.

WHAT DID YOU DO?

I DIDN'T DO ANYTHING, EXCEPT...

IT HAS TO BE MANX'S BLOOD TRANSFUSION. IT'S CHANGED MY PHYSIOLOGY ENOUGH THAT THE ZONES NO LONGER AFFECT ME.

BUT I STILL CAN'T GET ALL THE WAY IN. WHY?

WHY?!

BRONNIS, CUT OFF ALL BITLINK CONNECTIONS. I'M POWERING DOWN THE ZONE SUIT. ANY ELECTRONICS MIGHT INTERFERE WITH MY BIOELECTRIC SIGNATURE.

IT'S *WORKING!* I'M GOING THROUGH!

I'VE *DONE* IT!

I'VE BROKEN THROUGH THE ZONE PERIMETER!

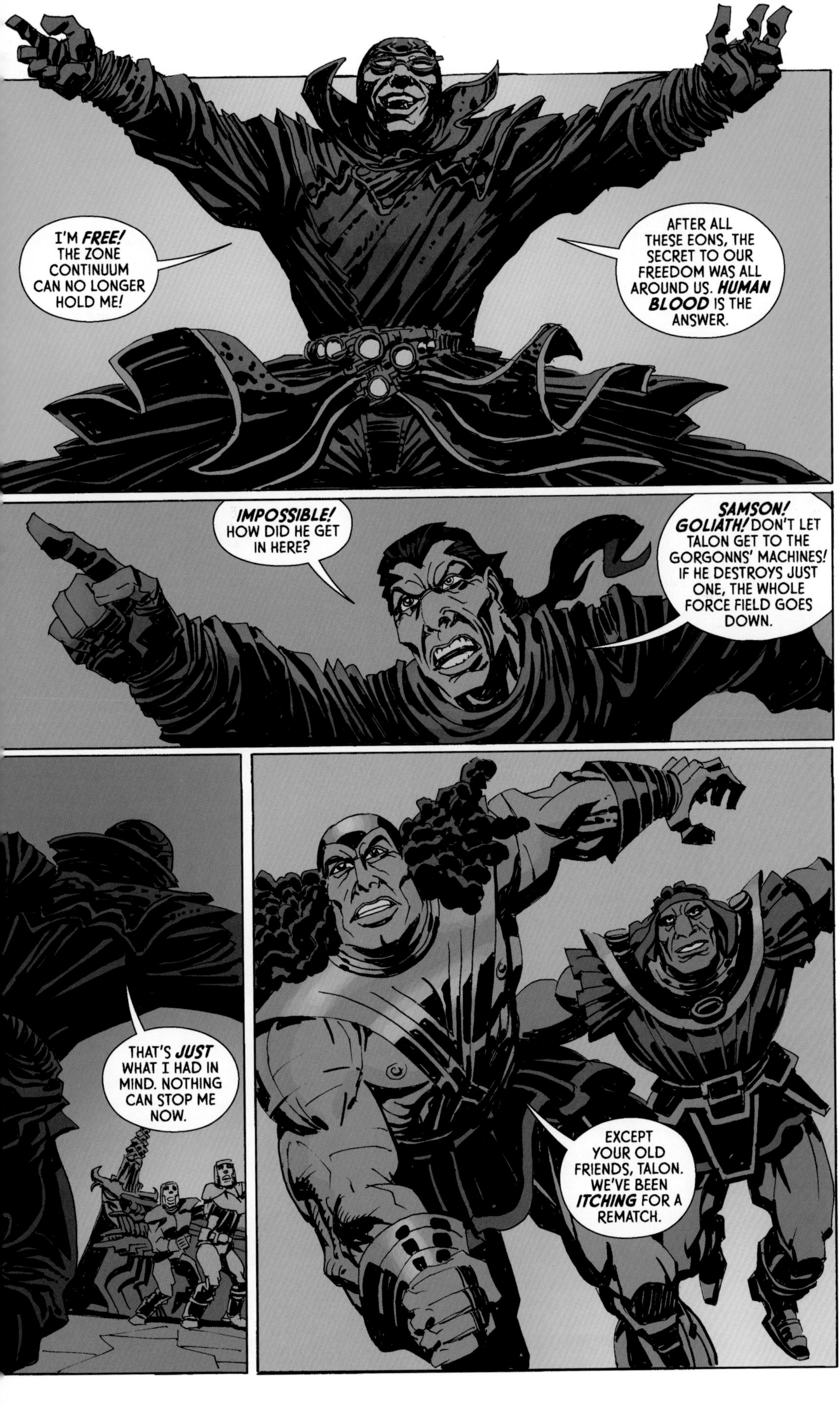
I'M *FREE!* THE ZONE CONTINUUM CAN NO LONGER HOLD ME!
AFTER ALL THESE EONS, THE SECRET TO OUR FREEDOM WAS ALL AROUND US. *HUMAN BLOOD* IS THE ANSWER.
IMPOSSIBLE! HOW DID HE GET IN HERE?
SAMSON! GOLIATH! DON'T LET TALON GET TO THE GORGONNS' MACHINES! IF HE DESTROYS JUST ONE, THE WHOLE FORCE FIELD GOES DOWN.
THAT'S *JUST* WHAT I HAD IN MIND. NOTHING CAN STOP ME NOW.
EXCEPT YOUR OLD FRIENDS, TALON. WE'VE BEEN *ITCHING* FOR A REMATCH.

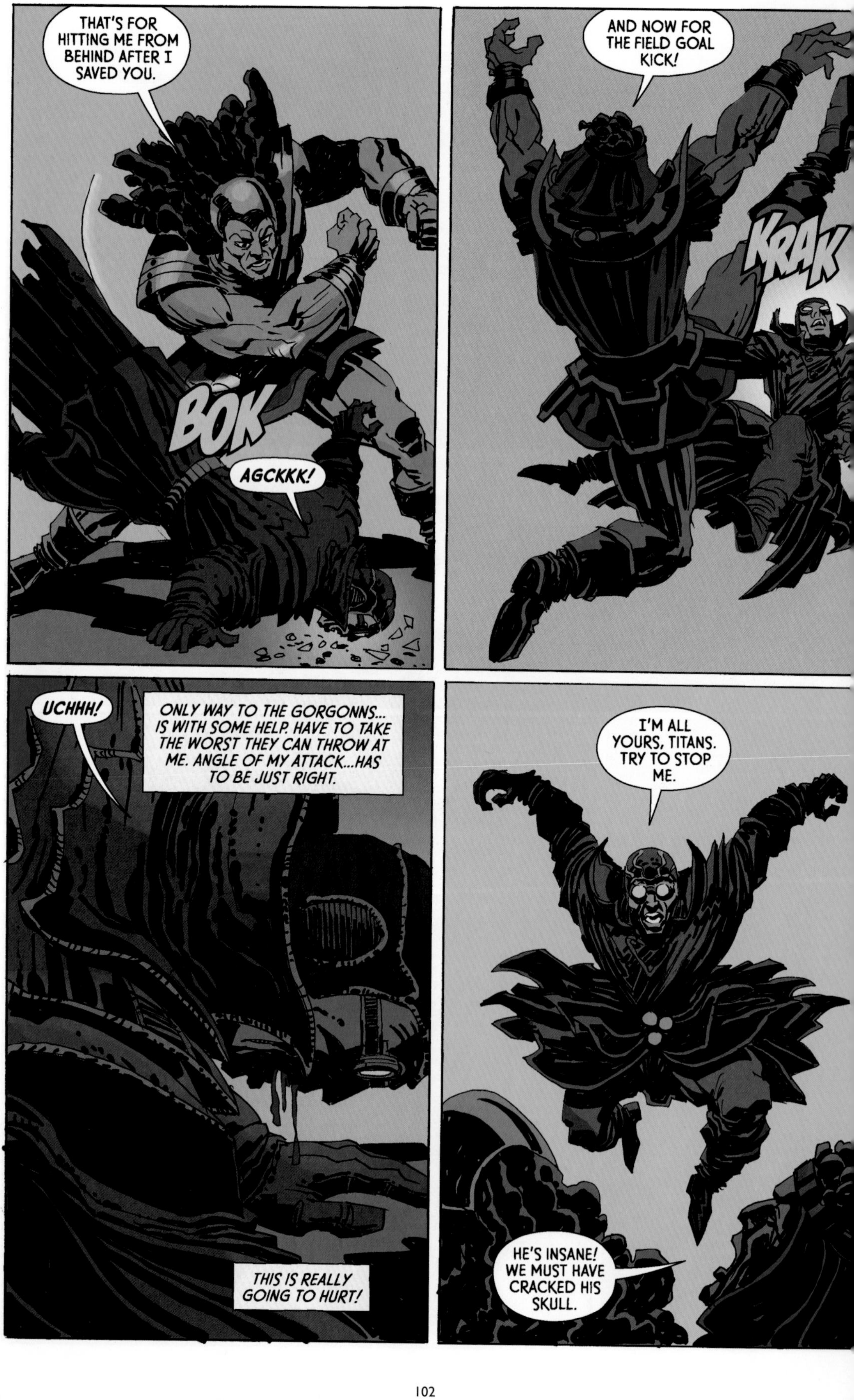
THAT'S FOR HITTING ME FROM BEHIND AFTER I SAVED YOU.
BOK
AGCKKK!
AND NOW FOR THE FIELD GOAL KICK!
KRAK
UCHHH!
ONLY WAY TO THE GORGONNS... IS WITH SOME HELP. HAVE TO TAKE THE WORST THEY CAN THROW AT ME. ANGLE OF MY ATTACK...HAS TO BE JUST RIGHT.
THIS IS REALLY GOING TO HURT!
I'M ALL YOURS, TITANS. TRY TO STOP ME.
HE'S INSANE! WE MUST HAVE CRACKED HIS SKULL.

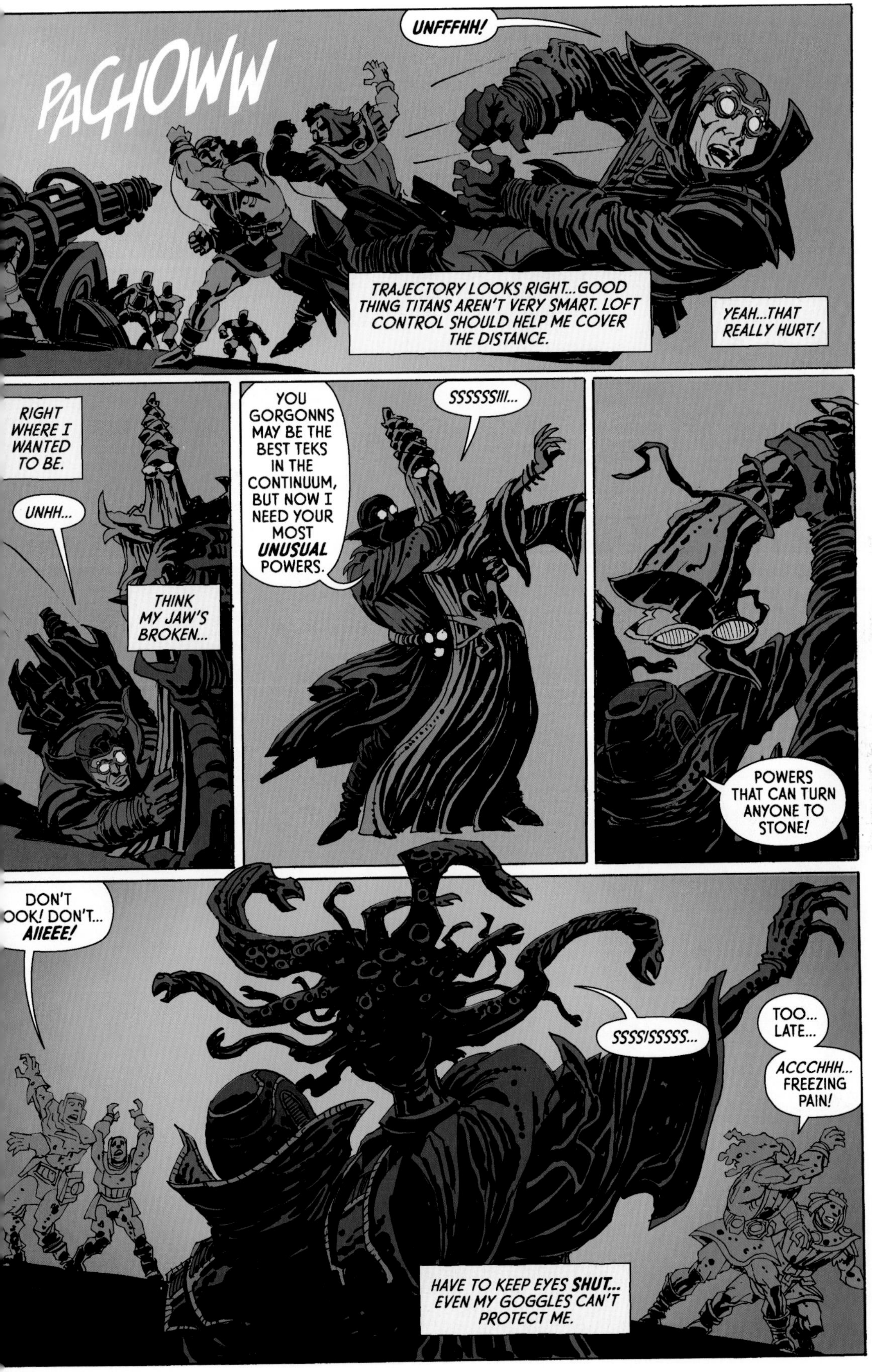

PACHOWW
UNFFFHH!
TRAJECTORY LOOKS RIGHT...GOOD THING TITANS AREN'T VERY SMART. LOFT CONTROL SHOULD HELP ME COVER THE DISTANCE.
YEAH...THAT REALLY HURT!
RIGHT WHERE I WANTED TO BE.
UNHH...
THINK MY JAW'S BROKEN...
YOU GORGONNS MAY BE THE BEST TEKS IN THE CONTINUUM, BUT NOW I NEED YOUR MOST UNUSUAL POWERS.
SSSSSSIII...
POWERS THAT CAN TURN ANYONE TO STONE!
DON'T OOK! DON'T... AIIEEE!
SSSSISSSSS...
TOO... LATE...
ACCCHHH... FREEZING PAIN!
HAVE TO KEEP EYES SHUT... EVEN MY GOGGLES CAN'T PROTECT ME.

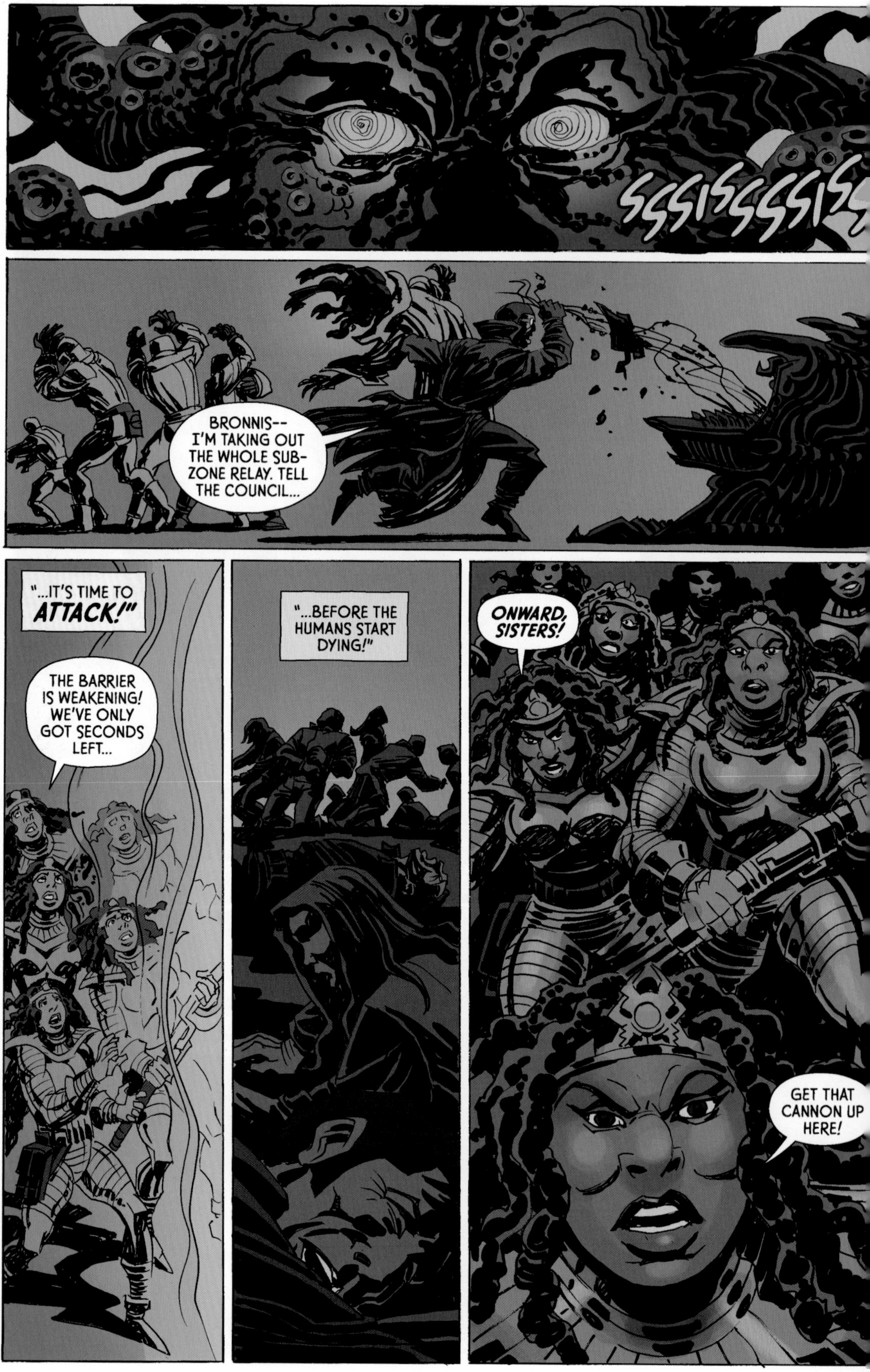
SSSISSSSSISS
BRONNIS-- I'M TAKING OUT THE WHOLE SUB-ZONE RELAY. TELL THE COUNCIL...
"...IT'S TIME TO ATTACK!"
THE BARRIER IS WEAKENING! WE'VE ONLY GOT SECONDS LEFT...
"...BEFORE THE HUMANS START DYING!"
ONWARD, SISTERS!
GET THAT CANNON UP HERE!

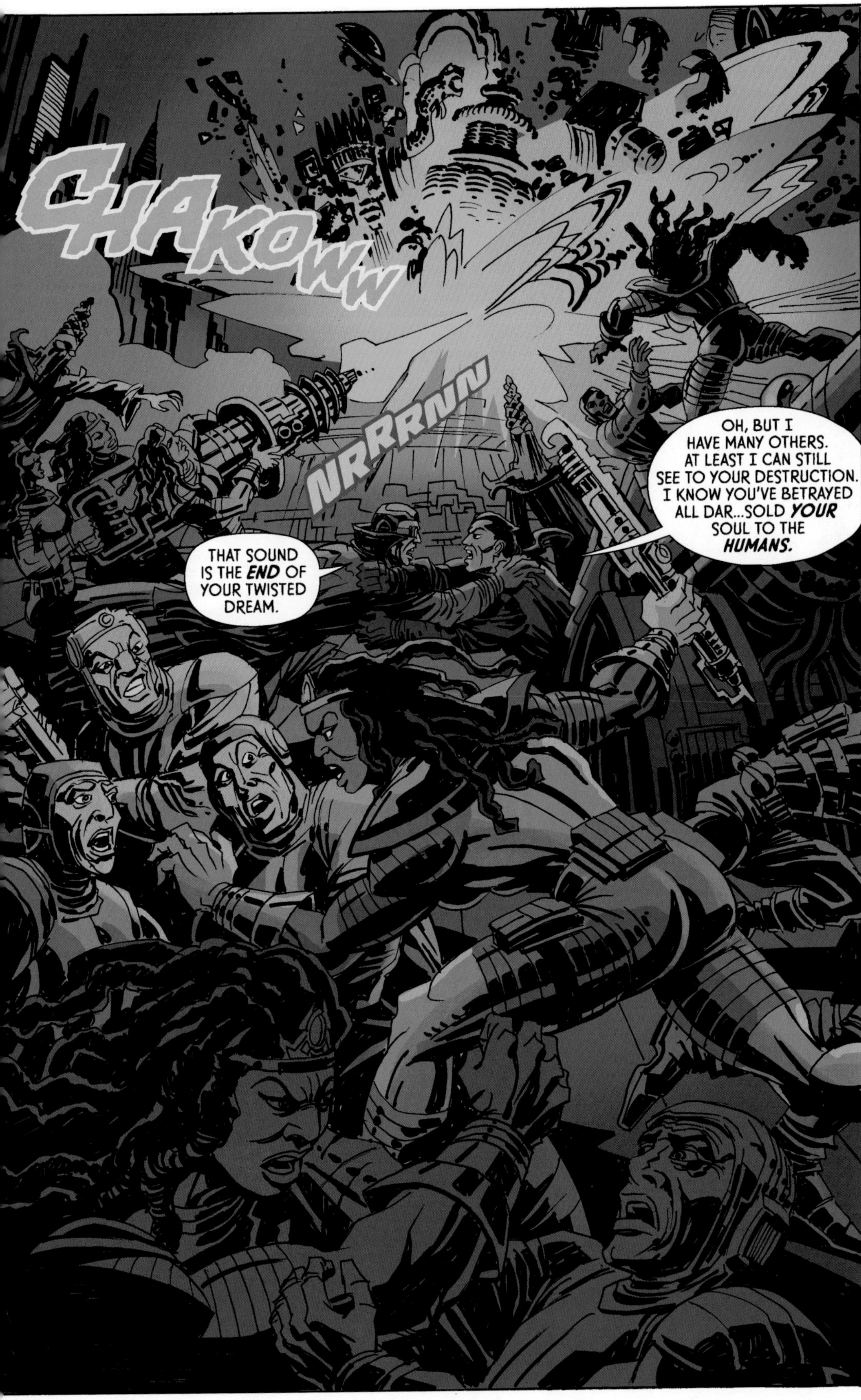
CHAKOWW
NRRRNN
THAT SOUND IS THE END OF YOUR TWISTED DREAM.
OH, BUT I HAVE MANY OTHERS. AT LEAST I CAN STILL SEE TO YOUR DESTRUCTION. I KNOW YOU'VE BETRAYED ALL DAR...SOLD YOUR SOUL TO THE HUMANS.

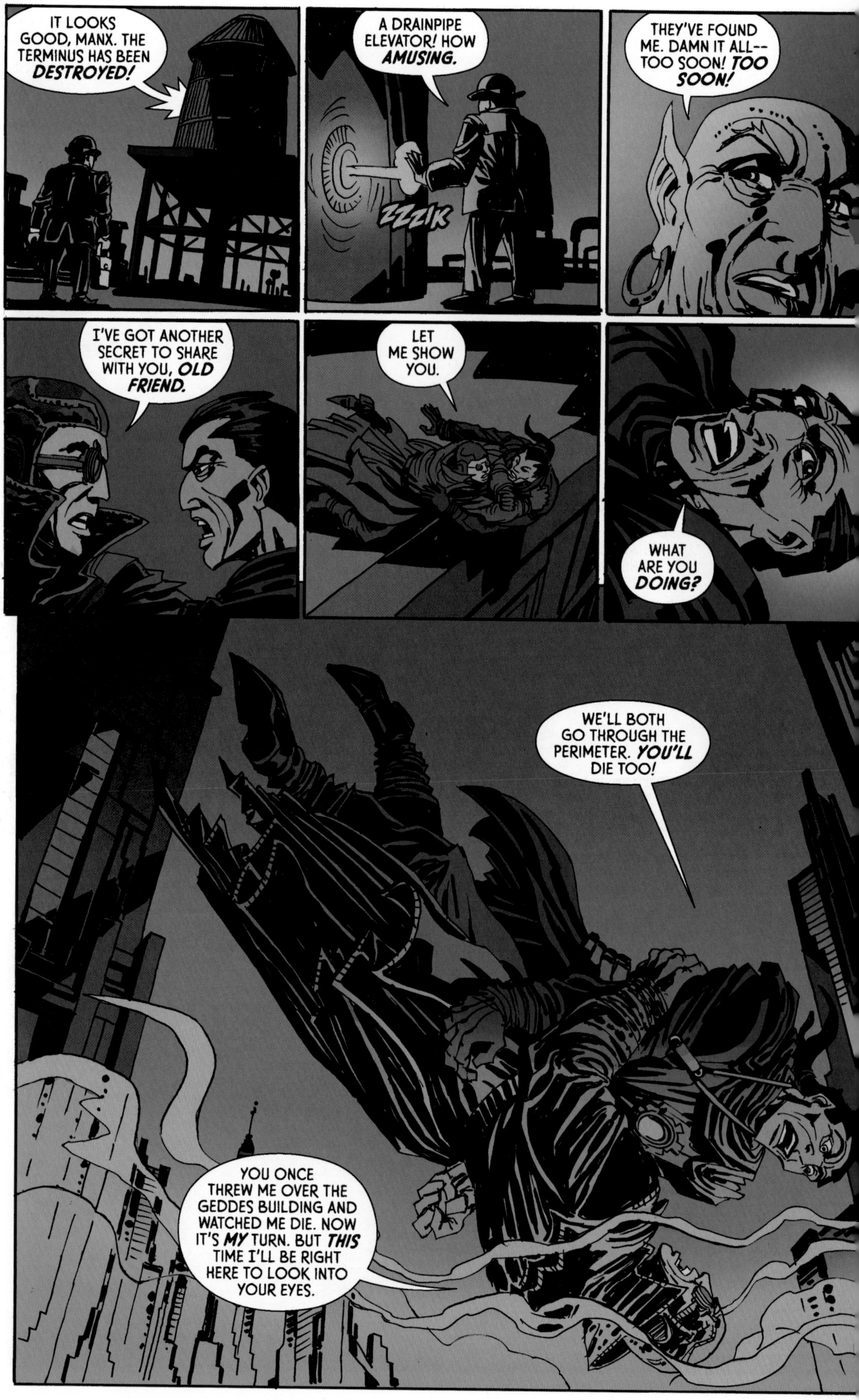
IT LOOKS GOOD, MANX. THE TERMINUS HAS BEEN DESTROYED!
A DRAINPIPE ELEVATOR! HOW AMUSING.
ZZZIK
THEY'VE FOUND ME. DAMN IT ALL-- TOO SOON! TOO SOON!
I'VE GOT ANOTHER SECRET TO SHARE WITH YOU, OLD FRIEND.
LET ME SHOW YOU.
WHAT ARE YOU DOING?
WE'LL BOTH GO THROUGH THE PERIMETER. YOU'LL DIE TOO!
YOU ONCE THREW ME OVER THE GEDDES BUILDING AND WATCHED ME DIE. NOW IT'S MY TURN. BUT THIS TIME I'LL BE RIGHT HERE TO LOOK INTO YOUR EYES.

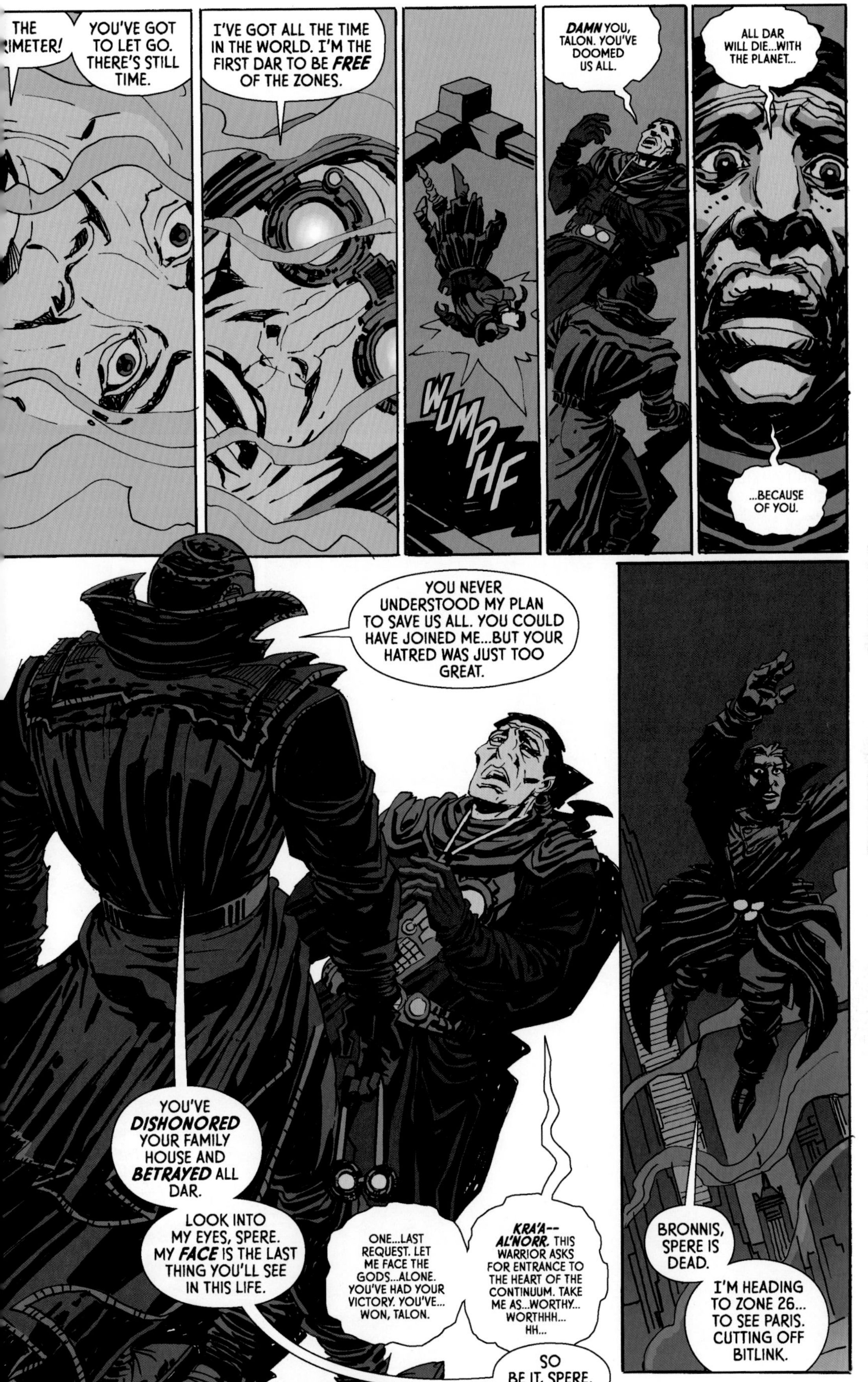

...IMETER!
YOU'VE GOT TO LET GO. THERE'S STILL TIME.
I'VE GOT ALL THE TIME IN THE WORLD. I'M THE FIRST DAR TO BE FREE OF THE ZONES.
WUMPHF
DAMN YOU, TALON. YOU'VE DOOMED US ALL.
ALL DAR WILL DIE...WITH THE PLANET...
...BECAUSE OF YOU.
YOU NEVER UNDERSTOOD MY PLAN TO SAVE US ALL. YOU COULD HAVE JOINED ME...BUT YOUR HATRED WAS JUST TOO GREAT.
YOU'VE DISHONORED YOUR FAMILY HOUSE AND BETRAYED ALL DAR.
LOOK INTO MY EYES, SPERE. MY FACE IS THE LAST THING YOU'LL SEE IN THIS LIFE.
ONE...LAST REQUEST. LET ME FACE THE GODS...ALONE. YOU'VE HAD YOUR VICTORY. YOU'VE... WON, TALON.
KRA'A-- AL'NORR. THIS WARRIOR ASKS FOR ENTRANCE TO THE HEART OF THE CONTINUUM. TAKE ME AS...WORTHY... WORTHHH... HH...
SO BE IT, SPERE. FAREWELL.
BRONNIS, SPERE IS DEAD.
I'M HEADING TO ZONE 26... TO SEE PARIS. CUTTING OFF BITLINK.

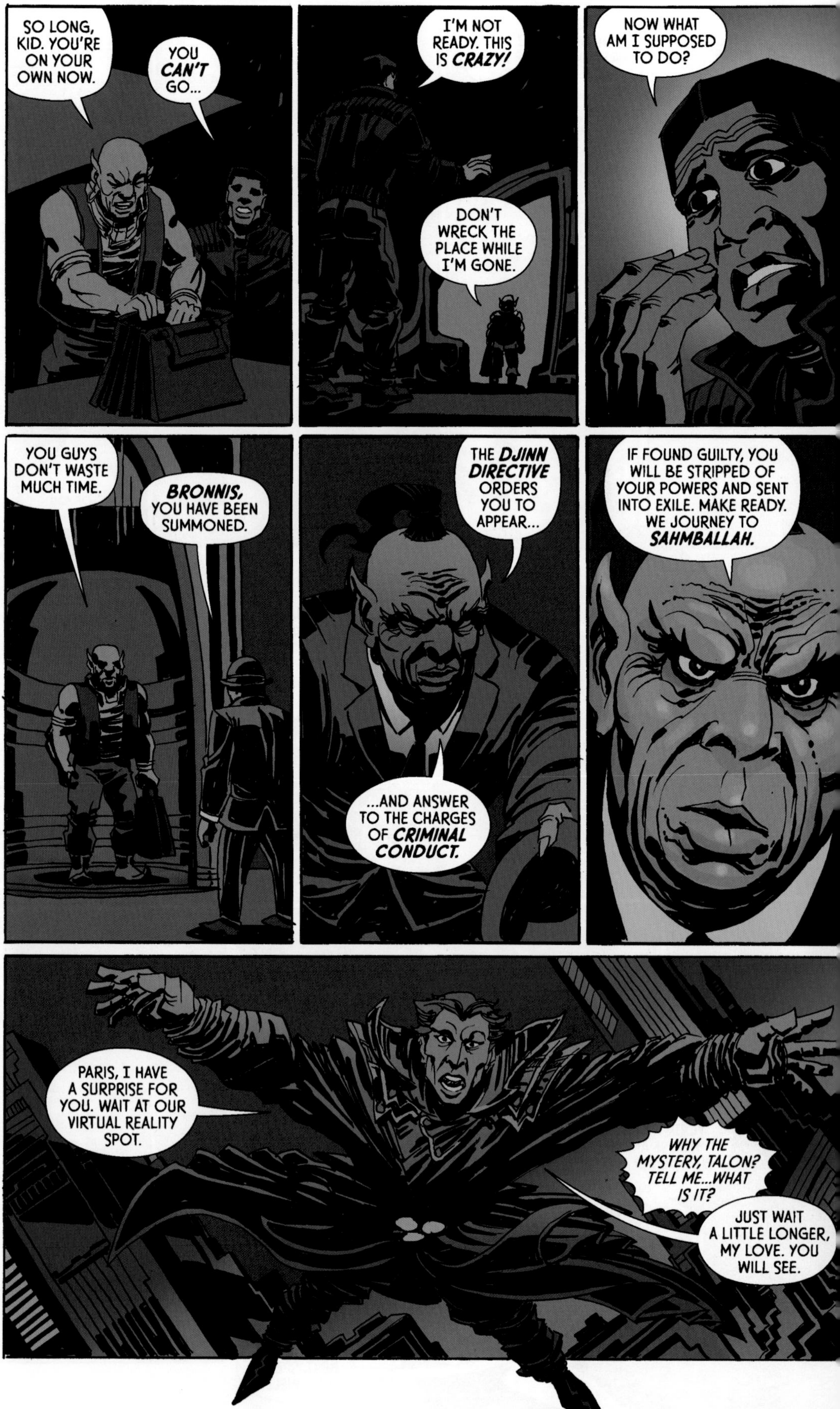
SO LONG, KID. YOU'RE ON YOUR OWN NOW.
YOU *CAN'T* GO...
I'M NOT READY. THIS IS *CRAZY!*
DON'T WRECK THE PLACE WHILE I'M GONE.
NOW WHAT AM I SUPPOSED TO DO?
YOU GUYS DON'T WASTE MUCH TIME.
BRONNIS, YOU HAVE BEEN SUMMONED.
THE *DJINN DIRECTIVE* ORDERS YOU TO APPEAR...
...AND ANSWER TO THE CHARGES OF *CRIMINAL CONDUCT.*
IF FOUND GUILTY, YOU WILL BE STRIPPED OF YOUR POWERS AND SENT INTO EXILE. MAKE READY. WE JOURNEY TO *SAHMBALLAH.*
PARIS, I HAVE A SURPRISE FOR YOU. WAIT AT OUR VIRTUAL REALITY SPOT.
WHY THE MYSTERY, TALON? TELL ME...WHAT IS IT?
JUST WAIT A LITTLE LONGER, MY LOVE. YOU WILL SEE.

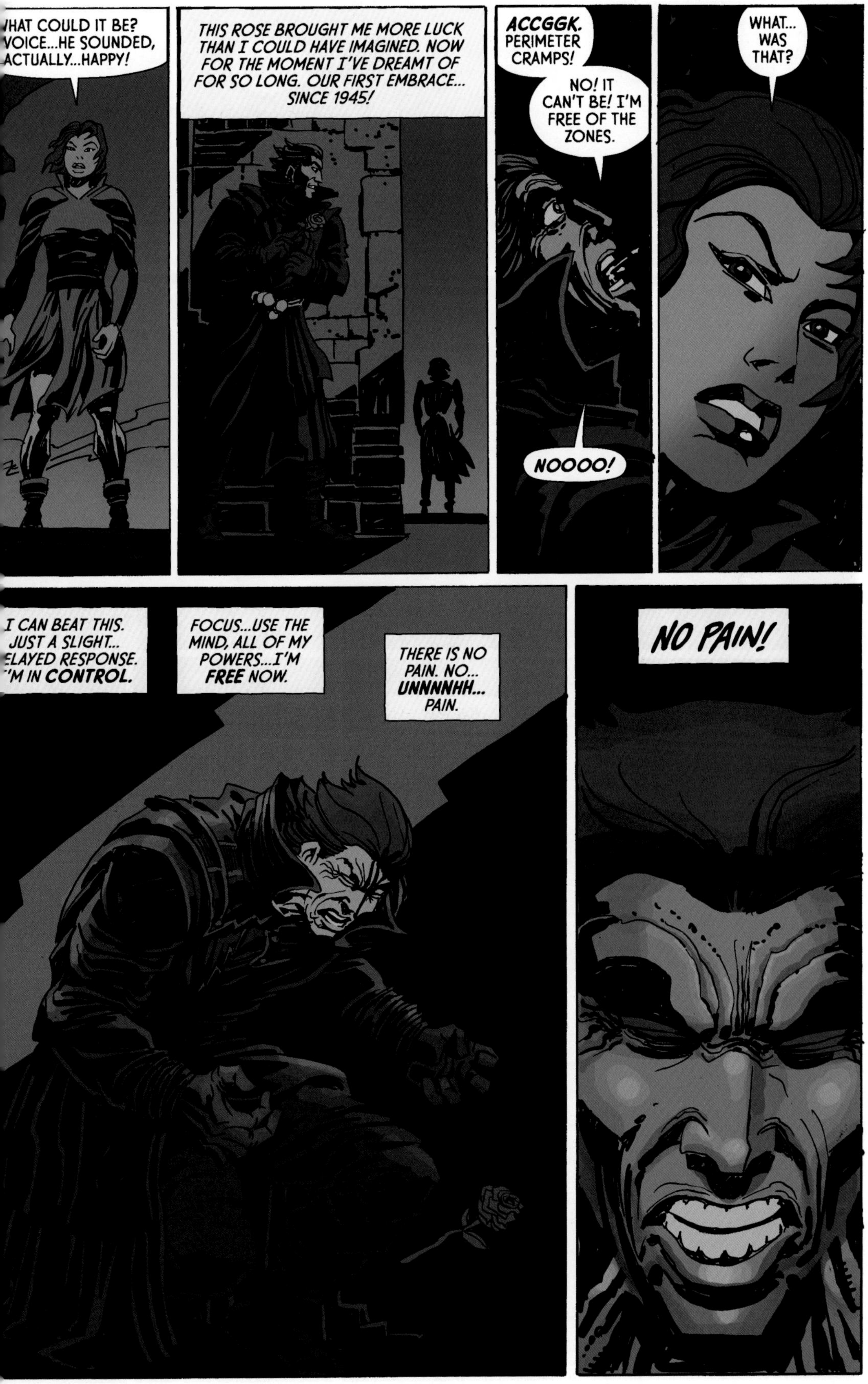

HAT COULD IT BE? VOICE...HE SOUNDED, ACTUALLY...HAPPY!
THIS ROSE BROUGHT ME MORE LUCK THAN I COULD HAVE IMAGINED. NOW FOR THE MOMENT I'VE DREAMT OF FOR SO LONG. OUR FIRST EMBRACE... SINCE 1945!
ACCGGK. PERIMETER CRAMPS!
NO! IT CAN'T BE! I'M FREE OF THE ZONES.
NOOOO!
WHAT... WAS THAT?
I CAN BEAT THIS. JUST A SLIGHT... ELAYED RESPONSE. 'M IN CONTROL.
FOCUS...USE THE MIND, ALL OF MY POWERS...I'M FREE NOW.
THERE IS NO PAIN. NO... UNNNNHH... PAIN.
NO PAIN!

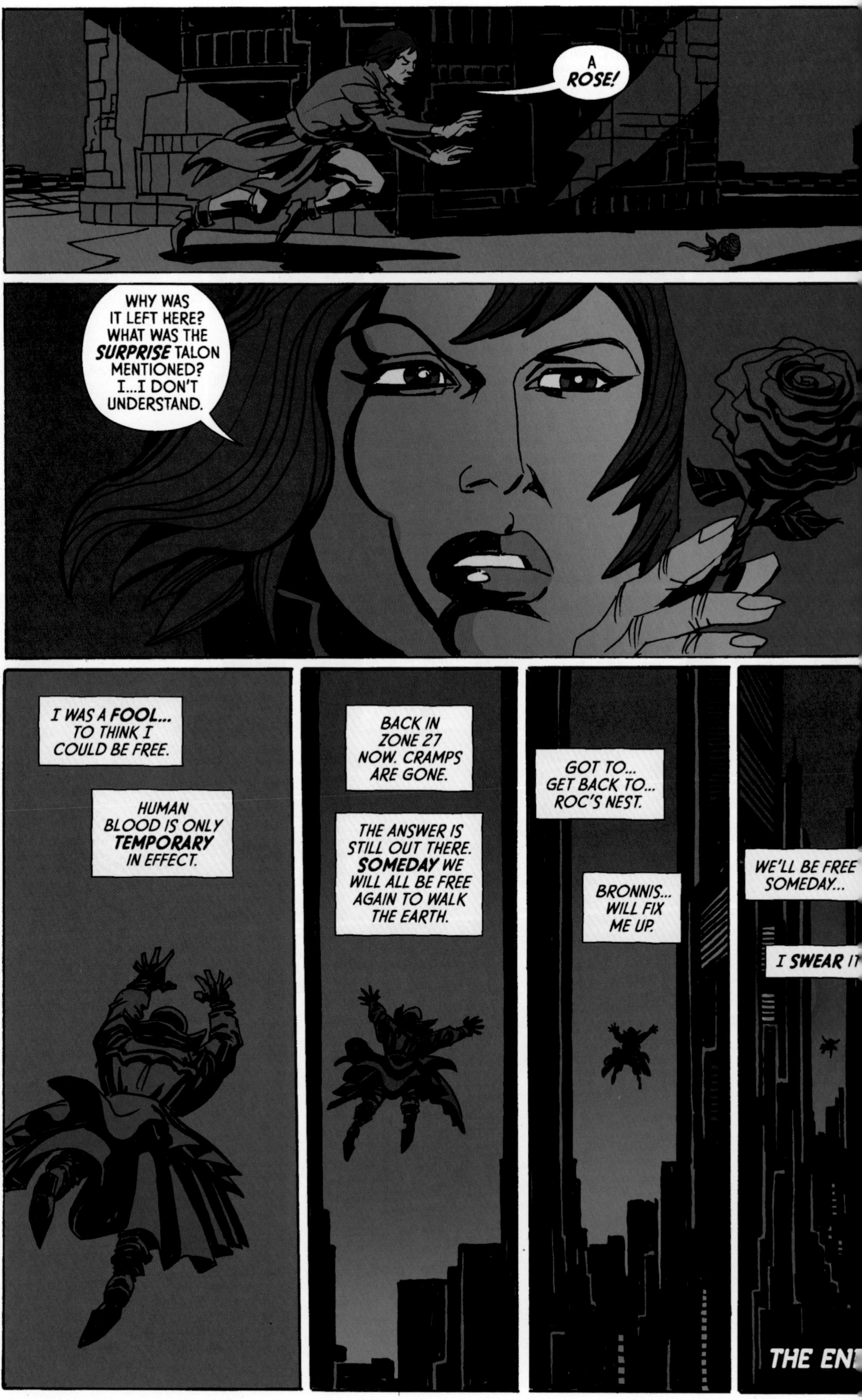
A ROSE!
WHY WAS IT LEFT HERE? WHAT WAS THE SURPRISE TALON MENTIONED? I...I DON'T UNDERSTAND.
I WAS A FOOL... TO THINK I COULD BE FREE.
HUMAN BLOOD IS ONLY TEMPORARY IN EFFECT.
BACK IN ZONE 27 NOW. CRAMPS ARE GONE.
THE ANSWER IS STILL OUT THERE. SOMEDAY WE WILL ALL BE FREE AGAIN TO WALK THE EARTH.
GOT TO... GET BACK TO... ROC'S NEST.
BRONNIS... WILL FIX ME UP.
WE'LL BE FREE SOMEDAY...
I SWEAR IT

GLOSSARY OF TERMS

ANTHRO-ENERGY SURGE: An instability which results in energy bursts that take on an animal-like shape, such as a cephalopod, an ophidian, or a quadruped. These surges are typically short lived but can cause terrible injury to the Dar. See also Continuum instability.

BI-TALIC AMPLIFIER: A microdevice smaller than a computer chip that directly converts magnetic energy into electrical power. The internal components are constructed from various reactive metals, such as cobalt, platinum, and C_{60}, which are separated by a thin metallic gauze. When an amplifier is placed in a magnetic field, magnetic current flows in from one side, and electricity flows out from the other.

BITLINK: A data transmission system integrated into a variety of Zone technologies. Environmental measurements and other information are broken down into bit streams and transmitted at extremely high rates either to centralized servers at Roc's Nest or to other portable data processing equipment.

CONTINUUM INSTABILITY: Fluctuation in the Zone Continuum due to human interference in the global environment (such as deforestation, microwave transmission, and air and water pollution) that has adversely affected its delicate ecology. Zones may shrink or rise and fall, forcing the Dar inhabitants to adapt to the challenging living conditions. Beast-like aberrations may also form that affect Dar inhabitants but cannot be seen, heard, or felt by human senses.

CYBERGRID: The communications interlink carried by the Continuum that unites the Dar and all Zone technology (e.g., computers, medidocs, Neuralnets) into a single cybernetic entity.

DAR: A humanoid inhabitant of the Zone Continuum. Each Dar is a sentient biological counterpart of negative and positive magnetic polar energy. A minimum of two are necessary to sustain a Zone's energy balance, but more may be present depending on an individual Dar's flow strength or psychomagnetic density. When a Zone is destabilized by an

Continuum Instability

imbalance in the Dar, then one or more destabilizing Dar must be ritually returned to the foam.

ETHER SNAKE: A variety of anthro-energy surge that forms in the shape of long, snaking tendrils. This type of Continuum instability can last for hours and is attracted to the Dar, making escape almost impossible. *See also* Continuum instability.

FEEDBACK LOOPING: A process by which collected data is integrated into a system's actions and decisions. In addition to monitoring information, a looped system also stores it in an accessible array for future interactive use.

FOAM: The infinite matter-antimatter sea originally predicted by Paul Dirac's 1928 theory in which matter and antimatter are constantly being created and annihilating each other. This sea of particles creates the space-time foam and provides the basis for the universal Magnetic Continuum.

FORGE (FORCE GENERATION ENHANCEMENT FEEDBACK): A feedback response between Talon's Neuralnet and the Roc's Nest biotelemetry activator. The system measures Talon's exertion and environmental variables and responds by micro-stimulating the optimum muscle groups and nerves for maximum physical efficiency under all conditions.

HOT GLOVES: Primary control component of the Zone suit, constructed mainly of an acrylic polymer composed of wavelite and C_{60}. Each glove features a customizable high-resolution microdisplay that can offer information on the Zone suit's function, condition, and power consumption, or environmental data pertinent to the suit's capabilities, such as local magnetic levitation field strength. The fingers and palm are laced with a complicated series of micro-electromagnets, which serve

Hot Gloves

double duty as the gloves' primary sensor apparatus and as ancillary Zone loft stabilizers in concert with the Wave Rider Belt. The gloves also incorporate a defensive magnetic countermeasure projector, providing the wearer with a limited degree of magnetic invisibility.

INNATE (ITERATIVE NUMERICAL ASSIMILATION TECHNOLOGY): The hardware and software used by Talon's computers, whose technology is based on genetically altered DNA, designed for information storage and programming. INNATE takes raw data and, like the human brain, assimilates that information into an ever-changing decision array. Compared to today's supercomputers, INNATE is 10^4 times faster and exhibits exponential capability expansion.

NEURALNET (NEURAL BODY NETWORK): A form-fitting mesh material of tritium-141 and C_{60} that covers the entire body except the face. The Neuralnet transmits various environmental and body-function variables to an interactive database in the Roc's Nest computers. Optimum body functions are controlled through the processes of INNATE, FORGE, and SPAR.

PLASMA FOUNTAIN: An instability that is typically caused by microwave transmission. The energy shapes are not anthropomorphic, instead taking the shape of fountain-like bursts. *See also* Continuum instability.

RITUAL LANGUAGE: Here, a group of terms used in an ancient form of combat designed to deal with either the selection of or the death of a Dar. The various stages of combat are *trono-kra'al, tal'truul, zur'kra'no'shi, taras'al, quar'al'nor, tor'al'k'norr*, and *nor'al'tros*.

ROC'S NEST: Laboratory, lair, and control center of Talon, the Dar leader of Zone 27.

SPAR (SUSTAINABLE PATH RESISTANCE): The fatigue-management system that is one of the biological-function parameters measured by the Neuralnet and controlled by the INNATE combat and control system. SPAR readouts are analyzed by the computer and automatically corrected by Neuralnet stimulation.

SYREN: An ancient form of Continuum instability caused by human deforestation of precious cypress trees on the Mediterranean islands during the Greco-Roman and Minoan eras. Syrens are known to utilize a high-pitched frequency to mesmerize victims before turning them to stone. While Syrens were previously considered uncommon in the modern Zone Continuum, numerous Syren appearances have recently been reported. *See also* Continuum instability.

VIPER: A perimeter disturbance taking the form of a highly dangerous bolt of pure mega-intensity wave energy which penetrates into the Zone from outside the Zone perimeter. *See also* Continuum instability.

Wave Rider Belt

WAVE RIDER BELT: A harness which straps around the waist of a Zone suit. Its controls manipulate the suit's ability to glide by adjusting the fabric's density and receptiveness to magnetic energy.

Plasma Fountain

Zone Perimeter

ZONE CONTINUUM: The electromagnetic envelope encasing the earth that is subdivided into smaller units ad infinitum. Woven throughout the Continuum is a psychospiritual energy that is the sum total of all past Dar. Zone locations are affected by their distance from the magnetic poles, the natural connective currents of the earth's molten interior, natural deposits of metallic ores, and manmade distortions, such as buildings, power plants, and plumes of factory emissions.

ZONE GOGGLES: Ocular-augmentation apparatus employing the principle of static field hyperization, capable of sensitizing the lenses to either a specific selected wavelength in the command mode or an optimum local wavelength via autoselect sensor array. The goggles also incorporate an environmental sensor array to detect and measure small pitch shifts in magnetic field conditions, and an OZMOS (over-the-horizon Zone magnetic oscillation sensor) that allows for the remote observation of any Zone on planet Earth. All functions are visible to the wearer in the goggles' heads-up peripheral input display.

ZONE PERIMETER: The boundary between Zones, composed of intense and unstable psychomagnetism. Though invisible and undetectable to normal humans, Zone boundaries are visible to the Dar as shimmering curtains of pure energy which separate Dar of different psychomagnetic signatures. For the Dar, passing through the perimeter is fatal.

Zone Goggles

ZONE PERIMETER EDGE FLIRTATION: The act of drawing energy and strength from the very edge of a perimeter. The Dar flirt with the edge in order to gain clarity of mind and optimum psychomagnetic power. Edge flirtation can produce perimeter storms and vipers.

ZONE SPECTRUM: The energy of the Zone made visible by special devices that measure electromagnetic intensity and convert it to a color scale in which blue is usually the highest magnetic energy and red the lowest.

ZONE SUIT: The protective outer dress and functional equipment system of the Dar made from di-poly lodestrand, a synthetic lodestone-based polymer. The suit fabric collects the microfilament magnetic energy of the Continuum and creates a significant amount of loft to aid in wave-gliding. Suits utilize camouflaging polymer compounds that blend suit colors with the nearby environment.

ZONE TEK: A technician who carries out research and development as well as systems-control functions for the Dar. Teks are sequestered in high-security sanctums where they compete against other Teks in the race for technological advancement. Of the Tek orders, Talon is partial to Syklops, who are gregarious yet extremely earnest, as has been their tradition for thousands of years. Conversely, Spere typically employs Gorgonns, who, though fearsome, are capable of revolutionary advances that accelerate the race for technological superiority.

ZONE 27: The Zone that occupies a ten-square-mile area of downtown Manhattan. Its bottom boundary is at an altitude of 150 feet. Zone 27, like all the other Zones, is in a constant state of change and is shrinking at an alarming rate.

ZONE WAVE (OR Z-WAVE): A spherical wave of power oscillation caused by variations in the strength of the magnetic field. The Zone waves create momentum forces that can carry a Dar in any direction, much like a hang glider can navigate over air currents. As with other Continuum phenomena, the waves are only visible to the Dar.

Zone Suit

SKETCHBOOK

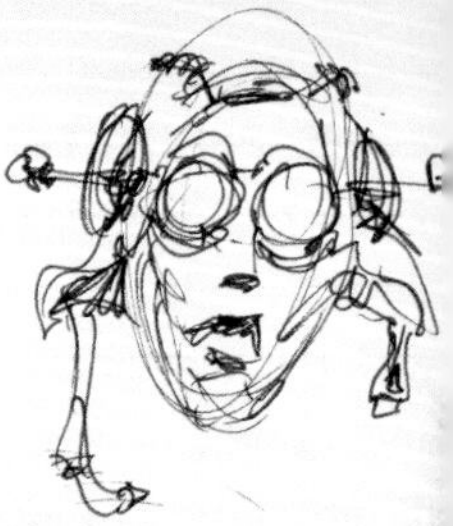

Early Zone suit ideas. It starte
a big, puffy trench coat and ev
from there.

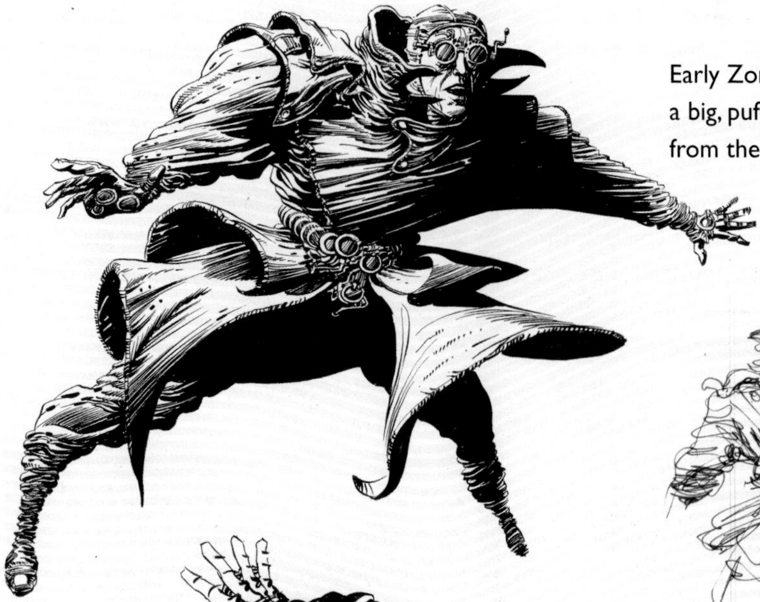

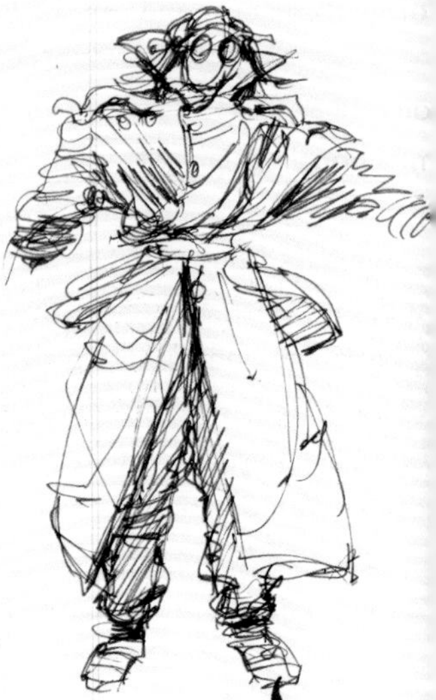

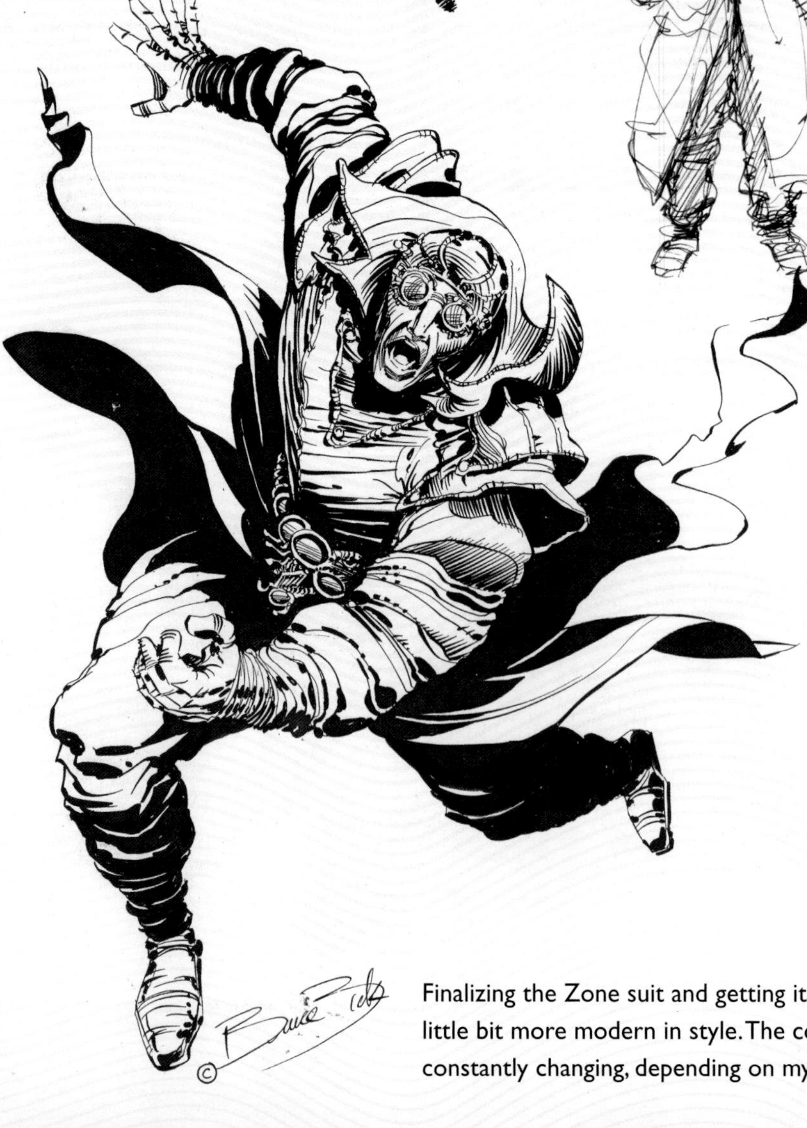

Finalizing the Zone suit and getting it to feel a little bit more modern in style. The coattails ar constantly changing, depending on my mood.

The headpiece went through many itera-
tions. It started as a hood and turned into
a skullcap inside an exaggerated, pointy
collar, which also changes depending on
my mood.

This became the iconic design for me. All the pieces
fit together just perfectly. The Zone goggles, which
I love here, are way too complicated to draw over
and over again, so I eventually simplified them just
to save some time. But I still love the clunky, retro,
almost steampunk look of them.

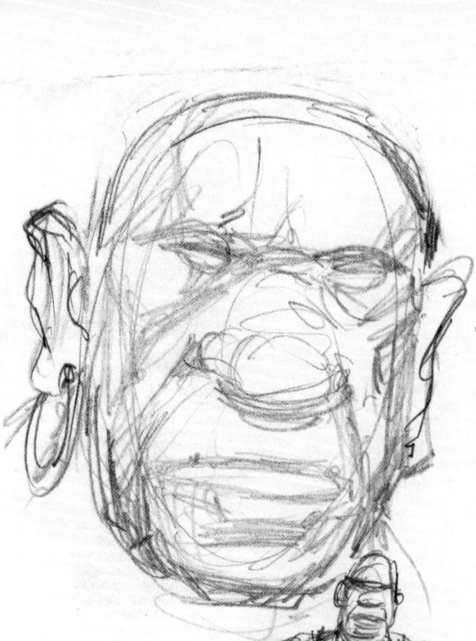

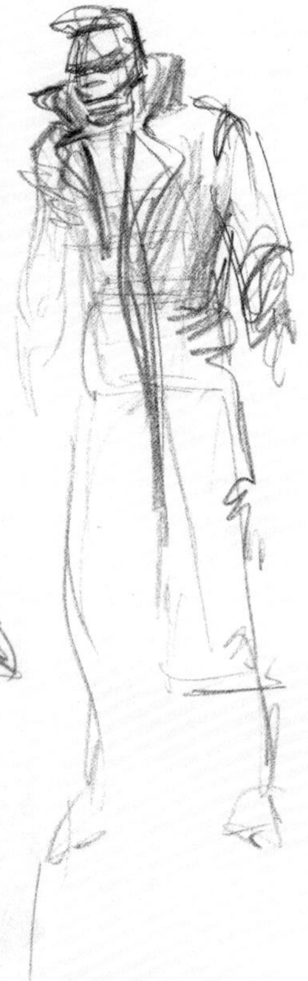

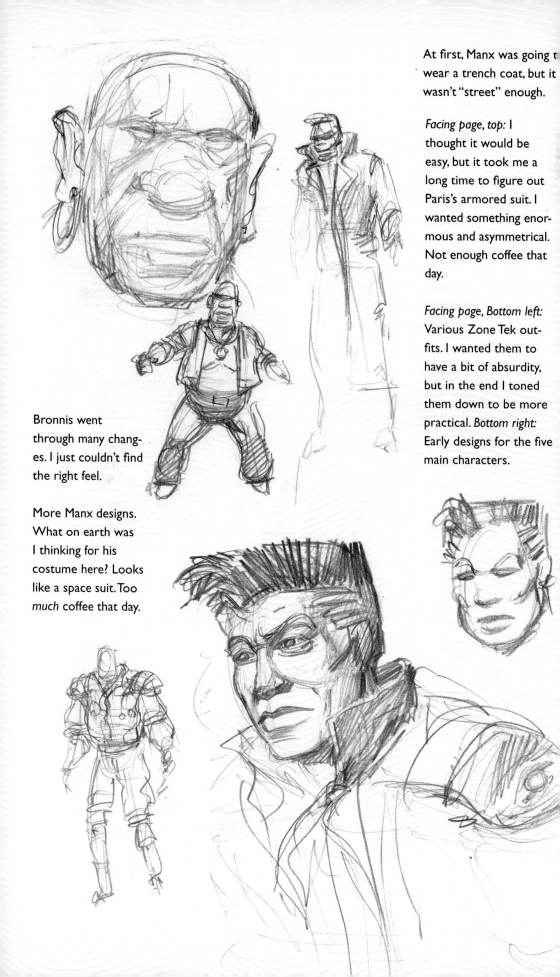

At first, Manx was going t
wear a trench coat, but it wasn't "street" enough.

Facing page, top: I thought it would be easy, but it took me a long time to figure out Paris's armored suit. I wanted something enormous and asymmetrical. Not enough coffee that day.

Facing page, Bottom left: Various Zone Tek outfits. I wanted them to have a bit of absurdity, but in the end I toned them down to be more practical. *Bottom right:* Early designs for the five main characters.

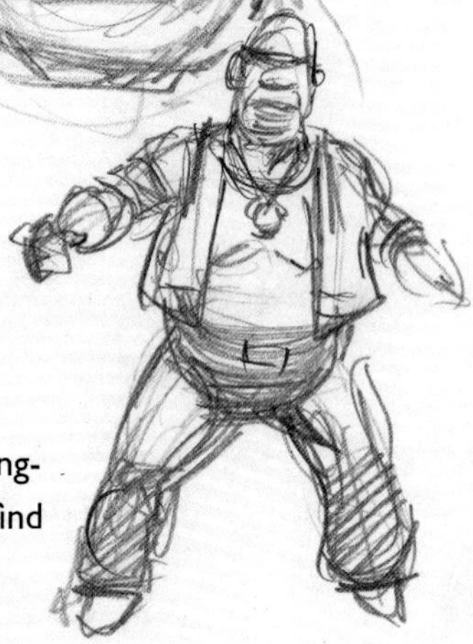

Bronnis went through many changes. I just couldn't find the right feel.

More Manx designs. What on earth was I thinking for his costume here? Looks like a space suit. Too *much* coffee that day.

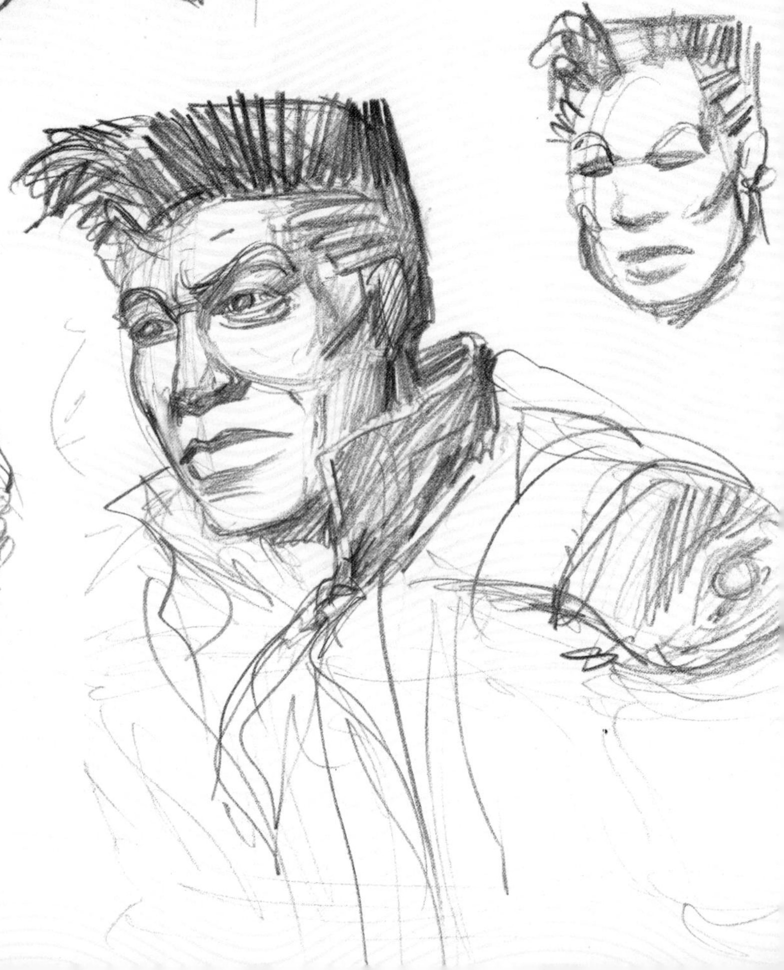

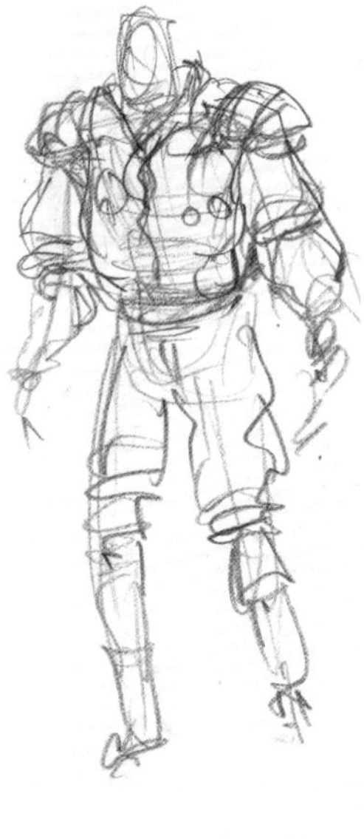

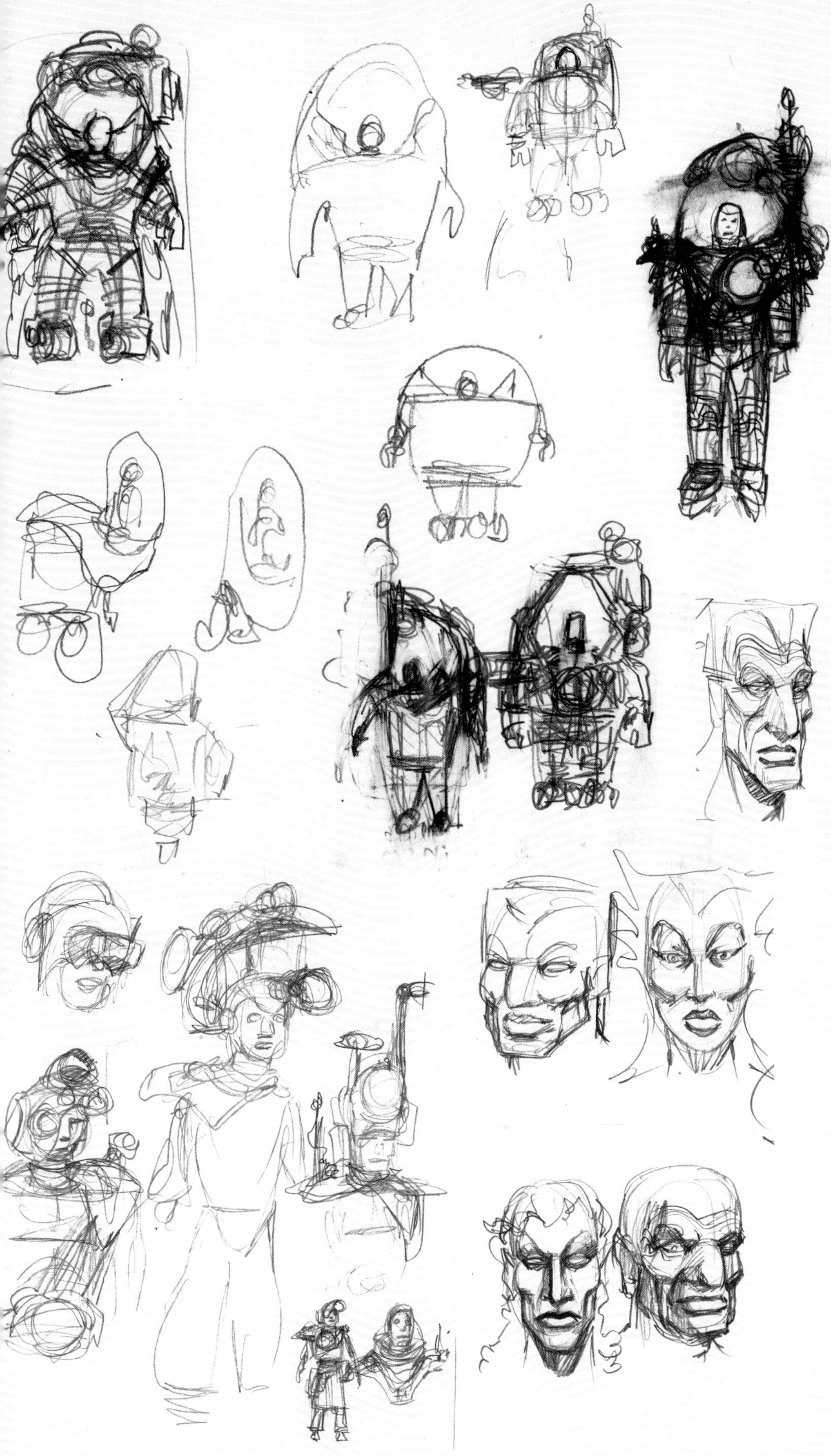

MORE FROM BRUCE ZICK AND DARK HORSE BOOKS!

AN ATOMIC COMIC
The ATOMIC LEGION
WRITTEN BY
MIKE
RICHARDSON
ILLUSTRATED BY
BRUCE
ZICK

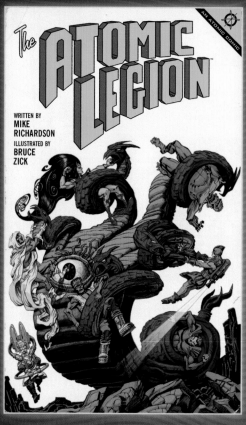

THE ATOMIC LEGION HC
MIKE RICHARDSON, BRUCE ZICK

In a hidden fortress near the North Pole, the greatest heroes of a past age live secluded from the world that rejected them. But when their benefactor—a mysterious scientist known only as the Professor—is kidnapped, it's up to a young boy to rally the robots, monsters, and superheroes in the fortress to come to the rescue as the Atomic Legion!

$29.99 ISBN 978-1-61655-312-8

mandala
STUART MOORE BRUCE ZICK

MANDALA TPB
STUART MOORE, BRUCE ZICK

Earth—here and now. Humankind is secretly enslaved by a global mind-control system called the GRID. Mike Morningstar and his spiritual spec-ops unit, the Thirteen, must alter time and take down the GRID before it's too late. As fiction meets reality, the Thirteen need your help if they are to succeed in awakening humanity and changing the future. Are you awake?

$24.99 ISBN 978-1-61655-389-0